Cloud Native Applications with Docker and Kubernetes

Design and Build Cloud Architecture and Applications with Microservices, EMQ, and Multi-Site Configurations

Jonathan Bartlett

Apress®

Cloud Native Applications with Docker and Kubernetes: Design and Build Cloud Architecture and Applications with Microservices, EMQ, and Multi-Site Configurations

Jonathan Bartlett
Tulsa, OK, USA

ISBN-13 (pbk): 978-1-4842-8875-7
https://doi.org/10.1007/978-1-4842-8876-4

ISBN-13 (electronic): 978-1-4842-8876-4

Managing Director, Apress Media LLC: Welmoed Spahr
Acquisitions Editor: Celestin Suresh John
Development Editor: James Markham
Coordinating Editor: Mark Powers

Cover designed by eStudio Calamar

Cover image by Fullvector on Freepik (www.freepik.com)

Distributed to the book trade worldwide by Apress Media, LLC, 1 New York Plaza, New York, NY 10004, U.S.A. Phone 1-800-SPRINGER, fax (201) 348-4505, e-mail orders-ny@springer-sbm.com, or visit www.springeronline.com. Apress Media, LLC is a California LLC and the sole member (owner) is Springer Science + Business Media Finance Inc (SSBM Finance Inc). SSBM Finance Inc is a **Delaware** corporation.

For information on translations, please e-mail booktranslations@springernature.com; for reprint, paperback, or audio rights, please e-mail bookpermissions@springernature.com.

Apress titles may be purchased in bulk for academic, corporate, or promotional use. eBook versions and licenses are also available for most titles. For more information, reference our Print and eBook Bulk Sales web page at http://www.apress.com/bulk-sales.

Any source code or other supplementary material referenced by the author in this book is available to readers on GitHub (https://github.com/Apress). For more detailed information, please visit http://www.apress.com/source-code.

Printed on acid-free paper

Table of Contents

About the Author

Jonathan Bartlett is a senior software developer at McElroy Manufacturing. His career has had a primary focus on developing data models and web APIs for both internally and externally facing business applications. He has worked with a large variety of languages, platforms, and development styles in his more than 20 years of experience in the industry.

Jonathan has been educating programmers for well over a decade. His first book, *Programming from the Ground Up*, is an Internet classic and was endorsed by Joel Spolsky, cofounder of StackExchange. It was one of the first open source books and has been used by a generation of programmers to learn how computers work from the inside out, using assembly language as a starting point. After more than 15 years, *Programming from the Group Up* was recently updated and rereleased as *Learn to Program with Assembly: Foundational Learning for New Programmers*.

Recently, Jonathan released *Programming for Absolute Beginners* which is focused on teaching brand new programmers about computers, the Internet, and JavaScript programming, based on his experience teaching programming to high-school and college students. Additionally, Jonathan has written several books on the interplay of philosophy, math, and science, including *Calculus from the Ground Up*, *Engineering and the Ultimate*, and *Naturalism and Its Alternatives in Scientific Methodologies*. For those interested in the more physical aspects of computing, he wrote *Electronics for Beginners*.

Jonathan also writes developer-focused articles for a number of technology websites. He is currently a writer for the technology blog *MindMatters*, and you can find his articles at `https://mindmatters.ai/author/jbartlett`. He has also written for IBM's DeveloperWorks, Linux.com, Medium.com, and Classical Conversations.

Jonathan also participates in a variety of academic work. He is an associate fellow of the *Walter Bradley Center for Natural and Artificial Intelligence*. There he does research into fundamental mathematics and the mathematics of artificial intelligence. He also serves on the editorial board for the journal *Bio-Complexity*, focusing on reviewing information-theoretic papers for the journal. Jonathan also served as editor of the book *Controllability of Dynamic Systems: The Green's Function Approach*, which received the RA Presidential Award of the Republic of Armenia in the area of technical sciences and information technologies. Jonathan also spends time teaching at a homeschool co-op through Classical Conversations.

Jonathan is married to his wife Christa. They have been together for over 20 years and have had five children.

About the Technical Reviewer

Shivakumar R. Goniwada is a chief enterprise architect, technology leader, and inventor with more than 24 years of experience focusing on Cloud Native Elements, Enterprise Architecture Setup, and Big Transformation Projects. He currently works at Accenture and leads a highly experienced technology enterprise and cloud architects. In his 24 years of experience, he has led many highly complex projects across industries and geographic regions. He has ten software patents to his name in the areas of cloud, microservices architecture, software engineering, and IoT (a few yet to publish). He has been a speaker at multiple global and in-house conferences. He holds Master Technology Architecture Accenture, Google Professional, AWS, and data science certifications. His executive MBA is from the MIT Sloan School of Management.

Source Code

All source code used in this book is available to readers at github.com/apress/cloud-native-applications-docker-kubernetes.

Acknowledgments

There are a lot of people I would like to thank for this book. However, the most influential people that inspired this book were Clark Ritchie and Tyler Brown (and Chris Zenthoefer for introducing me to them). Both Clark and Tyler helped me to think more explicitly about clouds and cloud services and move my thinking from traditional forms of system administration and system architecture to more cloud native ways of thinking. I actually want to thank all my friends at Specialized Bicycles for the time I spent with them. You all were a great crew to work with, and I am extremely thankful for the time I spent with you all.

CHAPTER 1

Introduction

There has been a very large shift over the last several years in the way that web applications are built and deployed. The modern approach is termed "cloud native," and it is an approach that is geared toward maximizing the benefit and ease of development and scalability that modern cloud computing offers. Whether you have spent years building applications "the old way" or you are just starting out and want to start building applications the right way, this book will set you on the right track to become a cloud native master.

1.1 A Brief History of Web Service Hosting

Oftentimes it is hard to understand why something is the way that it is unless you understand its history. To start with, I want to present a quick overview of the history of web infrastructure hosting to give you a better feel for what sorts of problems cloud native development solves.

1.1.1 The Old Way

Way back in the early days of the Internet, web applications were hosted on specific server machines. That is, when you wanted to host a web application, you had to purchase a physical machine, install Linux or some other operating system on it, and then pay an Internet Service Provider to put your machine on their network. This process was both time-consuming and expensive, often costing hundreds of dollars a month just to rent the space where you install your own server.

If you needed more capacity, this process was equally painful. You had to buy another server, install another copy of Linux on it, make sure it was configured exactly like your other server, and then pay to host that one as well.

1

© Jonathan Bartlett 2023
J. Bartlett, *Cloud Native Applications with Docker and Kubernetes*,
https://doi.org/10.1007/978-1-4842-8876-4_1

Additionally, you had to do quite a bit of work to share the load between servers. You either had to implement a DNS trick to get clients to split their time between machines, or you had to buy *another* piece of equipment, a load balancer, which took incoming traffic and balanced it between machines.

If one machine had faulty hardware, well, you are back to the drawing board. If you needed to upgrade the operating system, you had to log in to each machine, take it out of the lineup, and manually upgrade components. This was ridiculously hard work, and the system administrators who performed these tasks also cost a lot of money. Systems were eventually built to make the task of synchronizing such systems easier, but those had their own complexities to learn.

1.1.2 The Virtual Private Server

The first move to "the cloud" is known as a Virtual Private Server, or VPS. What happened is that advances in processors and operating systems allowed administrators to run virtual machines (VMs) underneath a host machine at essentially the same speed as a non-virtual machine. A virtual machine is simply a "fake" machine running under a real machine. For instance, you can run a Windows operating system within a Macintosh operating system using a virtual machine. The Windows operating system "thinks" it is a real computer, when actually it is just acting like a sub-computer of the Macintosh.

Virtual machines have been around since the 1970s. However, it was not until much later that virtual machines on standard processors were able to function at a speed that is close to "bare metal" and simultaneously be sufficiently secure that you don't have to worry about two VMs on the same host spying on each other. The way that a virtual machine works is that the actual hardware runs a slimmed-down operating system called a hypervisor. The hypervisor is in charge of creating and running virtual machines under it and making sure the resources of the computer (RAM, CPU, hard drives, and input/output operations) are properly distributed between the various VMs that are running under it.

Figure 1-1 shows a conceptual view of how physical machines were broken up into virtual machines (VMs). The hypervisor is in primary control of the machine and can partition the machine to run VMs underneath it. Each VM has the full functionality of a computer and runs its own operating system and applications. They even have their own IP addresses and disk drives (though likely these are virtual as well). The VMs have no idea that they are virtual machines, and, from the point of view of the VM itself, it thinks that it is a full computer. Its operation and usage of system resources, however, is governed by the hypervisor.

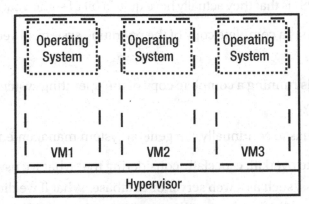

Figure 1-1. *A Physical Machine Hosting Multiple VMs*

Virtual machines paved the way for all sorts of innovations. To start with, system administrators no longer had to worry about getting the right size machine for the task. They could just purchase a high-powered machine and then later decide how to divide the computing power up. If they bought a machine with eight CPUs, 64GB of memory, and 10TB of drive space, they could decide to give two CPUs, 1GB of memory, and 3TB of drive space to one VM, three CPUs, 2GB of memory, and 1TB of drive space to another VM, and so forth. Individual CPUs can even be split—with a VM being given only a portion of a CPU's time.

Since the actual running operating system was virtualized, this made installation and maintenance a lot easier. If one physical host was having hardware problems, you could pause the VMs running on that physical machine, move them to another physical host, and start them back up. It is easy to replicate VMs, because their hard drives are all visible to the hypervisor. Thus, management of the servers was greatly simplified.

Hosting companies were able to take great advantage of these advances as well. They would offer users the ability to buy VMs with just a click of a button. You just select which system image you want to install and what size of computer you want and click a button, and the hosting platform would find a machine with enough capacity for your needs, allocate a VM, and send you the IP address. These are known as virtual private servers, or VPSs. Additionally, VPS providers usually allowed you to request the allocation of a load balancer to distribute traffic to all of your different VPSs.

3

1.1.3 From Virtual Private Servers to Containers

The problem with VPSs is that they actually have quite a bit of somewhat needless overhead:

- Each VPS has a complete copy of the operating system stored on-disk.

- Each VPS is running a complete copy of the operating system in its memory.

- Each VPS has to continually run general system management tasks.

This all seems like overkill, especially considering that what we usually want to run is just a single process, such as a web server or database. What if we didn't really need all of that overhead? What if there was another way to give developers something similar to full access to a server, but didn't have the overhead of a full machine?

Enter the container. Containers are similar to virtual machines in that they give a developer something that feels like an isolated machine. However, a container actually shares its operating system and its filesystem with other containers on the same host *without affecting them.* That is, each container thinks and acts like it is an independent machine, but it is usually sharing both the operating system and the filesystem with other containers without the application even being aware of this. Figure 1-2 shows what this looks like. You can run many more containers on a single physical machine than you can run VMs, because the entire operating system is shared between all of the containers. We will describe the magic that manages to keep these containers from running over each other in Chapter 2. But, for now, just recognize that it works.

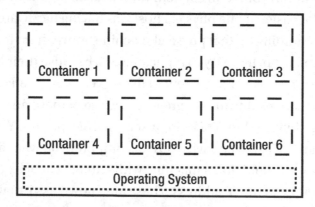

Physical Machine

Figure 1-2. *A Physical Machine Hosting Containers*

VMs and VPSs, while flexible, had quite a bit of overhead, as each instance required all the overhead of a regular operating system. Now, with containers, all of this overhead is shared by all or most of the containers running on a physical machine. Each container only adds the memory and disk space used by the specific process or processes that it was launched to run, but, for the process, it has the same flexibility as if it had control of the whole machine.

So, a typical Linux server usually has an installed footprint of 10-20 gigabytes of disk space. Such a server is usually running a bunch of kernel (operating system) processes, the `init` program, a system logger, a terminal program, an SSH service, and possibly other system services. These services typically use up about a half of a gigabyte of working memory (including disk cache). With containers, this price only has to be paid once per physical machine rather than once per VPS. Even so, containers still allow developers the option of making any modification they want on their own running instance.

Additionally, a set of standards developed around containers and container images which allow them to be created, manipulated, stored, and retrieved by tools from a variety of different projects or vendors. For instance, there might be a standard container image for a base install of Debian, and I can pull down that container image and install my application on top of it, and create a new container image out of the result, and store it back on the service.

Additionally, because running containers utilizes so little overhead, it is possible for developers to run multiple containers on their own personal computers. In fact, they can set up containers that are exact replicas of the setup used on the servers, and it often has minimal impact on the performance of their own computers.

This almost eliminates an entire class of issues caused by developer's local development environments. Historically, the configuration of a developer's personal computer does not exactly match what is on the server. They may be running a different version of the programming language, database, or any other component of the environment. With containers, developers can specify, run, and validate the precise operating environment on their local computers as will be running on the server. The entire operating system image itself can be the subject of development and testing.

1.1.4 Cloud Native Infrastructure

The move to containerized computing then paved the way for what is known as cloud native infrastructure. In cloud native infrastructure, entire application infrastructures are specified, created, and deployed using code. That is, you don't have to go ask for a bunch

5

of servers, install the image you want on them, and then add them to a load balancer. Instead, you tell a separate control service that you want to build a load-balanced system using a particular image and run between three and ten copies of it depending on the load. The control service then launches everything you need and keeps everything in sync.[1]

In a cloud native infrastructure, the control system does most of the routine management tasks that were previously done by system administrators. If a container dies, it gets cleaned up and restarted by the control service. If you start to get a higher load, depending on how the cluster is configured, the control service may launch more copies of your container. The control service will handle registering each of these containers with the load balancer, as well as finding which machines it should run the containers on.

Cloud native applications essentially turn infrastructure into code. You write code which specifies what your network infrastructure should look like, and the cloud makes it happen. This allows the incorporation of source control tools into the development of infrastructure itself. The configuration of your infrastructure can then be version-controlled, allowing easier tracing of configuration changes for diagnosing problems.

Today, there are a lot of choices for building cloud native applications. However, there is one system which runs on practically every hosting platform—Kubernetes, also known as K8s (pronounced "Kates"). Kubernetes is based on a system originally developed by Google for managing their own infrastructure. However, Kubernetes is an open source product and an open standard which is used by numerous different cloud providers, including the big guys like Google, Microsoft, Amazon AWS, and IBM, as well as the smaller players such as Linode and Digital Ocean. Additionally, you can create your own private clouds using software such as Red Hat's OpenShift and VMWare's Tanzu. Kubernetes essentially gives you the ability to build a scalable cloud infrastructure which doesn't tie you down to any specific provider.

---

[1] Just to note, you can run cloud native systems using traditional VMs instead of containers. Infrastructure as code can specify full-blown VMs to image and deploy. However, most agree that containers allow for the maximum amount of benefit of the cloud native approach.

1.2 An Overview of This Book

The goal of this book is to provide you with an understanding of the tools for cloud native development and how they are put together into a scalable web application. To this end, the book is divided into three parts. The first part will cover containers, how they work, and how to work with them. Without a good understanding of containers, it is hard to really understand what is really going on under the hood. The second part will be an introduction to Kubernetes. This part will cover the basics of Kubernetes and will show you how to get a small Kubernetes cluster up and running. The third part will show how to think about application architecture from a cloud native perspective.

1.3 Prerequisites

This book has very few prerequisites. Even if you aren't familiar with the specific tools we are using, this book has enough step-by-step instructions that you should be able to follow it fairly easily.

Since the book focuses on web applications, it assumes that you are familiar with the absolute basics of HTML, CSS, and the basics of how the Internet works (i.e., domain names, IP addresses, etc.). If you are not familiar with these topics, you should put this book down and pick up a copy of my book, *Programming for Absolute Beginners*. *Programming for Absolute Beginners* doesn't hit every topic you need to know, but if you understand its concepts, you should be able to work through most of the examples in this book.

This book doesn't focus on programming languages, as the details provided apply no matter what programming language you are using. For the example applications, this book will focus on Ruby and Sinatra, simply to make the examples small, self-contained, and easy to follow. There is nothing Ruby- or Sinatra-specific that we will be focusing on.

This book also presumes that you have a basic familiarity with databases and SQL. This is not an absolute requirement, but the database code itself is left largely unexplained. However, the SQL code is fairly simple and should be self-evident to anyone with even a passing knowledge of SQL.

Finally, this book uses Linux as the underlying operating system for its containers. However, even if you don't know anything about Linux, this book gives you every command you need to type, so you don't actually have to know a whole lot about Linux to use this book. Appendix A has a list of common Linux commands for reference if you want to know more or need a general introduction to command-line systems. The reason that Linux was chosen was because it is the most common operating system used in containerized environments. Additionally, most other operating systems can run Linux containers, but not the other way around (i.e., you can run Linux containers under Windows, but you can't run Windows containers under Linux). Also, because all of the components we will be using are all free and open source software, there are no licensing considerations for their use.

1.4 Typographical Conventions

Some commands in Kubernetes get kind of long. If a command goes longer than a single line, we will put a backslash (\) at the end of a line to indicate that it continues on the next line. The reason for this convention is that most command-line shells will interpret this the same way—if you add a backslash and go to a new line, then the shell treats that as if it were a continuation of the current line. However, you can put it all on the same line if you wish; just remove the backslashes.

For instance, we might ask you to type the following command:

```
echo this is a really long \
    command
```

That is identical to just typing the following:

```
echo this is a really long command
```

Also note that, when talking about Kubernetes, many things that you might speak about generically are actually proper names, so those names are capitalized. For instance, in Kubernetes, there is a resource called a Service, so, when referring specifically to a Kubernetes Service, the word "Service" will always be capitalized. Also, some Kubernetes resources combine two words together, like "ReplicaSet." This book follows the Kubernetes naming conventions and keeps these words together, capitalized in the same way that the Kubernetes documentation does.

PART I

An Introduction to Containers

CHAPTER 2

Containers Under the Hood

As businesses move more and more infrastructure off of their own premises to online services, finding the best way to manage that infrastructure becomes more and more important. As we will show throughout this book, containers enable development teams to have more reliable, repeatable, and testable services that can be easily deployed at any scale. Here, we are looking under the hood at containers, which will be used as the foundation for infrastructure management tools. Over the last decade, the popularity of containers for such tools has grown rapidly.

One particular tool stands out among others—Docker. Docker is a tool that enables easy management of the entire container ecosystem. Docker has a command-line tool that makes running containers easy, as well as creating, downloading, and managing container images. Docker also comes with a desktop application, Docker Desktop, that makes container management even easier. Finally, the company that built the Docker tool also runs Docker Hub, which makes it easy to store and access container images in the cloud.

Docker has been at the forefront of container management throughout its technological growth. Many of the modern standards around containers arose from features that originated in Docker, and even those that arose elsewhere were popularized by having an easy-to-use tool to make them accessible to the average developer. Docker is known as a "container runtime," as it contains the tools to make the containers boot up and execute in their own provisioned space.

In this chapter, we are going to take a look at the technologies behind containers generally (and Docker specifically) and where they came from.

© Jonathan Bartlett 2023
J. Bartlett, *Cloud Native Applications with Docker and Kubernetes*,
https://doi.org/10.1007/978-1-4842-8876-4_2

2.1 Answering Basic Questions About Containers

Let's start by looking at the basic questions that people have about containers themselves.

2.1.1 What Are Containers?

If you're not familiar with container technology, containers sit in a strange position in the technology toolchain. They are not something you develop with explicitly (applications in containers are rarely self-conscious of this fact). In fact, as a developer, you may never touch Docker or containers. A container isn't an operating system that you run things on. You still run on your normal server-side operating systems such as Linux. It isn't a hardware technology, either.

Essentially, containers wrap up both the application and the parts of the operating system's environment that the application uses into a single bundle that can be easily deployed anywhere. This is known as the container image. When it is deployed, it runs not as the primary system for the machine but as a process *within* your current operating system. That's right; you run a slimmed-down operating system inside your current operating system, which could either be your local development machine or a server. This running system is the container itself.

As far as the container is concerned, it thinks it is its own machine. It gets its own IP address, has its own filesystem, and even has its own isolated process tree. However, as we will see, it is actually sharing the core operating system with other containers on the system, but modern operating systems are able to sufficiently isolate processes from each other that they can't even see that they are sharing the operating system with others.

2.1.2 What Problems Do Containers Solve?

Containers solve two huge problems for deployments. The first is configuration management. Because Docker packages up both the operating system and the application into a single bundle, it allows for testing the app in the same configuration that it is going to run in when it is deployed on the server. The switch from staging to production can usually be handled entirely by changes to environment variables or runtime arguments.

Historically, developers have had the problem that they may be relying on a tool on their local machine that isn't available on the server or a version of something that is different on the server. With containers, both the operating system and the application are saved together before deployment, so the developers can be sure not only of their code but of the environment that it is running in.

The second problem is infrastructure management. Since containers run as a process under the main operating system, you can run multiple containers on a single machine. This means that, instead of choosing the exact right size for each machine, you can simply purchase or provision a large machine and run several containers on that machine. If you need more horsepower for one of your containers, you can simply move it to a bigger server.

Additionally, containers are becoming the standard for other infrastructure management tools. Amazon Web Services, which started out with their own infrastructure management tool (Elastic Beanstalk), has more recently been pushing containers instead, using their Elastic Container Service. Kubernetes, the open source cloud management system, also runs using containers and is available on Google Cloud, Linode, Azure, Amazon Web Services, and many other hosting services.

2.1.3 Does It Use a Lot of Disk Space?

It may sound like packaging up an entire operating system and shipping it to a server use a lot of disk space. Sometimes, in fact, it does. However, containers usually only contain the minimum of what is necessary to run the application, such as a minimal Linux distribution, the application runtime environment, and the application itself. Even further, some Docker applications don't need any of the operating system to run! For some programming environments (such as the Go programming language), the application and all its dependencies can be bundled together in a relatively small package that doesn't rely on any other operating system files.[1]

Many applications use the Alpine Linux distribution, whose base image currently uses less than ten megabytes of space. Most other distributions are more heavyweight, however, often being in the hundred megabyte range. Some container images, which

---

[1] These are known as "distroless" containers, since they don't contain an actual Linux distribution. There are, additionally, some distroless starter images which contain a few basic files, such as time zone listings and root SSL certificates, which may be needed even if the rest of the Linux distribution isn't needed.

require more of the operating system or themselves contain more files, can run into the Gigabyte range.

However, even with larger containers, the container infrastructure used by Docker and other container runtimes has a mechanism to limit the amount of space utilized by multiple containers running on the same system (more information on this is available later in the chapter).

2.1.4 What Is the Relationship Between "Docker" and "Containers"?

The systems we are talking about are known as containers. Docker is a set of tools for building, managing, and running containers and container images, combined with the standard registry of container images, known as Docker Hub. Docker is oftentimes used synonymously with containers, because for a while nearly every container was created, managed, and run using Docker or its components.

Now, however, containers and container images are largely standardized. Therefore, Docker, while it remains the most popular container development environment, is just one of many. There are differences between them, but, on the whole, containers made by one system are fully compatible with the others.

Personally I recommend Docker, and I recommend purchasing their paid subscription. They do a lot of work for the container community, and their Docker Desktop system is extremely easy to use. They even have tools to make developing for Kubernetes easier. However, if you prefer open source tools, Podman (available at `podman.io`) is almost fully command-line compatible with Docker. You can install Podman and then either replace all occurrences of `docker` with `podman` on the command line.[2] From that point, the commands will be mostly identical. The commands in this book were tested with Docker specifically, but I've also had a lot of success with Podman.

2.2 A Short History of Container Technology

To gain an even better understanding of containers, it is good to look into the history of where they came from, what problems they were built to solve, and what technological

---

[2] You can also symlink `/usr/local/bin/docker` to your `podman` command so that the command itself is also identical.

advancements allowed for containers to work so well for those problems. Some of this was covered in Chapter 1, but it is good to revisit it here to understand how the history impacted the technology itself.

2.2.1 From Emulators to Virtual Machines

Docker allows you to run numerous "containers" at the same time on a single computer. Each of these containers acts as if it were a separate computer. It knows nothing about what else is on the computer, and, for all it knows, it is the only thing on the computer. The computer, however, can manage multiple containers and allow the user to adjust which containers are running on which computers. How does this work?

One thing that has always been evident about computers is that you could run a virtual computer "inside" another. In fact, surprisingly, this was known before computers were technically invented. This notion, in inchoate form, originally appeared in Alan Turing's original paper describing computers. He noted that Universal Turing Machines (what we would call "general-purpose computers") have the ability to simulate any other Universal Turing Machine. In other words, you can get a computer to act as if it were another computer.

There are many ways that this virtualization can take place. The most general way is to have a program that literally reads the instructions that the processor would have executed directly and perform the steps within another program. This intermediate program is known as an emulator, because it emulates the way that a processor would act. The problem is that this technique is really slow. However, originally, this was the only way to achieve virtualization.

As processors progressed, the processors developed mechanisms that allowed the virtualized processes to run directly on the processors for most tasks but then run in a more roundabout way when executing operating system tasks. That is, you could tell the processor that certain parts of the code can be run directly, but other parts require more care. This is what allowed for systems such as VMWare to work so well. For the most part, the virtualized systems were just running as an ordinary process on your computer, making use of the processor directly for most tasks.

These virtualization technologies allowed for the growth of cloud computing, which allowed system administrators to purchase large computers and provision them into smaller ones. This greatly reduced the costs and overhead of system management and allowed for an entire ecosystem of servers which could be provisioned on demand.

For more information about developing applications in this sort of environment, see my book *Building Scalable PHP Web Applications Using the Cloud.*

2.2.2 Increasing Isolation Inside the Operating System

There was also progress that was made on the operating system side. Operating systems have long had a primary job of keeping different processes from interfering with each other. This first big leap in this was virtual memory, which isolates each process's access to your computer's memory. When using virtual memory, one process literally cannot access another process's memory.

Another interesting development in operating systems is known to system administrators as "chroot jails." This comes from the name of a command, `chroot`, which changes which parts of the filesystem a process is even allowed to see, usually relegating the process to a small, isolated subdirectory of the filesystem. This has long been popular with web server administrators. Oftentimes, administrators will increase the security of their systems by `chroot`ing the web service to a directory with a small set of files. Then, if a hacker manages to find a security flaw in the web service and break in, their access would be limited to the files available in the `chroot` jail.

Through the years, operating systems have added on more and more features which allow processes to isolate themselves from each other. Processes can be blocked from even seeing that other processes exist and can even be isolated onto a separate network than the rest of the computer!

The advantage of process isolation within a computer over virtualization is that, in virtualization, every virtual machine has the full overhead of running a complete operating system. However, an isolated process gets the benefit of sharing a lot more of the operating environment with the other programs. Thus, an isolated process is much more lightweight than a full virtual machine. However, they are much harder to manage. A virtual machine doesn't care that it is a virtual machine, and you can treat it exactly as if it were an ordinary bare-metal machine. A chrooted process, however, usually needs a bit of work to get it to run correctly.

2.2.3 The Birth of Containers

Eventually, programmers figured out a way to manage isolated processes in a way that is very similar to the way that virtual machines are managed. This new technique of isolating processes in a way that acts similar to a virtual machine is known as a *container*. The first system that implemented containers similar to what we think of them today was LXC, which stood for "Linux Containers." LXC pulled together all of the pieces and created a system which allowed a lightweight VM—a virtual machine that shared the core operating system between the different containers.

Because of the advances of process isolation, these containers were even able to create a virtual network and give each container its own location on this network.

2.2.4 The Union Filesystem

The early container systems had a problem, however. They still used a lot of disk space for each container. While the containers shared the core of the operating system (known as the kernel), each container wound up needed its own full copy of the other essential parts of the operating system. It needed all the support files copied into each container. This is a lot of essentially wasted overhead.

This was solved by the "union filesystem." The *filesystem* is the formatting that is applied to a hard drive. If you are on Windows, the filesystem is known as NTFS. If you are on a Mac, your hard drive is formatted to the Apple File System, or APFS. For most filesystems, every file in a directory (and, usually, every file on the same hard drive) is on the same filesystem.

The union filesystem works by creating a number of read-only layers on your operating system and overlaying them on each other. Only the top layer can be written to. You can actually modify (or even delete) any of the files in the read-only layers. However, the result of doing that is not to change the read-only part but rather to create a new entry in the topmost filesystem (which is read-write) which contains the changes. This allows you to share large portions of a filesystem, even in cases where the shared parts may need to be written to.

Figure 2-1 shows what this looks like. The container itself is running a read-only container image. This image consists of a number of filesystem layers, each stacked on top of each other. Each layer is immutable, but that doesn't mean there can't be changes. The changes are simply stored in the layer *above*. Finally, running on the top layer are the changes made by the container itself. Again, the container image is read-only, but the filesystem is read-write because the changes are simply stored in the container's own layer, not written to the layers below. The container itself only sees the results of combining all of the changes, not the individual layers themselves. This is what allows many containers which use the same image to run on the same computer with negligible per-container filesystem space. The container image only exists once, and each container only has to write its changes to the filesystem. Additionally, since the layers themselves are immutable, container images can themselves share layers.

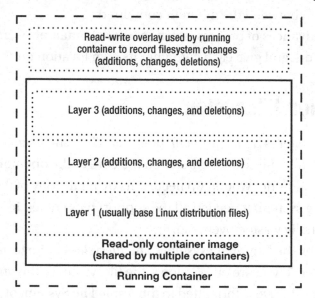

Figure 2-1. *The Layout of a Container's Filesystem Layers*

This is useful for containers because the read-only parts of a filesystem can be shared since they can't be modified. Therefore, the operating system files which don't change from container to container only have to exist once. They get put into a shared read-only filesystem, which is then used as a base layer for each container. Then, each container gets a read-write layer stuck on top of the base layer. Thus, to each container, it "feels" normal—each container has full authority to write to any part of its filesystem. However, since there is a large part that is shared and never ordinarily modified, you save a ton of disk space and can essentially have hundreds of full copies of an operating system running with practically zero overhead for doing so.

2.2.5 The Rise of Docker

These components—containers and union filesystems—became the core of the system known as Docker, which has now become almost synonymous with containers. The standards for container format and features are mostly derived from Docker itself.

Additionally, Docker, over and above the basic container technology, also provides a well-defined user interface for container management.

The essence of the Docker container format was how they defined the container images. An "image" is basically a starting point for a container. It's like a frozen hard drive that can be endless copied to be used as a starting point for each new system bootup.

Docker images contain a series of filesystem layers that are packaged together. Each layer is a set of changes which are built on top of the previous layer. The container itself is a combination of an image (with all of its layers) that is running with a top-level read-write filesystem. The top-level filesystem can record changes of any file at all (including those of lower layers). However, the lower layers *themselves* never change, but, to a user that has the top-level filesystem mounted, they see the files as having been changed.

Additionally, Docker provides a registry for housing these images as well as a standard protocol for retrieving them so that other registry providers can integrate seamlessly. Inside the registry, every layer is defined by a unique hash code, which allows images to share layers between them in order to save even more space.

To get a feel for how Docker containers can improve resource usage, imagine that you had three applications that you wanted to run in a virtualized environment—two of them running in a Ruby environment and one of them running in a Python environment. To run these on virtual machines, you would need a complete copy of the operating system, the environment, and the application for each virtual machine that you ran. With containers, however, you can have a base operating system layer that is shared by all of your images. So the operating system only has to be stored once. Then, the environment can be stored in another layer. This means that the layer containing the Ruby environment can be shared between the two applications. Finally, the applications themselves can sit on a layer at the top. Additionally, you can run multiple copies of each of these applications, and they all seamlessly share the same underlying layers, meaning that no significant additional disk space is used by launching numerous containers using the same images. Using containers essentially provides the isolation level of a virtual machine, but where the overhead is as minimal as running multiple processes on the same operating system.

2.3 Summary

In this chapter, we learned the following:

- Containers are a way of packaging up an application and an operating system together into a single package that can be easily deployed as a unit.

- Container images consist of a series of read-only filesystem layers which are built on top of each other.

- In a running container, the image is read-only, but a read-write filesystem layer is added on top which allows the container to make unlimited changes which are visible to the container itself without actually modifying the underlying image.

- This system of container image layers allows containers to be run with isolation levels similar to virtual machines, but with an overhead more similar to that of a single process.

- The Docker environment is the most common development environment for containers, but container standardization has allowed other tools to be used for containers as well.

CHAPTER 3

A Docker Interactive Tutorial

As businesses move more and more infrastructure online due to the effects of competition (not to mention workplace health scares), finding the best way to manage that infrastructure becomes more and more important. Containers enable development teams to have more reliable, repeatable, and testable systems that can be deployed at massive scale with the click of a button.

In this chapter, I will walk you through the process of using the Docker command-line tools to download, install, and run containers, as well as how to build your own. If you need direction for installing Docker, please see Appendix B.1.

3.1 Registries, Repositories, and Tags

Before we get started, I wanted to talk a little bit about how container images are stored and accessed over the Internet and some related terminology.

A container *registry* is a place on the Internet that stores container images. There are many registries around hosted by a number of companies, and you can even host your own registry. However, the most common registry available is Docker Hub, run by the same company that runs Docker itself. The URL for the registry itself (as seen by the container management system) is docker.io, but the URL for the registry search and management features is hub.docker.com.

Each registry contains a number of container image *repositories*. A repository is a named location where images can be stored. Normally, a repository contains a single type of container image, but possibly multiple versions of it. Each container image in a repository is identified by a *tag*, which identifies a specific image.

21

© Jonathan Bartlett 2023
J. Bartlett, *Cloud Native Applications with Docker and Kubernetes*,
https://doi.org/10.1007/978-1-4842-8876-4_3

The format of a *fully qualified image name* is `registry/repository:tag`. For instance, the container image for the latest version of a basic Ubuntu Linux distribution is available on Docker Hub at the repository `docker.io/ubuntu:latest`.

However, fully qualified image names are not always necessary. If you are pulling images from the standard Docker Hub repository, you don't need to specify `docker.io` (since it is the first and most widely used repository). Additionally, if you don't specify a tag, the `latest` tag is presumed. Therefore, you can actually refer to this same image as simply `ubuntu`.

If you wanted a specific version of Ubuntu, that's where the tags get helpful. Ubuntu 22 is known as "Jammy Jellyfish," and the tag for the latest incarnation of this version is `jammy`. So the fully qualified image name is `docker.io/ubuntu:jammy`. If you wanted the build that was specifically built on May 31, 2022, the fully qualified image name is `docker.io/ubuntu:jammy-20220531`. Note that an image can have more than one tag. So, if the latest version of Jammy Jellyfish *is* the May 31, 2022, build, then the `jammy` and `jammy-20220531` tags will refer to the same build.

Note that there are no rules as to how tags are named. Each repository can have its own naming scheme. The goal of most tag naming schemes is usually to help you identify a version with whatever level of specificity you are comfortable with. Additionally, the repository owner can change the meanings of tags at will. Therefore, when a new version of Jammy Jellyfish comes out, that manager will likely create a new, specific version tag (e.g., `jammy-somedate`) and change the general `jammy` tag to refer to the new image. That way, everyone who is just wanting Jammy Jellyfish in general can simply refer to the `jammy` tag, but, if you needed to make sure that each revision was specifically tested, you may be more comfortable with the build-specific tag.

Note also that not only does a repository owner have the ability to change the image a tag points to, but a repository owner is not required to keep images and tags at all. They are free to remove images and tags at any time. Therefore, for most production situations, most companies pay a registry to manage their own repositories or simply run their own registry. Docker Hub is a great place to manage your own repositories if you need one. Other popular registries include JFrog, Azure Container Registry, and Amazon Container Registry. All of the container images we will be using use Docker Hub as the registry.

One other note—sometimes the Docker command will refer to the full name of the image as a "tag," and not just the tag itself. This is an unfortunate confusion of naming, but unfortunately we are stuck with it.

3.2 Running Your First Container

In order to demonstrate different aspects of Docker containers, I built a few custom container images just for this chapter. The first one will be a "hello world" container, which just turns on, says `Hello world!`, and turns back off. To run this, just do the following:

```
docker run johnnyb61820/hello-world
```

The first time you run this, this will connect to the standard Docker registry and look for a repository named `johnnyb61820/hello-world` (`johnnyb61820` is my username on Docker Hub). It will then find the image tagged with the version named `latest` (meaning the most recent version of this image). It will pull down the image, save it locally, and then run it. It will display information about downloading the image, and then the last line will say `Hello World!`.

If you run the command again, since the image is now saved to your computer, it will just print `Hello World!` and exit. Run the command a total of three times to see how it works.

Now we will investigate what those commands actually did on your computer. The first thing it did was to install a Docker image onto your computer. You can see this by running the following command:

```
docker image ls
```

If you aren't familiar with Unix terminology (see Appendix A for a short introduction), ls (that's an L and an S if you are having trouble reading it) is a shortened form of "list," so this command lists the Docker images on your computer. If this is your first time using Docker, it should print out something like this:

```
Repository                           Tag     Image ID    Size
docker.io/johnnyb61820/hello-world   latest  4d1efc6684b5  2.07 MB
```

The repository is where the image is located. The tag is the version number (`latest` is the standard version for the most recent version of this image). The Image ID is the computer's name for the image. The size is how much space it takes up on your computer.

However, the image is just the unchanging part of a container. A container itself is a full virtual machine, and the uppermost read-write filesystem layer allows the container full access to modify its own files. In fact, if you ran the `hello-world` program three times, your computer now has three containers on it. You can see them by running the following command:

```
docker container ls -a
```

Without the `-a`, this command will only list running containers. But we want to see all of the ones that are on the computer, whether running or not. This produces what may be some surprising output (output shortened to fit the page).

```
Container ID  Image                        Status      Names
771c5e65d8db  johnnyb61820/hello-world     Exited (0)  vibrant_panini
eb7ade7aef2a  johnnyb61820/hello-world     Exited (0)  lucid_kalam
d725bdd2fdf2  johnnyb61820/hello-world     Exited (0)  gifted_keller
```

Every time we ran the command, the system started up a new container (i.e., a new "virtual machine"), created a read-write filesystem layer on top of the specified image for the command to run in, ran the code in the container, and exited. Even though they exited and are no longer running, the containers still "exist," and these are they. So what do these columns mean?

The Container ID is the computer's internal name for your container and is generated at random. The "names" on the right-hand side are also generated but are meant to be more human-readable. You can refer to containers by either name. The "image" is the name of the underlying read-only image that the container is running on.

Most containers contain entire operating systems that have several commands available. However, this container only has one file—the program to execute. Additionally, containers specify either an "entrypoint" or a "default command" (or both), and this is the command that they run when they are started. In our case, the `johnnyb61820/hello-world` container had one file in it, `/hello`, which is run when the container starts.

To restart the container (i.e., to rerun the command in the container without creating a new one), we will issue a `start` command to the container with the following command:

```
docker container start -ai CONTAINER_ID
```

In this command, replace CONTAINER_ID with one of the Container IDs that returned when you listed the available containers (or you can use the friendlier name as well). This will rerun the command within the existing container, rather than creating a new one.

Now, first you might be wondering why these containers are staying around. The reason is simple—in most cases, these are full applications, so, even when they aren't running, we don't want the container to be deleted! However, in this case, the program doesn't save any information, so we are fine deleting the container. We can tell Docker to auto-delete a container when it is done running by adding --rm to the docker run command, like this:

```
docker run --rm johnnyb61820/hello-world
```

This will do all of these functions—create the container, run the command, and then remove the container when the command is done, so it is not listed in the list of containers.

Note, however, that containers are not expensive! Since the underlying image is read-only (even though the uppermost filesystem permits changes to these files), the containers all share the image that they use to start with. In our case, the application does not create, delete, or modify any files, so that means that the amount of disk space that each container uses is extremely small (about 200kB per container). That doesn't count the image itself, but the image is only stored once for all containers using it.

To delete your non-running containers, run the following command:

```
docker system prune
```

You can add a -a to the end of that command to also delete all the images that are not presently used.

If you want to try out another simple Docker command, run the following:

```
docker run johnnyb61820/roll-dice
```

This will simply simulate the roll of a dice.

3.3 Running a Docker Service

More often than running individual commands, Docker is usually used to run services. In this next example, we will run a Docker app that simply runs as a very simple HTTP service, which runs on port 8070 inside the container. As you will see, we can map that port to a port on the main server (the example will use port 8080).

To run it, just run the following:

```
docker run -p 8080:8070 johnnyb61820/simple-web-server
```

While it is running, you can use your web browser to access the service running on your machine at `http://localhost:8080/`. It should give you back a plain-looking web page that says, "Hello from Docker!" You can push control-c at any time to stop the service.

So what does this command do? This is almost identical to our previous commands, with the exception that there is a `-p 8080:8070` added to the command. Remember, each container acts almost exactly like a full virtual machine. That means that each container has its own networking, too. The `-p` flag says to take the port 8080 on the real machine and proxy it to port 8070 on the Docker virtual machine. Note that these can actually be the same value since they act like completely separate machines, but I put different values so that you can see that you can map the ports however you like.

Now, most services are actually run in the background. To run a Docker image as a background service, add a `-d` flag like this:

```
docker run -d -p 8080:8070 johnnyb61820/simple-web-server
```

It will print out the Container ID (which is a longer form of the same name you get from `docker container ls`) and return to you. Now, if you do `docker container ls`, you can see it running (output shortened to fit on the page):

```
CONTAINER ID    COMMAND           PORTS            NAMES
0422ab9b8c7f    "/http-service"   8080->8070/tcp   hopeful_payne
```

Note that without the `-a`, `docker container ls` only shows actively running containers. It shows the ports that have been proxied from the main host to the container. We can then stop the container with `docker container stop CONTAINER_ID`. We can restart it again with `docker container start CONTAINER_ID`. We used the `-a` flag earlier because, otherwise, `docker container start` runs the container in the background (which we now want to do). After a container is stopped, it can be removed altogether by `docker container rm CONTAINER_ID`. Remember, the `CONTAINER_ID` can be either the raw ID that the computer generates or the more user-friendly name.

3.4 Running a Whole Operating System

So far, the containers we have been looking at are extremely lightweight, as they only contain one single file with the command in them. However, most Docker instances actually contain a minimal operating system on them, often based on some Linux distribution (usually Ubuntu, Debian, Alpine, or CentOS).

If you want to run a container as essentially a full machine, run the following command:

```
docker run -it ubuntu
```

This loads a standard image which is essentially a Dockerized version of the Ubuntu Linux distribution. Docker Hub has a number of images which are considered "standard," so you don't have to specify a username prefix for them.

The `-it` will allocate an interactive terminal. The default program that is run with Ubuntu is the shell. That means that running this command will (a) download a fairly minimal Ubuntu distribution (about 75MB), (b) create a container, and (c) start up a shell that you are now typing in. Again, this is a real Linux distribution, so you can use `apt-get` to install whatever additional packages you like. However, don't forget to `apt-get update` first to retrieve the list of packages that are available to install. To learn more about Linux and about installing packages, see Appendix A.

Note that, in the container, you can do anything you want: create files, run programs, anything! When you leave, the container will stop. However, you can get back to it by finding the container's name with `docker container ls -a` and then starting it again with `docker start -ai CONTAINER_ID`.

Note that, since your containers act essentially as full virtual machines, anything you do inside the Docker container won't affect other containers or the main operating system. If I install a package, it is only installed within the container, not on the underlying image. If I add a user, that user is only added within the container.

3.5 Copying Files to and from the Container

With Docker, you can easily copy files in and out of the container from the host computer using the `docker cp` command. If there is a file on your computer, say `myfile.txt`, you can copy it to your container using the following command:

```
docker cp myfile.txt CONTAINER_ID:/path/to/destination/file.txt
```

If there is a file on your container, say /path/to/file.txt, you can copy it out of your container using the same command:

```
docker cp CONTAINER_ID:/path/to/file.txt file.txt
```

No extra options are needed for copying directories. Just specify the name of the source and destination directories, and the entire directory tree is copied, maintaining permissions if possible.

You can copy files from a container whether it is running or stopped.

3.6 Creating a New Docker Image

Let's say that you have taken the Ubuntu package and done modifications to it, and now you have a container that you want to replicate to other containers. This can be done easily by converting your container to an image.

As a simple example, we will create a container from the Ubuntu image, install a single package, and then create a new image out of our container. Run the following commands:

```
docker run -it --name mycontainer ubuntu
apt-get update
apt-get install uuid
exit
```

The --name parameter tells Docker that we will decide the name of the container rather than having Docker autogenerate one for us. Then, inside the container, we run those commands to install a single additional package, the uuid package (this was chosen just because it is a small package that supplies an easy-to-run command, uuid). Finally, we exit out of the container.

Now, to create an image out of our new container, we run the following:

```
docker commit mycontainer ubuntu-with-uuid
```

This will take the Container ID mycontainer and create an image out of it called ubuntu-with-uuid. Additional changes can be made with the --change flag (such as what program gets run when the container starts), but that is outside the scope of this chapter.

Now, we can run new containers using this image as a base with the command:

```
docker run -it ubuntu-with-uuid
```

Note that the image for this container as given in `docker ls` is 98MB. However, it actually uses much less than that. Since our new image is based on the Ubuntu image, it actually shares the underlying files with that image, so only the differences take up additional disk space.

If you want to know the changes you have made to a container before converting it to an image, you can run `docker diff CONTAINER_ID`, and it will give you a list of all the files that have been added, changed, or removed on the container.

3.7 Creating Docker Images Using a Recipe

While you can create images by just messing around with an existing image, that can lead to problems with configuration management. Let's say that there is a new release of the Ubuntu image, and you want to rebuild your environment using the new image as a base. Do you remember all the steps you did to configure your environment? Chances are you won't. I've been building operating system images practically my whole life, and I can tell you that I never remember.

Therefore, a better and more systematic approach is to use a recipe, known as a Dockerfile, to create your image from a previous image. An example Dockerfile (which should be named `Dockerfile`) is shown in Figure 3-1.

```
FROM ubuntu
RUN apt-get -y update
RUN apt-get -y install uuid
COPY some-file-in-current-directory /path/to/container/destination
CMD ["/bin/sh"]
```

Figure 3-1. Example `Dockerfile` Creating a Modified Ubuntu Image

The `FROM` command tells Docker what the base image should be. Any `RUN` command causes Docker to run those commands inside a container with that image. In this case, we are running installer commands and using the `-y` flag so that it doesn't ask us any questions. Any `COPY` command copies the given file in the current directory to the given location in the container (a recursive copy in the case of a directory). Finally, the CMD specifies the default command to run when the container is started, but these can be overridden by arguments to the docker run command.[1]

To build the new image, go to the directory with the Dockerfile and run the following:

```
docker build -t NEW_IMAGE_NAME -f Dockerfile .
```

This will create a new image called NEW_IMAGE_NAME based on this recipe. The period (.) at the end of the command means to use the current directory as the main source directory when working with the Dockerfile.[2]

3.8 Pushing the Image to Docker Hub

If you have an account on a container registry such as Docker Hub, if you name the container the same name as one of your repositories, you can push it with docker push IMAGE_NAME. For instance, I created a repository on Docker Hub called johnnyb61820/example-from-recipe. I then built the previous recipe with the following:

```
docker build -t johnnyb61820/example-from-recipe -f Dockerfile .
```

Since I did not specify a version (which I would have done by adding :my-version-identifier to johnnyb61820/example-from-recipe), it uses :latest as the default. I can then push my new image up to Docker Hub by first logging in with docker login and then giving a push command like this:

```
docker push johnnyb61820/example-from-recipe
```

This will push my image up to my repository. I can add a version tag onto it if I want to push a version other than the latest.

---

[1] If an ENTRYPOINT is specified, these arguments are *prepended* to the CMD command/arguments when running the container. Essentially, the ENTRYPOINT is the mandatory part of the container start command, and the CMD is the optional part. If the ENTRYPOINT is not specified, then the whole thing can be overridden.

[2] You may be wondering why the command is specifying the Dockerfile with the -f flag, since Dockerfile is the default name. The reason is that, under Podman, the default filename is actually Containerfile. By making the filename explicit, it works for both systems.

3.9 Logging into a Running Docker Container

Many times when running a service using a Docker container, it is helpful to have a login to the box and look around. If a Docker container is running, you can run other processes within that container using `docker exec`. Since many Docker containers contain at least a minimal Linux operating system, you can usually run `docker exec -it CONTAINER_ID /bin/sh` to get an interactive shell within a running Docker container.[3] However, `docker exec` only runs on actively running containers, not on stopped containers, so if your container stops, you will not be able to get a shell on it. Nevertheless, for interactively checking on and diagnosing problems in a running service, this trick is a lifesaver.

3.10 Summary

In this chapter, we learned the following:

- Docker will download and run images you specify on the command line and then save those images for when you request to run them later.

- Docker images can be as small as a single file, but most of them contain a stripped-down installation of a Linux distribution.

- Docker creates both a computerized and friendly name for each container so that you can manage them with various Docker commands.

- Container images can be either created from running containers or scripted through recipes called `Dockerfiles`.

- Container images can be pushed to Docker Hub where they can be accessed by other users or services.

---

[3] This does not work on the containers shown at the beginning of the chapter, since they only contained a single file and not a full distribution. Most containers you will encounter, however, include full distributions.

3.9 Logging into a Running Docker Container

3.10 Summary

CHAPTER 4

Best Practices for Building Containers

Container-building is an art form in and of itself. Ultimately, the goal of a container is to create an ultra-slim, single-task process.[1] However, while containers look a lot like virtual machines, we have to take a different approach and mindset to building containers than we normally apply to building virtual and physical machines.

In short, the principles we will be looking at in this chapter include the following:

- Containers are fundamentally different than virtual machines and should be treated as such.

- Containers should be limited to a single, unified task.

- Base images should be chosen with care.

- Container images should include as little of the operating system as is possible.

- All dependencies should be explicitly named in your `Dockerfile`.

- Care needs to be taken to avoid image bloating.

- Containers should be made to be easily configurable to the environment.

---

[1] By "task" here I don't mean the operating system concept of a task, but rather the Docker container should only do one thing.

33

© Jonathan Bartlett 2023
J. Bartlett, *Cloud Native Applications with Docker and Kubernetes*,
https://doi.org/10.1007/978-1-4842-8876-4_4

4.1 How Not to Build a Container

The best way to describe good container-building methodologies is to start by describing bad ones. The biggest (and probably most common) bad methodology for building containers is to treat a container as a slimmed-down version of a virtual machine (VM). This is a natural way of thinking because containers are indeed the successors of VMs in the data center. However, importing VM thinking into building a container will reduce your effectiveness considerably.

VMs are the successors of physical machines, and, in fact, they work essentially just like physical machines except for the ability to maintain hardware and software independently. Therefore, most of what worked when thinking about servers running on physical hardware transferred directly to thinking about servers running on VMs. It's tempting to continue to bring that information forward to the next step, but, at heart, it's a bad idea.

4.1.1 Don't Make a Container Perform Multiple Tasks

Essentially, when managing servers, system administrators or developers typically "organized" the server—adding a caching server, adding a proxy service, running file synchronization jobs, running scheduled tasks, etc. However, in cloud native architectures, this organization is done at a higher level—at the cluster level. As we will be discussing in Part 2, the Kubernetes system will essentially be acting as your cluster's operating system. You will organize Pods, Deployments, Services, and other Kubernetes workloads, which are all made up of containers. However, in order to enable this sort of orchestration to be maximally flexible and take advantage of all that Kubernetes has to offer, each container really needs to do only a single "thing."

Now, I recognize that "thing" is inherently a fuzzy concept. However, the way that I think about it is this—if you would naturally manage it separately, it's a separate thing. For instance, scheduled jobs are usually managed separately from the main service. Therefore, scheduled jobs are a separate "thing." Caching servers have their own configuration, their own command-line options, run on their own port, and run in a separate process than your main task. It is a separate "thing."

For larger systems such as the PostgreSQL database, even though it technically runs several very different processes under its main task (an autovacuumer, a stats collector, a log writer, etc.), it all follows from a single configuration file, all run under a single start/

stop command that manages the whole thing. Therefore, since *you* are only managing one thing (the PostgreSQL configuration as a whole), you can consider larger systems like this a single "thing."

4.1.2 Don't Include an Entire Operating System

The second thing that is tempting is to build your container images with lots of additional tools. Some people take a base Linux distribution, add every package they can imagine, and then build all of their containers on top of that.

The problem here is that it ultimately hurts your containers in several ways:

- The more things you include in your container image, the more things an attacker can take advantage of. This is known as the "attack surface" of your container image. The more things you install just give attackers one more potentially buggy tool that can be exploited.[2]

- Bigger containers hide dependencies. One of the goals of containerization is to be more explicit about our operating system dependencies. If we throw the whole operating system into our container, then we may miss the fact that our container depends on having ImageMagick installed, or some other dependency. Containers usually come with only the bare minimum, and you should add each dependency explicitly so that you have documented what is needed to run your application. The "bare minimum" usually includes a shell, a few standard system utilities, package management tools, and the most common system libraries and configuration files.

- Bigger containers tempt developers to *add* hidden dependencies. If it is already on the container, why not make use of it, right? Developers are usually quick to use anything and everything that is available to them. Making slim containers forces developers to make choices and explicitly log them in the `Dockerfile`. This means that all developers

---

[2] This is somewhat mitigated by Kubernetes itself—your containers aren't generally going to be running as root in the host system, so attackers are limited by what they can do *already*. However, it is a best practice just not to give them a handle anyway.

are more likely to use the same tools for similar tasks, because they will recognize which specific tools are already present (since they are there explicitly).

- Bigger containers require more maintenance. One thing I've learned in life (both in computing and in my personal life) is that everything requires maintenance at some point. If you have a bigger house, you have more rooms to clean. Another bathroom also means more pipes that can break. The same is true of computers. Every package you add will have to be monitored and updated due to security vulnerabilities or will eventually stop working with something else you have installed. Overall, it's best to go for the minimalist approach.

- Bigger containers are, well, bigger. The nice thing about containers is that, even with a bigger container, running multiple of the same image doesn't add *additional* disk space. However, it does use the space once, and that can be wasteful. This is especially true if you have different applications which don't share much of the same base image running on the same host. Additionally, it takes time and network traffic to transfer images as well as disk space in the container registry to store them.

- Bigger containers make it hard to switch base images. If you have a lot of hidden dependencies, switching Linux distributions can be quite a pain. The tool doesn't work exactly the same, or the paths used are different. Having slim images with explicit dependencies means that you know everything that is in your image, so you also know what you will have to test or possibly modify if you switch Linux distributions.

A good, achievable goal for most containers is to keep them under 100MB. Most of my containers are significantly smaller.

Now that we know how *not* to build containers, let's look at some good container practices we should be adopting.

4.2 Base Images

For most development platforms, there is a base image available that only contains (a) the minimal operating system install and (b) the minimum install of the language and platform needed to pull in other dependencies. For instance, the standard ruby image on Docker Hub contains the base operating system, Ruby, RubyGems (the package system), and Bundler (the dependency manager). Your container build script can then use this standard image to pull in additional dependencies, both from the operating system and from the platform.

I highly recommend using the standard base images wherever possible. Using standard images allows for better maintenance, because the actual platform maintenance will be handled by the platform itself. If you need to update the version of your platform, it usually just means updating the base image version at the top of your Dockerfile and moving on. The container images for the standard platforms are generally very high quality, and I highly recommend them.

Additionally, you should think about the version tags you are using for your base image. Using latest (or not specifying one at all) means that every time you rebuild your image, you will get an up-to-date version. The problem, however, is that sometimes your project may not run correctly on the latest upgrade. On the other hand, if you use a tag that is specific to the latest point release, you might find that this base image gets removed if a security bug is found.

You should basically balance two things—how specifically you are relying on version-specific features and how problematic a broken build process is. Most of the time I try to target only major-level releases. This gives me pretty good flexibility for upgrading easily just by rebuilding containers, but doesn't run the risk of breaking the build when the project does a major overhaul.

Also remember that you don't actually know exactly what is on someone else's container image. Therefore, I would caution against using images except from known good sources. Just because some user has an image that they claim works well for a task does not guarantee that the image doesn't also contain malware. I tend to stick to official Docker Hub images, Bitnami images, and ones from the official organizations that run the projects.

4.3 Alpine Distributions

The Alpine Linux distribution started life as the Linux Router Project (LRP)—a project whose goal was to get Linux to run on tiny Wi-Fi routers in order to pack in additional features. The LRP enabled you to take a cheap Wi-Fi router and turn it into a VPN server or any of a number of complicated network tools. They created a specialized Linux distribution because the devices they were trying to fit Linux onto had so little memory and disk space.

While the Linux Router Project no longer exists, the distribution they built eventually became the Alpine Linux distribution—an ultrasmall Linux distribution which works as a *perfect* base for containers. The base image clocks in at only five megabytes (*megabytes*, not gigabytes)! Yes, that's the entire OS, including shell and all.

To fit in such a space, Alpine Linux has several differences from typical Linux distributions, however. First of all, most of the applications in Alpine are actually a single application called busybox. The actual application names, sh, vi, mv, rm, etc., are all symlinked to this one application. The application uses the name that it is called by in order to know what command to execute. That allows Alpine to fit its entire command structure in a single megabyte application. Second, rather than using the enormous GNU C Library, Alpine uses a smaller, stripped-down C library, known as musl.

Note that, on the whole, you won't notice too many differences between Alpine Linux and any other distribution, but occasionally you may run into slight differences dealing from either differences in the commands themselves or small differences in the C Library, though these are usually very rare and technical differences.[3]

Most major container images are available as both a regular image (usually based off of Debian) and an Alpine version. The Alpine versions usually have -alpine in their image tag names. So, for instance, for a basic webserver, there is an official nginx image. If you want to run the Debian-based image for version 1.21 of nginx, you would use the image nginx:1.21, but for the Alpine build you would use nginx:1.21-alpine. The Debian-based one is about 56 megabytes, while the Alpine one is only 10!

Ultimately, the differences are not huge (remember, the container image is only stored *once* on any given host no matter how many containers are running it). However, the larger GNU C Library that comes standard in non-Alpine distributions uses more memory, which can cost money when running containers in the cloud.

---

[3] The one difference I've seen come into play is that Alpine has a very small thread stack size. So, if you run into stack errors on multithreaded apps on Alpine, that could be the cause.

4.4 Avoid Bloated Images from Deleted Files

The biggest surprise when building containers is that the RUN command builds a single layer which *cannot* be removed. That doesn't mean the *files* can't be removed—the next layer can remove them easily. However, the "deleted" files will still stay in your container image—forever.

Oftentimes, some stage of the build relies on having an entire development toolchain. The problem, here, is that you wind up carrying the entire development toolchain wherever you go, oftentimes *even if* you delete it later.

```
FROM debian AS builder

# Copy files from local directory
COPY . .
RUN apt install -y gcc make
RUN make

FROM debian
COPY --from=builder /PATH/TO/OUTPUT /DEST/PATH
```

Figure 4-1. *Multistage Build:* Dockerfile

Let's imagine the following snippet from a Dockerfile. Here, we are going to install gcc in one RUN command, use it in the next, and then remove it:

```
RUN apt install -y gcc
RUN gcc MY_C_FILES.c -o myapplication
RUN apt remove gcc
```

The problem here is that each RUN layer gets a *separate* layer. That means that we will install gcc in one layer and use it in the next to generate myapplication, and then the final layer will remove gcc. However, even though the containers running our image will not be able to see gcc (because it got removed in higher layers), it still *exists* in the lower layers! This means it has to be stored in the registry, transferred over the Internet when pulled, and stored on the final host machine, even though it is never used! I've seen images bloat more than an extra gigabyte through such processes.

There are three primary ways to avoid this tragic fate. The first is to put everything on the same RUN command. That's doable, but it makes the Dockerfile really messy. The second is to create a script in your build that contains (a) the setup installations, (b) the build, and (c) the teardown deinstallations all in one script. Either of these two methods will ensure that, by the end of the RUN command, only the files we wanted to add are in the layer.

The final mechanism is to use a separate container image for the build and then copy the specific, resulting files from the build into your main container image. This is known in the container world as a multistage build. Figure 4-1 shows an example Dockerfile implementing this. There, the build image is named builder, and we can then use the --from flag of the COPY command to load files from this build.

The different builds don't need to use the same container base, you can have as many stages you want, and only the last image gets saved and tagged.

4.5 Make Your Containers Configurable

The best containers are highly configurable through environment variables. Environment variables are the best way to pass information to a container from the outside. They are supported on every application platform and have thorough support in Kubernetes.

Anything that you might consider configuring should be exposed (and documented) as an environment variable. The location of every other service that your application needs to talk to should be configurable as an environment variable.

The end goal is to be able to take the exact same container image and use it locally in development, in the staging cluster, and in the production cluster, without any changes to the container image at all. This way, not only is production the same *code* as staging, but it is literally the same server image. Everything that is different between the two should be encoded in those environment variables. This makes mistakes not only rare but also easy to spot and diagnose.

Many containers for standard services come with shell scripts that read the environment variables and then do a number of pre-startup tasks (such as writing configuration files) and then hand off the actual operation of the container to the main service. The official postgres image is an example of an ideal system. You can set the data directory, the username and password, the authentication mechanism, and more through environment variables. On startup, the entrypoint is a shell script which puts together the configuration for the server and then runs an exec to start up the server itself.

The exec shell command causes the current shell process to be *replaced* by the given command. When a shell just invokes a command, both the shell and the command are taking up memory, while the shell waits for the command to complete. By finishing the setup with an exec, however, the shell process is physically replaced by the executed command, thus freeing up some additional memory. This is a very common startup pattern for containers.

For example, let us say that you are building an application that connects to a databases, a caching server, and a payment system. At minimum, you would want the hostnames and credentials for each of these services to be configurable via environment variables or similar mechanisms. If they needed to be written to a configuration file, then your startup script can take the environment variables, create the configuration file, and then start the application.

4.6 Be Clear About Your Statefulness

Managing state is an important task within a cluster. It is mostly important to be *clear* which containers are maintaining state, how they are maintaining it, and what are the effects of restarting those containers. One of the goals of a containerized infrastructure is to have no (or at least very few) containers which you actually care about. You care about the *system*, and, ideally, any particular container should be replaceable.

The easiest to manage containers are those that don't require any state. They don't need special disks allocated to them. They don't need any special setup or teardown. They just process, process, and process until we tell them to stop.

So, ideally, you want to not have state in your application. However, the fact is that the reason why someone uses your app at all is probably because it is holding some amount of state (data, files, etc.) that they care about. However, we should attempt to isolate the stateful aspects of our application as much as possible. In other words, we need to be clear about the statefulness of each container.

The following are some things to ask yourself for each container:

- Can the whole thing be shut down and replaced without any loss of function? (ideal)

- Does it need backing hard drive storage for its state?

- Does the backing hard drive storage need to keep on living after the container dies?

- Is there a good way for a new container to pick up where the previous container left off?

- What sort of coordination is required by these stateful activities?

- Is my application resilient enough to reconnect automatically if the stateful aspect goes offline, or will the whole cluster need to be individually restarted?

- What are the ordering considerations for any stateful components? What needs to be booted first? Second?

- How do you know when the stateful service is fully up and ready?

These are the types of things that a cluster administrator needs to keep in mind when thinking about stateful components. If a component is stateless, you don't have to think about these things—which is why statelessness is preferred as much as possible.

4.7 Final Tips

The following are a few final things to keep in mind for your containers:

- You should always be sure to run tests on a container running the image. Remember, containers are there because we are packaging *both* the operating system and the application as a single package. Therefore, we need to test to be sure that they run well together. Running your tests in a built container means that, if an upstream modification to a container image breaks your build, you are likely to catch it before sending it to production.

- Don't forget that, with the advent of Apple Silicon, a lot of developers aren't running the same CPU architecture anymore! Docker has the ability to create multi-architecture builds, or, more straightforwardly, you can specify `--platform=linux/amd64` in the `FROM` line of your `Dockerfile`, which will generate a 64-bit x86-compatible Linux image from either Mac or PC.[4]

- If, for some reason, you have a process that spawns children who don't get taken care of (they become "zombies"), you may need an init process to help. Docker containers don't have a standard init process to clean up zombie processes. However, there are packages such as `dumb-init` and `tini` that can help you out here. Normally, the presence of zombie processes is due to bad code or bad design, so always consider redesigning before switching to `dumb-init` or `tini` as a workaround.

- Scan your images. Most registries have the ability to regularly scan your images for vulnerabilities. Be sure to take advantage of this easy security boost.

- Get to know your distribution, and especially the package management tools. Most of your interaction with your distribution will be through its packaging tools, so be sure to get to know them well.

- Don't get too tricky. The Kubernetes infrastructure works best when everything works in an expected manner. The less "weird" your container image behaves, the more likely it will integrate into your cluster without causing headaches.

---

[4] Docker also has a tool called `buildx` for making both multi-distribution and multi-platform builds, but it is outside the scope of this book.

4.8 Summary

In this chapter, we learned the following:

- While containers are the next big advancement after virtual machines, there are a lot of differences between how containers and traditional servers are managed.

- Container images should be oriented to one, single task.

- Container images should be minimal, containing only the dependencies needed to run the application.

- Choose the base image for your container wisely.

- It is important to keep base images up to date with the latest security fixes, but you don't want new releases to break your application.

- Application tests should be run on a fully built container so that you test the complete operating system and application package.

- Containers should be made to be largely configurable through environment variables.

- Container images often contain an initial script which uses environment variables to create or modify configuration files and then runs exec to start the real service.

PART II

Introducing Kubernetes

CHAPTER 5

The Cloud Native Philosophy

Kubernetes is a cloud-level operating system which ties together multiple physical machines into a cluster and manages running and networking containers across these different machines. Before we dive into the details of how Kubernetes works, in this chapter, I want to take a step back and talk about the philosophy of cloud native applications. What is it that really makes Kubernetes (and other cloud native systems) tick? How is it that someone building a cloud native cluster thinks that is different from someone who is building a traditional server-side application?

5.1 Cloud-Level Operating System

The first difference in cloud native thinking is that the "operating system" has now moved. No longer is the operating system on the machine itself. I mean, technically, each machine must run an operating system, but we don't really care about the details of that—it's more of an implementation detail. What I mean is that the place where we actually perform regular development and maintenance tasks has changed.

In cloud native systems such as Kubernetes, Kubernetes essentially functions as a cloud-level operating system. I schedule containers on the cloud as a whole, not on individual machines. It is the Kubernetes system which takes this scheduling request and then makes the specific determination of which physical machine or cloud VM to run the container on. Take a moment to imagine a traditional bare-metal server that has a quad core CPU. If you run an application on that server, you don't care which core the operating system schedules a process on, do you? It is of no concern to you whether the process is running on core 0, 1, 2, or 3. That's the operating system's concern, not yours.

47

© Jonathan Bartlett 2023
J. Bartlett, *Cloud Native Applications with Docker and Kubernetes*,
https://doi.org/10.1007/978-1-4842-8876-4_5

Now, in this scenario, a well-written application will be able to *take advantage* of the fact that you have multiple cores, and a poorly written one will not. But, from an application level, or a system administrator level, the specific scheduling decisions of the operating system are not your concern. Likewise, in the cloud, any given container might be scheduled on any particular machine (called a Node in Kubernetes). Which particular machine that Kubernetes schedules the container to run on isn't really much more of our business than which core of the CPU the operating system schedules a process on.

Now, to be fair, when it comes to the cloud, since the containers are scheduled across the network (and possibly at different speeds, capacities, and latencies), which particular machine a container runs on winds up being *a little bit* our problem. Nonetheless, the mindset that you should employ as a default basis is that we are going to attempt to separate out responsibilities. The cloud administrator is responsible for telling Kubernetes what the pieces are and how they fit together. It is Kubernetes' job to figure out how that should work in practice. As much as possible, we should try to stick to our own roles in order to maximize the benefits from cloud native thinking.

In traditional server thinking, the operating system runs on the computer, and the system administrator handles processes. All networking and connections between machines are handled more or less manually and involve lots of configuration of the machines and processes involved. In cloud native thinking, the operating system runs on the cloud, and the system administrator handles containers. The networking and connections between the containers are simply declared, and the cluster itself figures out how to wire it all together.

5.2 Declarative Infrastructure

The next big idea in cloud native thinking is that the cluster is defined *declaratively*, not *imperatively*. What this means is that, on the whole, the way we will be managing the cluster is by defining files that tell Kubernetes what we *want* our end-state to be. We say what we want the end result to look like. It is Kubernetes job to figure out *how* to get there.

For instance, we would say, "Dear Kubernetes, I want to have a cluster that runs three instances of this container in a load-balanced configuration, and I would like an external IP address attached to the load balancer." Kubernetes is then responsible for getting it done. At the time you make your declaration, *you* are done, but Kubernetes is not. Kubernetes will continually check the state of its cluster and make changes to bring it into conformance with your requests.

Kubernetes will say, "the administrator asked for three instances of this container, but there aren't any running. I had better boot up a new one." Then it will say, "Oh yes—a load balancer was needed with an externally-facing IP address, and I haven't built one yet. I had better request one from the cloud provider and send traffic to these machines that I booted up." What IP addresses do those machines have that Kubernetes booted up? Frankly, you don't care. You don't have to know or configure them. You just tell Kubernetes that you want them load-balanced, and it will take care of figuring out how to tell the load balancer which IP addresses to send traffic to. That's entirely not your problem.

The classical approach of managing servers (which we try to avoid) is typically much more of an "imperative" approach. In such a mindset, you "do things" to your machines until they are in the correct state. Will you remember all of the steps for the next time you need to install them? Maybe, but probably not. Even worse is when certain situations may demand different steps, so you can't even necessarily script the list of commands to bring you to your goal. With a declarative approach, you are just saying what you want the *final* state to be and letting the system figure out the steps to get from where it is to where it needs to be.[1]

This brings a number of other advantages.

First of all, it allows you to treat your infrastructure as code. That is, the set of declarations of how we want our cluster to look can be put into files which are then checked in to a version-controlled system (we will get into this a lot more in Chapter 9). We have a readable, versioned declaration of what our cluster looks like that can be referenced (or changed) at any time. This means that newer system administrators don't need to know as much about the *history* of the cloud system, but only on its present configuration.[2]

---

[1] Now, some people talk about doing imperative Kubernetes management, but this is a bit of a misnomer. When people talk about doing imperative Kubernetes management, what they are usually talking about is creating Kubernetes resources directly through the command-line tool kubectl (as we will do in Chapter 7) rather than creating files and then applying them to the cluster (which we will do in Chapter 9). However, from a Kubernetes standpoint, both of these are actually declarative commands, as Kubernetes itself processes them identically. There are a handful of imperative Kubernetes commands, but they are generally geared toward debugging clusters.

[2] In traditional server management, much of a cloud's architecture is dictated by its history. This particular server may be running some process because it was the one that had the most memory available. That server is running an older version of the operating system because of a particular application that requires it. With cloud native development, these ideas are all baked into the containers themselves, and don't pose much of an issue for server management.

Additionally, since we are declaring end-states, this gives the cluster some amount of self-healing capabilities as well. If you said you wanted three instances of this container running, and one of them dies, the cluster will notice and boot a new one. The way Kubernetes works is with a *control loop* (actually a whole set of control loops). This loop continually performs the following steps:

1. Look at the state of the cluster itself.

2. Look at what the cluster configuration says the cluster's state needs to be.

3. Take the next appropriate action to bring the cluster's state in line with what the configuration states.

4. Perform a short delay before performing the loop again.

Using a control loop to ensure the cluster state is in line with our declarations allows for several benefits. First of all, our configuration commands are complete when the configuration is stored. We don't have to keep our software connected while we wait for the cluster to bring everything inline. Second, this gives Kubernetes some amount of self-healing power. Since Kubernetes is continually looking at the cluster's real state and comparing it to its configuration, it will detect misalignments, often even when the misalignment is due to a failure, and correct them.

5.3 Containers Are "Cattle" Not "Pets"

Another change in mindset that comes with a cloud native perspective is the way that we treat servers and containers. The analogy that is typically used is the difference between treating something as "cattle" compared to "pets." Historically, system administrators would treat their servers like pets. Each server was individually known and given a special name. If the server was having problems, the system administrator's goal was to nurse it back to health.

In a cloud native view, we view containers as being more like cattle. We don't expect our containers to be around forever, we don't care enough about each individual one to give it a name, and, if it gets sick, we shoot it and replace it with a new one.[3]

---

[3] This might sound like a harsh metaphor until you realize that, in the server world, the metaphor we use for a service restart involves demons killing their own children.

This means that administrators spend much less time on transient issues that are occurring and can instead focus their attention on the more architectural aspects of cloud administration.

In fact, even the servers (Nodes, in Kubernetes parlance) are replaceable. The actual server code is minimal, and if a Node is having hardware problems, it is easy enough to mark it as unavailable, drain the containers off of the Node, and then replace the server. Nothing complicated is involved with reconfiguring the cluster—everything will automatically shift to other hardware. When the Node is fixed, it will simply receive new jobs as they come in. This generally makes a cleaner separation between the roles of server management and cluster management.

Overall, the cloud native philosophy greatly improves the productivity of cloud administrators and makes the management of clouds much more straightforward.

5.4 A Note on Costs

One thing you should keep in mind while going through this book is that almost everything costs money. Thankfully, most cloud-based services on the Internet are charged by the hour, so as long as you shut everything down in a timely manner, the costs aren't problematic. However, you need to keep in mind that many of the things that are done on a Kubernetes service do in fact add charges to your monthly bill. The things that cost money depend on your cloud provider but tend to be anything which requires provisioning something from your cloud provider. Load balancers, disk volumes, and physical hardware generally all cost additional money, so, when you add them to your cluster, you are adding to your monthly bill. Just keep that in mind and be sure to delete resources that are not being used. Additionally, you should be sure that deleting any resource fully removes it from your account. Sometimes resource deletion only deletes it from the Kubernetes system itself, not from your cloud account.

In any case, it is always a good practice to watch your billing every month and know what you are spending money on. Don't leave things on that you aren't using, as it will just cost you money every month. Cloud services these days are fairly inexpensive, but the cost of leaving on systems you don't use adds up. Also remember, if you delete something from Kubernetes, always be sure to check that it was deleted *all the way* on your cloud account and you aren't still being charged for it.

5.5 Summary

In this chapter, we learned the following:

- Kubernetes is a cloud-level operating system. Kubernetes handles scheduling container-based applications across a number of physical machines similar to how your operating system schedules processes across multiple CPUs.

- Kubernetes allows you to focus on your cluster as a whole and not worry about details such as which service is running on which machine.

- Kubernetes operates declaratively, not imperatively. This means you tell Kubernetes the end-state of your cluster, and Kubernetes is responsible for determining how to get it there.

- The declarative approach has a number of advantages, including reduced reliance on the history of your implementation, the ability to version control your infrastructure, and the ability of Kubernetes to have some amount of self-healing.

- In the Kubernetes philosophy, containers are "cattle" not "pets," so each container should be developed to be disposable.

- The Kubernetes philosophy allows for a strong distinction in the roles of cloud architect and server management. Server management takes care of the physical machines and connecting them to the cluster, and the cloud architect takes that cluster and deploys containerized applications onto it.

CHAPTER 6

Getting Started with Kubernetes

Before we start covering the theory of Kubernetes in Chapter 8, this chapter will get you up and running with a real, live Kubernetes cluster. If I start talking about Kubernetes theory first, it tends to be pretty meaningless. If you start with some concrete Kubernetes usage, then, when I start talking about the theory, you will have a more concrete grasp of how things go together.

We are going to use Linode to create the cluster, because Linode's Kubernetes service is easy, low-cost, and reliable. You will need to sign up for an account on `Linode.com` to get started.

6.1 Setting Up Your First Cluster

Setting up a Kubernetes cluster in Linode is incredibly simple. From the Linode dashboard (`cloud.linode.com`), click the "Create" button and choose Kubernetes from the drop-down menu. This will bring up a screen that will ask you a few basic configuration questions to get your Kubernetes cluster running:

> **Cluster Label** This is the name of the cluster but can only take certain characters. I called mine `my-test-cluster`.
>
> **Region** This is the physical datacenter that you want your cluster running in. You can choose wherever you wish, but I used "Dallas, TX" for mine.
>
> **Kubernetes Version** We will be using the latest iteration of version 1 (1.23 at the time of writing).

53

© Jonathan Bartlett 2023
J. Bartlett, *Cloud Native Applications with Docker and Kubernetes*,
https://doi.org/10.1007/978-1-4842-8876-4_6

The next section is about the machines which will be running your cluster. These are organized into "Node Pools." We are only going to make a single node pool. You can find the lowest-cost machines under the "Shared CPU" tab. For this demo, I recommend adding three of the lowest-cost machine available. At the time of writing, this was a "Linode 2 GB" which costs $10 per month (each) or $0.015 per hour (each). Click the "Add" button to add those machines to your cluster.

At the bottom of your page, it will give you a monthly total and a button that says "Create Cluster." Click that button and Linode will begin creating your cluster!

It may take a few minutes for your cluster to be fully created. When it is done, the dashboard will have a downloadable "Kubeconfig" file available for you. Figure 6-1 shows what this looks like. Click the download link to download the Kubeconfig file to your local machine. This file contains the information you will need to access your cluster.

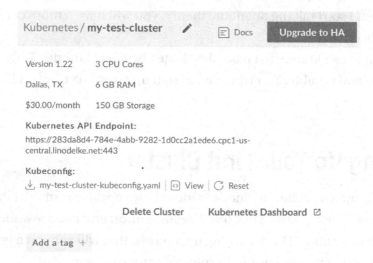

Figure 6-1. *Your Deployed Kubernetes Cluster*

Linode comes pre-equipped with a Kubernetes application called the Kubernetes dashboard, which gives you a web-based interface for managing your Kubernetes cluster. To access this, just click the "Kubernetes Dashboard" link shown in Figure 6-1. This will ask you for an authentication method. Choose "Kubeconfig", and then, in the box below, upload the Kubeconfig file you previously downloaded to your computer. Then, click "Sign In."

The starting dashboard is shown in Figure 6-2. On the left are the different types of resources (called "objects" in Kubernetes terms) that Kubernetes can manage. At the top is a "namespace" selector, which is currently set to `default`. The main part of the screen says, "There is nothing to display here" because we haven't deployed anything yet.

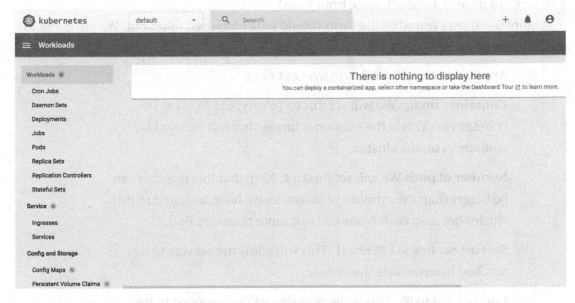

Figure 6-2. *The Starting Kubernetes Dashboard*

To see the machines that are included in your cluster, on the left-hand menu, go down to the "Cluster" section and click "Nodes." This should give you a list of three entries representing the machines that we originally added to the cluster.[1] With Kubernetes, however, we don't care too much about the physical hardware, as long as there is enough available for everything we want to do. How the applications are distributed on that hardware is managed by Kubernetes itself. Nonetheless, this section will show you Kubernetes' view of your hardware.

6.2 Deploying Your First Application

Normally in Kubernetes, deployments are managed by YAML manifest files which can themselves be under source control. However, to get started quickly, the Kubernetes dashboard provides a simple web interface to deploy a basic application.

---

[1] Note that these are themselves likely to be Virtual Machines, not bare-metal hardware. However, the point is that they represent some real resource the cluster has available to it.

To start the process, click the "+" icon on the top right of the screen. That will bring a new screen which gives you three options: "Create from input," "Create from file," or "Create from form." Choose "Create from form."

Figure 6-3 shows you what the form should look like when filled out. We are going to set the following:

> **App name** We will set this to my-test-app.
>
> **Container image** We will set this to johnnyb61820/simple-web-server. This is the container image that will be used for containers on the cluster.
>
> **Number of pods** We will set this to 4. Note that this number can be bigger than the number of instances we have assigned to this cluster because each Node can run more than one Pod.
>
> **Service** Set this to External. This will allow the service to be reached from outside the cluster.
>
> **Port** Set this to 80. This is the port that will be exposed to the external world.
>
> **TargetPort** Set this to 8070. This is the port that our containers are listening on. The container specified here listens on port 8070.
>
> **Protocol** Set this to TCP.

Create from input   Create from file   Create from form

App name *   An 'app' label with this value will be added to the
my-test-app   Deployment and Service that get deployed. Learn
                                              more ☑

                                11 / 24

Container image *   Enter the URL of a public image on any registry, or a
johnnyb61820/simple-web-server   private image hosted on Docker Hub or Google
                                              Container Registry. Learn more ☑

Number of pods *   A Deployment will be created to maintain the
4   ⌄   desired number of pods across your cluster. Learn
                                              more ☑

Service *   Optionally, an internal or external Service can be
External   ▼   defined to map an incoming Port to a target Port
                                              seen by the container. Learn more ☑

Port *   Target port *   Protocol *
80   ⌄   8070   ⌄   TCP ▼   🗑

                                  Protocol *
Port   ⌄   Target port ⌄   TCP ▼

[Deploy]   Cancel   Show advanced options

Figure 6-3. *Creating a Deployment with a Form*

Once all of that is set, click the "Deploy" button. At the time of this writing, there was
a bug in the dashboard which says you have unsaved changes and asks if you really want
to leave. Just click "Yes." You should now wait a few minutes (probably five minutes to be
safe) for Kubernetes to get your app started.

That's all there is to it! You now have a (small) web application deployed to
Kubernetes. To access your web application, click the "Services" tab on the left-hand
side. One of the services listed should be your my-test-app service, and to the right
there should be a column titled "External Endpoints" which has a link to where your
application was deployed. Click that link, and it should say, "Hello from your container!"

6.3 Looking Around the Kubernetes Dashboard

Now that you have an application deployed on Kubernetes, it's time to take a short tour of the Kubernetes dashboard. All of this information can be accessed from the command line, but the visual dashboard helps to guide you about what is available.

Our deployment in the previous section essentially created four types of objects: Services, Deployments, ReplicaSets, and Pods. Figure 6-4 shows how they relate to each other.

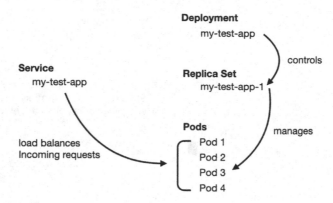

Figure 6-4. *Kubernetes Cluster Objects*

At the top of the chart, we have a "Deployment." Deployments have one basic job—controlling "ReplicaSets." A ReplicaSet is essentially an image which the cluster wants multiple identical instances of. When we specified our container image, that is what the ReplicaSet replicates. It will create many containers from this image. The deployed containers are called "Pods." A Pod can technically have more than one container, but for right now we can view them as roughly the same thing. We asked for four Pods, which are created and managed by the ReplicaSet.

You might be wondering why we need both Deployments and ReplicaSets. The reason is that if we change versions of our application, then the Deployment will manage creating the new ReplicaSet (we will need a new one since it will be a different container image) and then turning off the old ReplicaSet once the new one is up and running. In general, we directly interact with Deployments in Kubernetes, and the Deployments then creates, manages, and removes ReplicaSets as needed, and those ReplicaSets in turn manage creating and running the Pods themselves.

We now have several Pods running our application, but we need a way to access them. A "Service" is a named endpoint (internal or external) in the cluster. Services can load balance between multiple Pods that implement the same service. Therefore, if someone requests a Service endpoint, the service then routes that request to an appropriate Pod for processing.

So how does the Service know which Pods can handle which requests? Imagine if you had multiple different Deployments running, each doing different things. How would the Service know which one to point to? Most objects in Kubernetes have "Labels" attached to them. Labels are essentially arbitrary key/value pairs attached to objects. While they can be arbitrary, there are some predefined standard ones as well which can be used. The Service implements a "selector" which finds Pods based on their labels. The labels for the Pods are initially defined in the Deployment, copied to the ReplicaSet, and then copied to the Pod. The Service then uses the label to know which Pods can handle requests. Since the Service was created as an "External" service, a load balancer was created for it, which also gives it an IP address that can be accessed from outside the cluster.

Now that we know what was deployed, we can look around the Kubernetes dashboard and find these things. You can find Deployments, ReplicaSets, and Pods in the "Workloads" section and Services under the "Service" section. Feel free to click around these different areas.

As you click around, notice that nearly everything has a name and a set of labels. The name only has to be unique to the object type. Note that in our current deployment, both the Service and the Deployment are named my-test-app. Personally, I don't like giving things the same name, but that is what the form-created service deployments do automatically.

Each object in Kubernetes can be modified through a YAML manifest file. To the right of each object is a button with three dots. Clicking that button will give you the option of editing the object. If you click the "Edit" button, you can see what the YAML manifest for that object looks like. Taking a look at these different object configurations will give you a preview of what we will be learning in subsequent chapters.

6.4 Summary

In this chapter, we learned the following:

- A Kubernetes cluster can be easily created with a few clicks.

- The Kubeconfig file contains the information needed to access the cluster.

- The Kubernetes Dashboard is a web application that helps you view information about your cluster.

- A simple Kubernetes application consists of a Deployment (which manages ReplicaSets which manage Pods) and a Service (which manages creating an endpoint to access and load-balancing between the Pods).

- Pods are what actually run on the hardware, and they consist of one or more running containers.

- ReplicaSets manage groups of identical Pods.

- A Deployment is essentially a versioned ReplicaSet. It allows releasing new versions of a container image, and then creates a new ReplicaSet with that image, and destroys the old ReplicaSet.

- Labels are used for a variety of tasks within Kubernetes. They are used by ReplicaSets to manage Pods and by the Service to find Pods for load-balancing.

- External Services create a load balancer which has external IP addresses that can be used to access the containers from outside the cluster.

CHAPTER 7

Managing Kubernetes with `kubectl`

In this chapter, we are going to take the Kubernetes cluster we put together in Chapter 6 and learn how to control it from the command line using the Kubernetes administration tool, `kubectl`. See Appendix B.4 if you need help installing this tool.

7.1 Setting Up Your Connection

In Chapter 6, you downloaded a Kubeconfig file from your Kubernetes cluster. This file has all of the information needed to connect to your Kubernetes cluster. The file is a YAML file which includes information such as the following:

- The location of the Kubernetes API server that can be used to control your Kubernetes cluster

- Certificates used by your Kubernetes cluster for verification

- A user of the system

- A token that the user can use to access the system

Technically, the Kubeconfig file can hold information about a variety of Kubernetes clusters and users. Therefore, the Kubeconfig file also has a list of "contexts" which define the user-to-server mappings available and a "current context" which tells `kubectl` which mapping to use currently. The one you downloaded in Chapter 6 only has a single server, user, and context and sets that context to be the current context.

There are three ways to get `kubectl` to find your Kubeconfig file:

1. Every time you run `kubectl`, specify `--kubeconfig=/PATH/TO/KUBECONFIG` as part of the command line.

© Jonathan Bartlett 2023
J. Bartlett, *Cloud Native Applications with Docker and Kubernetes*,
https://doi.org/10.1007/978-1-4842-8876-4_7

2. Set the environment variable KUBECONFIG to be the location of the Kubeconfig file.[1]

3. Copy the Kubeconfig file to the standard location, which, from your home directory, is .kube/config.

The commands given going forward will assume that you did option 2 or option 3. If you chose option 1, you will need to modify the commands to reference the Kubeconfig file.

To see if you have downloaded and configured everything properly, issue the following command:

```
kubectl get nodes
```

This should return a list of the physical nodes that were originally created in Chapter 6. My output looks like this:

```
NAME                          STATUS    ROLES     AGE    VERSION
lke56032-87892-623e0e04d72b   Ready     <none>    20h    v1.23.6
lke56032-87892-623e0e04dfc4   Ready     <none>    20h    v1.23.6
lke56032-87892-623e0e04e7ca   Ready     <none>    20h    v1.23.6
```

If you get similar output and no errors, you are ready to move on.

7.2 Basic kubectl Commands

While the kubectl command manages a lot of different aspects of your cluster, there is a general format to the command that covers a large portion of its usage.

The general format is as follows:

```
kubectl COMMAND RESOURCE [NAME-OF-OBJECT] [OPTIONS]
```

In our starting example, the command was kubectl get nodes. Here, the command was get and the resource was nodes. Note that the resource name is not case-sensitive or even plural-sensitive (you can call the resource node, nodes, NODES, or NoDeS). In

---

[1] Remember that environment variables disappear when you end your current session. So, if you want your computer to remember this value past your current session, you need to modify your profile to set the environment on session startup.

Kubernetes, a "resource" is a pool of objects of the same type. The Node resource refers to all of the Node objects in the Kubernetes system.

Additionally, resources have shorter names which can be used instead. The short code for node is no. Therefore, the command could have been written as kubectl get no.

In the preceding example, one of my nodes was named lke56032-87892-623e0e04dfc4. Therefore, I can ask about that specific node object using the following command:

```
kubectl get node lke56032-87892-623e0e04dfc4
```

Note that this returns the same data as before, since it was using the same command (get). If you wanted more data, you can use the describe command:

```
kubectl describe node lke56032-87892-623e0e04dfc4
```

There are several kubectl commands available for most resources. These include the following:

> **get** Returns a list of the objects in that resource.
>
> **describe** Describes the details of an object in that resource.
>
> **create** Creates an object in that resource.
>
> **set** Updates an object in a resource by setting certain values. This command adds a SUBCOMMAND argument after the command.
>
> **edit** Starts an editor containing a YAML file describing the object for you to edit and updates the object when the file is saved and the editor exits.
>
> **delete** Removes the specified object from the resource.
>
> **explain** Gets documentation about a resource and the fields it supports.

There are a lot of other commands available for kubectl which deal with highly specific actions for various resources. For instance, the cordon command is used on Nodes to tell Kubernetes to no longer schedule new Pods to this Node. Appendix C has a lot of additional commands, but you will need to read more of this book before you fully understand what they do.[2]

So, in my case, I could prevent new Pods from being scheduled to one of the nodes by typing the following:

```
kubectl cordon lke56032-87892-623e0e04dfc4
```

Note that this command, since it is specific to Nodes, does not require me to specify node in the command and in fact gives an error if you do.

7.3 Playing with `kubectl`

Play with your cluster by retrieving information about different resources and objects in your system. Some commands to get you started are as follows:

```
kubectl get services
kubectl get deployments
kubectl get replicasets
kubectl get pods
```

You can then use the `describe` command to get further information about the objects that are returned. This will give you more information than you know what to do with, but it will help you to get a glimpse of what we will be talking about in later chapters.

Another thing we can do is show how the ReplicaSet objects work. Remember that in Chapter 6 we created a Deployment, which created a ReplicaSet which created a group of identical Pods. The `kubectl get pods` command will show you a list of Pods. Type in the command `kubectl delete pod PODNAME` using one of the Pods retrieved. This will destroy the Pod, its container, and any other associated pieces of the Pod. However, since the Pod was started as part of a ReplicaSet which wants four Pods to be running, the ReplicaSet will notice that the Pod is missing and create a new one. If you now run `kubectl get pods`, you will find that there are still four Pods, but the one you deleted has been automatically replaced. This is the self-healing power of declarative programming in action.

---

[2] Additionally, the reference guide for `kubectl` is available at `https://bit.ly/kubectl-reference`.

7.4 Creating Another Deployment with `kubectl`

Now let's create a second deployment that is essentially identical to the one we created in Chapter 6 but created manually using `kubectl` instead of through the user interface.

The user interface created two objects in Kubernetes—a Deployment and a Service. There were other objects as well, but they were created by the Deployment—the Deployment created a ReplicaSet which created the Pods.

So, let's start with a Deployment. We will name it `my-test-deployment`. Create it with the following command:

```
kubectl create deployment my-test-deployment \
    --image johnnyb61820/simple-web-server \
    --replicas=2
```

Now, there are two ways of creating the Service. There is a specialized command called `kubectl expose` which creates a Service for a Deployment in one step. However, we are going to do this the longer way by creating the Service manually. The reason for this is that it will better match the final approach we take in later chapters.

The first step for exposing your deployment to the world is simply creating the Service. Service creation has an extra argument sandwiched between the resource and the object's name, which is the type of Service we want. We won't go through all the types of services here, but the type we want is `LoadBalancer`, as that will create an externally facing load balancer that we can reach from outside the cluster. Create the service using the following command:

```
kubectl create service loadbalancer my-test-service --tcp=80:8070
```

This creates an externally facing load balancer Service which will listen on port 80 and forward that to port 8070 on the target Pods. However, right now, it doesn't know *which* Pods to send requests to. Running `kubectl get services` would show you the external IP address, but if you tried to access it you would get nothing.

Services find Pods by their label. To find the label being used by the Pods under our Deployment, run `kubectl describe deployment my-test-deployment`. There will be a section titled "Pod Template," which will show the labels used for pods created by this deployment. In my case, it says `app=my-test-deployment`. Therefore, we need to tell our Service to look for that label by setting the Service's label selector:

```
kubectl set selector service my-test-service app=my-test-deployment
```

Now you can access the load balancer Service via its external IP address which will be sending requests to our deployment.

7.5 Accessing Multiple Clusters

If you run more than one Kubernetes cluster, you will need to set up your environment to work with them. Of course, you can append the `--kubeconfig` option to each command to specify which cluster you are accessing, but no one really wants to do that. However, the `KUBECONFIG` environment variable can refer to multiple Kubeconfig files, separated by a separator. On Linux and Mac, the separator is a colon (`:`), and on Windows it is a semicolon (`;`). Essentially, the `kubectl` command merges these files into a single file that it uses as your configuration.

You can manipulate your configuration using `kubectl`'s `config` command. If you have more than one Kubeconfig file set, then you can show the contexts that are available to you by issuing the command `kubectl config get-contexts`. I have two setups, and it returns an output that looks like this:

```
CURRENT    NAME          CLUSTER      AUTHINFO         NAMESPACE
           lke55986-ctx  lke55986     lke55986-admin   default
*          lke56032-ctx  lke56032     lke56032-admin   default
```

The output shows the name of the context and, next to it, the cluster and the user it is associated with. The star (*) indicates which context I am currently using.

To switch contexts, I just use the `use-context` command:

```
kubectl config use-context lke55986-ctx
```

Now when you use `kubectl config get-contexts`, it will show the other context as being the current context.

You may be wondering how common it is to be running multiple clusters. In fact, it is very common. To begin with, most people run separate staging and production clusters. Additionally, you might have multiple clusters set up in different datacenters. This can give you high availability (if one datacenter goes offline), or it can give you geographical-based services (responding to requests using a geographically closer datacenter). Additionally, many organizations separate applications into different clusters.

In any case, even if this is your first (and currently only) cluster to administer, trust me, you will eventually be managing more!

7.6 Summary

In this chapter, we learned the following:

- `kubectl` is the tool used for command-line management of Kubernetes clusters.

- The Kubeconfig file contains access information for your Kubernetes cluster, and the `kubectl` command relies on this file to access the cluster.

- `kubectl` commands have a basic structure that is largely consistent across various Kubernetes resources.

- Kubernetes objects can be created, listed, described, modified, and deleted using `kubectl`.

- The current user/cluster combination is called a "context," and `kubectl` allows you to switch between contexts for managing multiple clusters.

CHAPTER 8

An Overview of the Kubernetes Environment

Now that you have some concrete experience using Kubernetes, this chapter will present the basic theory of how a Kubernetes cluster works. We won't talk about *how* to accomplish these things in the present chapter—the goal is to provide you with a broad understanding of the components of Kubernetes. In later chapters, we will discuss how to actually set up Kubernetes to make use of these ideas. I imagine you will return to this chapter frequently to remind yourself of how all of the pieces fit together.

8.1 Basic Kubernetes Components

Kubernetes comes with a lot of different components, and it is hard to get them all shown on the same diagram, so we are going to just do a few at a time. The first figure we are going to look at is a high-level picture of what a Kubernetes cluster looks like. Figure 8-1 shows the basic setup, which we will cover in this section.

You will see here a separation between the internal Kubernetes network and the Internet. Note that this separation is not necessarily physically enforced. That is, depending on your cluster provider, this traffic may or may not be cordoned off from the rest of the Internet. When running on Linode, Kubernetes traffic is only seen by nodes within the cluster, but that is not a general Kubernetes guarantee.

© Jonathan Bartlett 2023
J. Bartlett, *Cloud Native Applications with Docker and Kubernetes*,
https://doi.org/10.1007/978-1-4842-8876-4_8

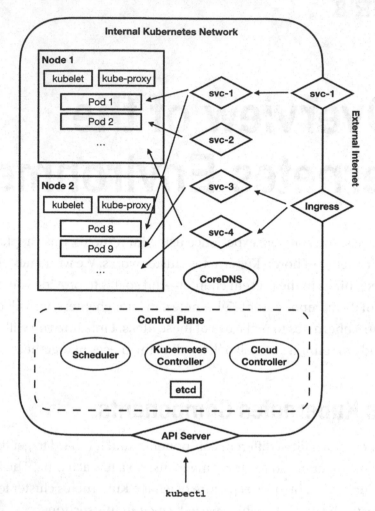

Figure 8-1. *Basic Kubernetes Components*

8.1.1 The Control Plane

Within the Kubernetes cluster, there is a control plane. This is the cluster management center. All of the decision-making about the cluster occurs here. What is the present state of the cluster? Do we need to launch more Pods for a Deployment? Those sorts of decisions are made by the control plane.

You can think of the control plane as being divided up into several pieces:

- The cloud controller is used for interacting with native resources from your cloud provider. While Kubernetes provides a lot of functionality, some features (such as load balancers, physical hardware, and disk drives) are rooted in the cloud's platform itself.

- The Kubernetes controller is used for interacting with Kubernetes-provided resources. The Kubernetes controller performs the physical actions associated with launching Pods, Services, and other features that run on top of the cloud-provided resources. There are usually separate controllers for various different aspects of Kubernetes.

- The scheduler figures out what needs to be done. The scheduler figures out when Pods need to be deployed and what Nodes they need to be deployed on.

- etcd stores the configuration and state of the entire cluster. All of the other services use etcd to know what they should be doing.

The control plane is accessed through the API server, which acts as the gateway into the Kubernetes cluster. Essentially, whenever you use kubectl, it talks to the API server, which then tells the control plane what to do. You will rarely if ever need to directly worry about what happens on the control plane itself. Just realize that Kubernetes is running several processes to keep your cluster working the way that you have requested it.

8.1.2 Nodes and Pods

Within the cluster are Nodes. A Node is essentially a physical or virtual machine allocated to the cluster. Each Node runs two required processes—kubelet, which physically launches Pods as requested from the control plane, and kube-proxy, which keeps the networking rules on the Node up-to-date with those specified in the cluster and makes sure that the Pods can access all of the cluster resources they are permitted to.

The kubelet process launches Pods, which are the basic unit of management in Kubernetes. A Pod usually consists of a single running container, but they can actually be configured to be running more than one container for more advanced use cases. We will talk more about Pods in Section 8.2.

8.1.3 Workloads

A workload is a management tool for launching Pods. While a Pod can be managed and launched individually, usually they are launched as part of a workload, which provides additional visibility for making sure that the Pod is up and running when it is supposed to be.

There are a few basic workload types in Kubernetes:

Pod: A pod is the smallest workload unit. Pods are rarely created/managed directly by the cloud administrator (except for debugging purposes). Pods are usually managed by other workload objects in the system.

Deployment/ReplicaSet: A ReplicaSet manages a number of Pods which should all be running the same containers and configuration. As we saw in Chapter 6, ReplicaSets are usually themselves managed by Deployments, which handle gracefully deploying and migrating between versions of the ReplicaSet.

StatefulSet: A StatefulSet is like a ReplicaSet, but the member Pods are not necessarily identical and may require some amount of ordering to properly boot up. These usually also have some sort of permanent storage attached to them (see Appendix D.4 for more information on StatefulSets).

DaemonSet: A DaemonSet is used to schedule Pods that run per Node in your cluster (for instance, an intrusion detection monitor).

Job/CronJob: A Job defines a process that runs to a completion point and then stops. A CronJob is a Job that recurs according to a set schedule.

8.1.4 Kubernetes Services

A Service is used to identify a feature of the cluster. Services provide stable endpoints to hit, even when the underlying Pods may be continually recycling. A Service, when it is first deployed, receives a stable IP address on the cluster that the cluster uses to access that Service as long as it is deployed. Whether the Service is served by one or many underlying Pods, the rest of the cluster does not worry about the specifics of the Pods; it just directs traffic to the Service.

There are several types of Services as well:

> **ClusterIP**: A ClusterIP service is simply an IP address internal to the cluster which routes traffic to one or more underlying Pods. You can think of it as a load balancer that is internal to the network. For ClusterIP services, the load-balancing is generally done at the networking layer, with no usage of actual load-balancing hardware. In other words, creating a ClusterIP service usually won't incur monthly charges for using a load balancer from your cloud provider.

> **LoadBalancer**: A LoadBalancer service is like a ClusterIP, but the IP address is exposed outside of the network, usually using a load-balancing technology that is native to the cloud platform you are using. Since this relies on the native cloud implementation, if you have set up Kubernetes on your own personal hardware, you may not have access to this service type. However, it is available on most cloud providers.

> **NodePort**: A NodePort sets up an externally facing port on every Node which proxies that port to the Pods that implement the service. This is useful if you have set up your own Kubernetes cluster yourself and don't have access to load balancers.

> **ExternalName**: An ExternalName service simply gives an internal name to an external DNS name. For instance, one could imagine setting up a service named `search-service` to refer to `customsearch.googleapis.com`. These do not generally refer traffic to Pods within the cluster.

In Figure 8-1, several Services are shown. The Service `svc-2` is a ClusterIP service—it is an internal-only service that is available only to Pods on the cluster. The Service `svc-1` is a LoadBalancer Service—it is exposed externally to the public. However, it also operates internally to the cluster like a ClusterIP service.

The Services `svc-3` and `svc-4` are ClusterIP services but are made available to the external world through an Ingress. An Ingress is similar to a Service but is HTTP-specific and layered on top of existing Services. An Ingress is primarily used for allowing access to cluster Services from the outside.

Ingresses are different from LoadBalancer services because they offer several features unique to HTTP services. First of all, an Ingress handles TLS/SSL termination. What this means is that certificate handling only has to be set up on the Ingress, and traffic can flow and be handled unencrypted throughout the rest of the cluster. This makes managing and updating certificates much easier than trying to make sure each Pod has the right setup. Additionally, since this is handled on the Ingress (and not in the Pod itself), certificate management becomes an infrastructure issue, not an application issue.[1] This allows your developers to worry about the application, and your devops/sysadmins/netadmins worry about the certificates. However, this presumes that traffic flowing inside your Kubernetes network is either isolated or encrypted, which depends on your provider. On Linode, the network traffic is isolated from other clusters.

Another purpose for an Ingress is to manage URL paths that are developed and maintained as separate applications. Many APIs are structured so that certain hostnames and paths are really separate Services. Ingresses provide a way to say, for instance, that /my-app gets forwarded to one Service and /my-other-app gets forwarded to another. This allows the individual Services to be managed and updated separately (perhaps by separate teams) but merged into a unified API when accessed by the external world.

8.1.5 CoreDNS

So, if we deploy a Service in Kubernetes, how do the Pods find the Service? In Kubernetes, a Service is given a fixed name and a fixed *internal* cluster IP address. Then, it stores the name-to-address mapping in CoreDNS, which is the local DNS provider for all Pods on your Kubernetes cluster.[2]

---

[1] Depending on how your cluster is ultimately configured, some certificates (such as database access certificates) may still need to be managed on the application level. However, I usually advocate for avoiding this where possible, implementing Kubernetes on networks where the interior of the Kubernetes network is generally trusted. In any case, an Ingress at least allows you to minimize the amount of application-level certificate handling that is needed.

[2] You might hear this referred to as KubeDNS sometimes, because that was the name of the previous DNS implementation. KubeDNS was replaced by CoreDNS as the default DNS several years ago, and full support for KubeDNS was removed in version 1.21. Nevertheless, the Service name kube-dns still exists in the kube-system namespace for legacy purposes.

CoreDNS allows you to simply give your service a name and know that the name will be respected in all Pods within the cluster. Because the cluster creates a unique internal IP address for the Service, it is fine if your Pod caches the resolved address of the Service—that IP address will be fixed as long as the Service exists on the cluster.

There is very little about Kubernetes itself that your Pods need to know. Rarely do Pods interact with the Kubernetes API Server or even the kubelet running on its own Node. For the most part, the structure of the Kubernetes cluster is relayed to Pods as hostnames. Simply because CoreDNS is the default resolver for the cluster, all name-based Service lookups will automatically find the right IP address.

8.1.6 The Structure of a Pod

Usually, we think about Pods as just being containers. However, the actual Pod structure is a little more complicated than that.

A Pod can actually run multiple containers. However, the containers all share the same basic system context. Normally, containers have a completely isolated view of things—for all they know, they are by themselves on a machine and have total (and unique) access to all ports, filesystems, sockets, and other system resources. However, with Pods, many of these resources are actually shared.

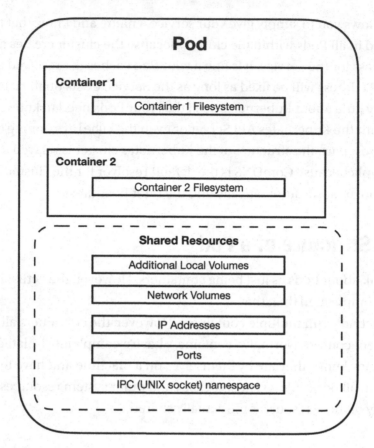

Figure 8-2. *Pod Structure*

Figure 8-2 shows the basic layout of a Pod. For a single-container Pod, nothing is surprising—it is just a container with normal container resources. However, for a multi-container Pod, while they each have their own local container filesystems (based on their container image), they can share volumes (either local or remote) that get mounted into their filesystem.

Additionally, since the containers share IP addresses, they can talk to each other over localhost. Since they also share an interprocess communication (IPC) namespace, they can also communicate using standard UNIX IPC mechanisms.[3]

Why would you want to run multiple containers on a Pod? Generally speaking, this happens when you want a secondary process to be a "helper" to your primary process. Some examples of this include the following:

---

[3] Note that in order to do UNIX-domain sockets, both containers would need to mount a shared local volume.

- One container runs your main service while the other container runs a caching service such as `memcached` or `redis`.

- One container generates logs to a shared volume, and the other container regularly copies those logs to a standard logging server.

- One container serves HTTP requests, while the other container synchronizes static files from an external source. Essentially, they would share a local volume where one container wrote to the volume and the other container served the files via HTTP.

These types of helper containers are often referred to as *sidecars*. They perform an important system service but are essentially running "off to the side" of the main application. Another set of uses of multiple containers are known as *adapters* or *ambassadors*. An adapter essentially provides some essential bridge—either between users and the main container or between the main container and the rest of the network. Examples of adapters include the following:

- A web application firewall put in front of your main web application to prevent abuse

- A VPN bridge/proxy to open up ports/networking to another network

- A service discovery proxy, which allows the main container to always connect to all services (such as the database) via `localhost` but then routes the request to the proper place on the network

Unfortunately, Kubernetes does not have a way to synchronize container startup. Essentially, Kubernetes starts all of the containers at once, and it is up to the containers themselves to wait for the required services to be up and running if a specific ordering is needed. However, as we will see in Chapter 10, Kubernetes does allow for `initContainers` to be run *prior* to the main application containers. These will run in the specific order specified, and the main containers will run after they are all completed.

8.2 Kubernetes Storage

The final piece of the Kubernetes architecture we will consider is the Kubernetes storage system. Obviously, containers themselves have a filesystem. However, there are other container storage needs that Kubernetes can handle.

While there are quite a number of variations and nuances in Kubernetes storage (and many of them vary based on your cloud provider), you can generally think of storage as existing in three basic tiers:

1. The container filesystem itself (which only exists while the container exists)

2. Pod-specific volumes that are shared by multiple containers in a Pod (which only exists while the Pod exists)

3. Persistent volumes which have fixed names and roles in the system and survive the lifetime of individual Pods

The first tier is handled automatically by the container system—you don't need to specify anything here at all. The second tier is often handled through a volume type called `emptyDir`. Essentially, this creates a new, empty volume at Pod start which can be shared to any or all of the containers in the Pod.

The third tier is more interesting. This is the tier which holds database storage, uploaded files, and other data that needs to stick around for a long time. Historically, each cloud provider essentially had their own storage service type, plus a few generic ones for standard protocols such as iSCSI and NFS volumes. These are essentially volumes that are configured and deployed outside of Kubernetes and then mapped in directly to Pods.

However, the problem with this approach is that it too closely tied the definition of a Pod with a specific physical aspect of the cloud. This made it hard to move between cloud services or even move between local, staging, and production instances of your cloud. So, if you were running Kubernetes on the Azure cloud, and if you said that a Pod mounted an Azure Disk, you would have to change that definition when you wanted to run the Pod locally, since Azure Disk is specific to that cloud service.

To resolve this, Kubernetes implemented Persistent Volume Claims. A Persistent Volume Claim (PVC) is essentially a notation on a Pod that it wants access to some form of persistent storage. The actual persistent storage used is defined elsewhere. This allows for developers to fulfill the PVC with their own local storage during development and for cloud administrators to fulfill the PVC with provisioned storage from the cloud provider, all using the same Pod definition.

PVCs can be fulfilled in two ways—using either statically provisioned resources (where a cloud administrator creates a volume on the cloud ahead-of-time) or dynamically provisioned resources (where Kubernetes will do this for you on-demand).

Using statically provisioned resources is useful because it forces cloud administrators to think clearly about their cloud needs ahead-of-time and makes sure they are aware of the costs the cloud will incur. Using dynamically provisioned resources is useful because it allows application developers to simply specify what their storage requirements are, and the cloud will automatically make provisions for them.

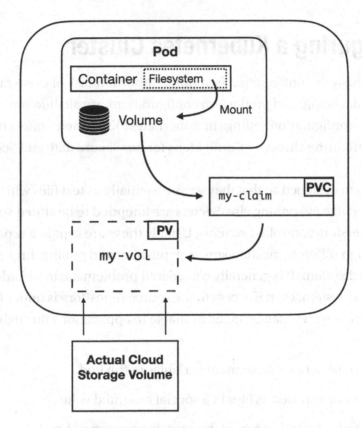

Figure 8-3. *A Persistent Volume on Kubernetes*

Statically provisioned resources are defined as Persistent Volumes (PVs). Essentially, you create the volume using your cloud provider's tools, and then the Persistent Volume object imports the volume into your Kubernetes cluster to be used.

Figure 8-3 shows how Kubernetes sees the relationship of Pods, Persistent Volume Claims, and Persistent Volumes. The Pod consists of a single container with a filesystem. The filesystem mounts a volume specified in the Pod's configuration. This volume refers to the Persistent Volume Claim (PVC) called my-claim. This PVC then refers to the Provisioned Volume called my-vol, which is just the Kubernetes name for existing storage created in your cloud provider outside of the Kubernetes setup.

Dynamically provisioned storage is similar, but, rather than the PVC referring to a specific volume, it refers to a Storage Class, which you can think of as a storage space factory. Each Storage Class merely defines the parameters for building the storage, and the PVC will auto-create a volume if one does not already exist based on the details of the Storage Class.

8.3 Configuring a Kubernetes Cluster

Managing your cluster's configuration is another important task of cluster management. Usually your local, testing, and production configurations are all different, so how do you manage different configuration settings in Kubernetes? Kubernetes offers two primary resources for configuring clusters—ConfigMaps for nonsecure data and Secrets for secure data.

ConfigMaps are designed so that they work essentially as text files which can be version-controlled like everything else. Secrets are intended to be stored separately and not included in version-controlled systems. Usually these are kept in a separate directory and shared through different mechanisms than pushing and pulling through your version-controlled system. It is generally considered problematic to include a Secret in a version-controlled system, even if access to the source repository is under tight control.

ConfigMaps and Secrets can be made available to applications through four mechanisms:

- They can be set as environment variables in the Pod.

- They can be exposed as files in a special mounted volume.

- They can be passed as part of the container command and arguments.

- They can be read directly through the Kubernetes API (rare).

For configurations that are simple key/value pairs, setting environment variables is probably the most straightforward way to send configurations to your applications and likely requires the least amount of knowledge that your application needs about your Kubernetes environment. However, for larger settings (like Java `.properties` files), having the settings written into a filesystem may be the easier route.

8.4 Application Interaction with Kubernetes

One of the design goals of Kubernetes is to minimize the amount that an application has to know about Kubernetes. Ideally, an application should have no idea that it is running on a Kubernetes cluster and should have no need to know about the cluster. The goal is for Kubernetes to provide configuration and context information to the running containers using "ordinary" means—means that are available whether or not you are running Kubernetes.

For example, in Kubernetes, Services are found using DNS lookups. DNS is a standard service that exists whether or not you are running Kubernetes, and DNS lookups are a standard way for services to look up information about other hosts. Therefore, finding a Service in Kubernetes doesn't rely on any Kubernetes-specific APIs or mechanisms. Kubernetes just simplifies the way that these DNS entries are defined and manages all of the networking and routing to get them to work. For the application, though, it is just a DNS lookup.

Likewise for configurations and secrets, these are generally exposed to your containers as environment variables or files. Applications normally receive configurations through environment variables or files. Therefore, the application doesn't need to know that the environment variables or files came from Kubernetes—there is nothing Kubernetes-specific about them.

In all, the goal of Kubernetes is to make life easier for the cloud administrator, but to get out of the way of the application itself. Kubernetes is generally invisible to the application and simply works to provide a configured environment for the application to run in.

8.5 Summary

In this chapter, we learned the following:

- A Kubernetes cluster consists of a control pane (which manages the cluster), an API server (which manages external requests such as from kubectl), workloads (which do the actual work of the cluster), and services-type objects (which manage routing requests to workloads).

- Kubernetes workloads include individual Pods, ReplicaSets which manage groups of identical Pods, Deployments which manage ReplicaSets, StatefulSets which manage groups of nonidentical Pods, DaemonSets which manage per-Node Pods, and Jobs, which are expected to run and finish.

- Kubernetes includes several types of Services, including ClusterIP services (which provide an internal load-balanced service) and LoadBalancer services (which provide an external IP address and load balancer).

- Services create a fixed IP address and a DNS entry in CoreDNS so that all Pods can locate the service by its name.

- An Ingress can be used to manage HTTP endpoints and can map different Services to different HTTP hosts and paths.

- Pods consist of one or more containers which share many resources together, including mounted filesystems, networking, and IPC mechanisms.

- In addition to storage that comes with the containers themselves, storage for a Pod can be Pod-specific (using `emptyDir` filesystems) or can be managed by the cloud using Persistent Volume Claims (PVCs) which allocate permanent storage from your cluster provider.

- Kubernetes clusters can be configured using ConfigMaps for nonsecure configuration items and Secrets for secure configuration items. These can be presented to the application as either environment variables or files.

- Overall, one main goal of Kubernetes is to make it so that the application doesn't have to care or even know that it is running in a Kubernetes cluster. Kubernetes provides configuration details using standard mechanisms such as DNS, environment variables, and files, so that the application doesn't have to concern itself with anything Kubernetes-specific.

CHAPTER 9

Basic Kubernetes Management

Now that we have our feet wet with Kubernetes (Chapter 6), have played with the
`kubectl` management tool (Chapter 7), and have looked at all the components that
make up Kubernetes (Chapter 8), it's time to really look at what Kubernetes cluster
management looks like.

9.1 Infrastructure as Code

Over the years, people have realized that application clusters require just as much
management as software projects. It used to be that system administrators would
deploy changes to the network and infrastructure and just remember how everything
was set up—what was installed on what machine, how the networking was set up, what
the firewalls looked like, etc. The problem with this method is that, as infrastructure
grows, all of the decisions are eventually forgotten. Nobody remembers that these two
machines had a firewall between them, or that a special routing change had to be made,
or that we installed a new version of ImageMagick to take care of some bug. Therefore,
system administrators and cluster administrators decided that they wanted what the
software people had—a total view of the configuration of their network at every point in
time, including notes as to why changes were made. In a word, version control.

In order to manage their infrastructure using version control tools, and to make
explicit how their network is set up, networking admins came up with the concept of
infrastructure-as-code, also known as IaC. What IaC does is record your system state
into a set of files and then uses standard source control tools such as `git` to manage
those files.

© Jonathan Bartlett 2023
J. Bartlett, *Cloud Native Applications with Docker and Kubernetes*,
https://doi.org/10.1007/978-1-4842-8876-4_9

While you can administer Kubernetes clusters using imperative commands such as those we performed in Chapter 7, the preferred way to manage a Kubernetes cluster is by making configuration files and then just telling Kubernetes to apply those configurations. Then, these configuration files can be version-controlled, and you can easily roll back to any version of the cluster you want. Additionally, it is trivially easy to rebuild your cluster from scratch, since you have all of the files required to do so.

Rebuilding the cluster from scratch actually comes in handy more often than you might realize. You might want to rebuild your cluster for any of the following reasons:

- Disaster recovery

- Creating additional development or staging instances

- Creating custom implementations of your system for special customers or other localities

Using infrastructure as code allows you to provision a new environment any time you wish. Want to do performance testing? Spin up a new environment. Want to give an environment over to an outside firm for penetration testing? Spin up a new environment. It really is that straightforward.

Even if you never rebuild your cluster (but trust me, you will, if only for getting development instances up and running), maintaining your infrastructure as a code base will help you be able to recognize and remember all of the decisions and configurations that went in to making your cluster work. This is especially useful as jobs change hands over the years, and the new guys need to get up to speed on what your cluster looks like. Having it all in a source code repository makes it trivial to look through and understand both the current state and its history of changes. If you are unclear as to why a setting is set the way that it is, you can simply use `git` to find the version where this was set and look at the date, the commit message, and the other changes that were made simultaneously with it.

9.2 A Short Introduction to YAML

Docker clusters are configured through text files which describe the desired end-state of the cluster. These files are written in a format called YAML, which is a pretty common configuration file format. Essentially, YAML makes it easy to write files that are mostly hashes of key/value pairs, where the keys are strings and the values can be strings, other hashes, or arrays. We won't offer a complete guide to YAML (it supports some pretty intricate features), but this section should be enough to get you going.

To get a feel for the YAML format, a simple YAML file is provided in Figure 9-1. Probably the easiest way to describe how this is parsed is to show the equivalent JSON for this code. That is provided in Figure 9-2.

```
mykey: myvalue
another-key:
  subkey: Another value
  another-subkey: Yet another value # This is a comment
  key-for-array:
    - array entry
    - another entry # leading/trailing whitespace removed
  people: # an array of hashes
    - name: Jim
      age: 20 # This is parsed as a number
      favorite color: blue
    - name: "Bob" # You can use quotes if you want
      age: 30
      favorite color: green
```

Figure 9-1. An Example YAML File

85

```
{
  "mykey": "myvalue",
  "another-key": {
    "subkey": "Another Value",
    "another-subkey": "Yet another value",
    "key-for-array": [
      "array entry",
      "another entry"
    ],
    "people": [
      {
        "name": "Jim",
        "age": 20,
        "favorite color": "blue"
      },
      {
        "name": "Bob",
        "age": 30,
        "favorite color": "green"
      }
    ]
  }
}
```

Figure 9-2. *The Example YAML File Translated into JSON*

As you can see, YAML is using indentation whitespace to determine the nesting level for its hashes and arrays. YAML doesn't actually care how many spaces you use to indent, but it does expect you to be consistent for each indentation level. Because of this, the group developing YAML has decided that only spaces should be used for indentation and *not tabs*.[1]

Note that YAML auto-interprets numeric data *as numbers*. So, the 20 and 30 above got translated into the *numbers* 20 and 30. If you wanted to write a number, but have it treated like a string, you can just put quotes around them. The values "20" and "30" would be interpreted as the *strings* 20 and 30.

Additionally, YAML allows more than one YAML document to be specified in a single file. The documents are separated by a triple dash (---) sitting alone on one line. Here is an example:

---

[1] As a tab enthusiast myself, this hurts, but I've had to learn to accept it.

```
a: b
c: d
---
e: f
g: h
```

This gets translated into two separate documents. The first document is a hash which looks like this:

```
{"a": "b", "c": "d"}
```

And the second document is a similar hash:

```
{"e": "f", "g": "h"}
```

This feature is very important for Kubernetes, as most people will group several related YAML documents into a single file, separated by these three dashes. Additionally, you can also put the three dashes *before* your YAML file and even provide some processing directives to YAML before this marker (e.g., to specify the YAML version being used), but we won't do that in this book.

There are many other features of YAML, but this is sufficient for getting started in it.

9.3 Defining Kubernetes Objects in YAML Manifest Files

As noted, we will no longer be using the kubectl command to directly create Kubernetes objects. Instead, we will be writing YAML files which describe them and then just telling kubectl to *apply* those files. The Kubernetes YAML configuration files are often referred to as *manifests* because they list out the things that the cluster should contain. The Kubernetes cluster is responsible for making it actually happen.

A very simple Kubernetes YAML manifest file is provided in Figure 9-3. Type it into a file called simple-pod.yaml.

```
apiVersion: v1
kind: Pod
metadata:
  name: simple-pod
  labels:
    my-label-name: my-label-value
spec:
  containers:
    - name: my-container
      image: httpd
```

Figure 9-3. *Simple Pod Configuration:* `simple-pod.yaml`

This is a description of a Pod. Normally, Pods are launched as part of some other types of workload (like a Deployment), not created directly. However, this allowed for a very simple YAML manifest file to start with.

The following keys wind up in pretty much every Kubernetes file:

apiVersion: This is the version of the Kubernetes API. This is going to be `v1` for many core objects. However, another format is `GROUP/VERSION`, and many standard Kubernetes objects which are layered on top of core objects are given a group such as `apps` or `batch`. For instance, Deployments are defined in the `apps/v1` version.

kind: This is the type of object we are describing. Here we are describing a Pod.

metadata: This is identifying information for the object. The `name` subkey is required. The `labels` subkey (optional) contains a hash of additional key/value pairs which can be used for categorization and grouping of objects. While there has been some attempt to standardize some labels, they are essentially whatever you want them to be to help you group Kubernetes components. There is also an option `annotations` subkey which is usually used to enable nonstandard features or used by external Kubernetes tools.

spec: This contains the details of how the object will be set up and varies by object type.

For Pod objects, the `spec` can contain a variety of keys, but the only one we are interested in here is the `containers` key, which is a list of containers that the Pod will be deploying. For the container, we have to specify a Docker image with the `image` key and a name for our container with the `name` key (the name only has to be unique within the Pod).

Now, to get Kubernetes to build our object into our cluster, use the following command:

```
kubectl apply -f simple-pod.yaml
```

Kubernetes will respond with something like `pod/simple-pod created`. We can check on the status of our Pod by doing the following:

```
kubectl get pod simple-pod
```

Once the status is `Running`, you are all set! You can also get more detailed information by using `describe` instead of `get`.

There's honestly not a lot we can do with this Pod. Launching Pods by themselves doesn't do a lot in Kubernetes—Kubernetes won't try to keep it running (you would need a ReplicaSet or Deployment for that), it doesn't provide a way to access it inside or outside the cluster (you would need a Service for that), etc. However, we can get logs for the Pod. If you run the command `kubectl logs simple-pod`, it will show you the logs for this Pod.

Now, what happens if we apply the same file again? Go ahead and try it! You will get back from Kubernetes `pod/simple-pod unchanged`. That's because we gave our Pod a name, and Kubernetes knows what we asked it to look like. Since we didn't change the specification, Kubernetes recognizes there is nothing to do. However, if you were to change the definition of the Pod (without changing the name), then applying the change would tell Kubernetes to modify or relaunch the Pod (depending on how drastic the change is) so that it matches its newly requested configuration.

By keeping track of all object names, Kubernetes provides a straightforward way of knowing when a file contains new cluster object or when the file contains updates of existing cluster objects. Kubernetes contains all of the logic needed to plan and execute the changes needed to get the cluster into the newly requested state. Note, however, that the changes are not instantaneous. The `kubectl` command finishes as soon as it tells Kubernetes what to do, *not when Kubernetes has completed the task!* You will have to ask Kubernetes for the status of your various objects in order to know when Kubernetes has completed its requests.

Part of the magic of Kubernetes is that it is continually monitoring and tracking your cluster to make sure that the cluster stays in line with your requested configuration and that it plans the changes necessary to move the cluster into new states upon request. Kubernetes will do things such as check which Nodes have enough capacity to add more Pods, add entries into CoreDNS to let everyone know about new services, and modify the networking configuration for allowing new ClusterIP, NodePort, LoadBalancer, and other services. For Deployments, Kubernetes will automatically manage migrating a Deployment from a ReplicaSet containing an old version of your application to a ReplicaSet of the new version of your application.

So, in summary, the preferred way to manage Kubernetes clusters is to do the following:

1.   Store cluster information in YAML manifest files.

2.   Give each cluster object a unique and permanent name.

3.   Use `kubectl apply` to send updates to Kubernetes.

9.4 Kubernetes Files for Our Walkthrough Deployment

In this section, I will present what the deployment we performed in Chapter 6 looks like if it were done via Kubernetes files instead of directly in the user interface. I think you will find that, now that you know how Kubernetes works a little better, doing it with files is actually *easier* than doing it in the interface (it is also the recommended approach for enterprise applications).

In the walkthrough, we basically created two Kubernetes objects—a Deployment and a Service. The Deployment did some additional work—it created a ReplicaSet, and that ReplicaSet created Pods. We don't have to do that ourselves because the Deployment will take care of it. But we do have to tell the Deployment *how* it should create the ReplicaSet and Pods.

The Deployment file (with some names changed to make it a new deployment) is shown in Figure 9-4. Here, the `template` is a template for how the Pod objects should be created. Note that the `name` is left out of the template, because each created Pod will need its own name (which is generated by the ReplicaSet). Other than that, it is just a description of a Pod.

```
apiVersion: apps/v1
kind: Deployment
metadata:
  name: my-file-deployment
spec:
  replicas: 3
  selector:
    matchLabels:
      my-label-name: my-label-value
  template:
    metadata:
      labels:
        my-label-name: my-label-value
    spec:
      containers:
        - name: my-http-container
          image: johnnyb61820/simple-web-server
          ports:
            - containerPort: 8070
```

Figure 9-4. *Basic Deployment File:* `my-deployment.yaml`

The Deployment knows which Pods it controls using the `selector` and `matchLabels` keys. The Deployment basically monitors all Pods which match *all* the labels specified (you can specify more than one label).[2] It uses the `replicas` key to know how many replicas to keep running.

The `containerPort` is primarily for informational purposes (however, you can also add a `hostPort` parameter to it to expose a specific `containerPort` on an additional, different port). This helps you to document which ports on the Pods you care about. However, ultimately, Kubernetes doesn't care what you set this to. It will expose any port that is listening on the Pod.

You can create the Deployment by doing `kubectl apply -f my-deployment.yaml`. You can watch the Pods get created with `kubectl get pods`. If you ask `kubectl` to describe a Pod, you will notice that each one is getting created with your label.

Next, we will configure the Service which will provide load balancing and also give us external access. Figure 9-5 shows what this file looks like.

---

[2] Note that the `selector` and `matchLabels` keys *cannot* be changed after creating the Deployment. You would have to delete the Deployment and recreate it to alter it.

```
apiVersion: v1
kind: Service
metadata:
  name: my-file-service
spec:
  selector:
    my-label-name: my-label-value
  ports:
    - protocol: TCP
      port: 80
      targetPort: 8070
  type: LoadBalancer
```

Figure 9-5. *Basic Service File:* `my-service.yaml`

This will auto-create a load balancer on your cloud platform. You can see the external IP address by doing `kubectl get service my-file-service`. The `selector` key tells the Service how to find the relevant Pods.

Now, let's say that you wanted to scale your cluster to have four replicas. How would you do that? Simple—just modify your `my-deployment.yaml` file so that it says `replicas:` 4. Then do a `kubectl apply -f my-development.yaml`, and it will modify the number of replicas to use. That's all there is to it!

Note that, since these two files logically belong together, we could combine them into one file and separate out the documents using YAML's triple dash (`---`) between them.

9.4.1 Organizing Your Kubernetes Files

How you organize your Kubernetes files is ultimately up to you. However, some common practices have emerged that are fairly useful. Ultimately, Kubernetes doesn't care how you organize your YAML manifest files—it just performs any task in any file you specify using `kubectl apply`.

First of all, it is good to keep your entire cluster setup contained within a directory tree that is version-controlled. You should always push your changes to your version-controlled system *before* applying them to your cluster. That way, you have a tracked notation of every state your cluster has been in. Some people go further and will have their Continuous Deployment (CD) pipeline automatically deploy changes when pushed to a specific branch. In such systems, people often auto-tag the change with a version number and then run `kubectl` to apply the changes. You don't have to go that far, but at least keeping your cluster configuration version-controlled will save you a lot of headaches.

As mentioned, YAML files can contain multiple YAML documents. Normally, cluster administrators keep related YAML documents together in the same file. For instance, you might put both a Service and its related Deployment into a single file. Having fewer files where each file pertains to one logical application or service makes maintaining a cluster a lot easier. If the services are complicated enough to warrant multiple files, some people create folders for each major service.

Additionally, many people create folders for each cluster environment. For instance, for a production environment, you might want a terabyte or more of storage for the database but only need a gigabyte in the staging environment. Therefore, the `environments/production` folder would have the storage details for production volumes, and the `environments/staging` folder would have the storage details for staging volumes.

The `kubectl` command provides some helpful behaviors for managing clusters in this way. First of all, instead of applying a specific file using a command like `kubectl apply -f myfile.yaml`, you can specify a whole folder. So, if I had all of my main cluster files in the current directory, I could perform the following command to update my entire cluster:

```
kubectl apply -f .
```

Note that this only specifies the files in that folder, *not in any subfolder*. This is great because if I had my environment-specific files in a subfolder called `environments`, this would not apply those files (otherwise, it would wind up applying the files from *all* environments to the current cluster, and that's not what we want!).

Additionally, Kubernetes supports invoking multiple instances of the `-f` parameter. Therefore, if we had our main cluster configuration in the present directory and our environment-specific configuration in the `environments/production` folder, I could update the entire cluster with a single command:

```
kubectl apply -f . -f environments/production
```

Again, it is not required, but having some amount of basic organization to your Kubernetes files will help you maintain control of your cluster.

9.5 Deleting Kubernetes Objects

Using kubectl apply only works for creating/updating Kubernetes objects. It does not help if we want to *delete* an object. This is good because you don't want anything to accidentally delete something on your cluster.

There are two ways to delete something on your cluster—by name or by label. Deleting by name is straightforward enough: kubectl delete RESOURCE NAME, where RESOURCE is the resource you are talking about (i.e., Pod, Deployment, Service, etc.) and NAME is the name of the object in Kubernetes. Additionally, to delete all Kubernetes objects in a file by their name, you can do kubectl delete -f MYFILE.yaml.

However, if you are getting rid of something bigger (say, an entire application), this may be tedious. Therefore, Kubernetes allows you to specify labels instead of object names. The following command will delete all Kubernetes objects which are Deployments or Services which have the label label1 set to the value value2 (note that there is no space after the comma):

```
kubectl delete deployments,services -l label1=value2
```

You can specify additional labels as well (separated by a comma without a space) to further narrow the list of things to delete.

In fact, most of the kubectl commands mentioned in Chapter 7 can use labels instead of names using the -l option. Most of them can also take multiple resource types as well (separated by commas but no spaces).

☞ A NOTE ON LABELS

As you have seen, labels are used for all sorts of things in Kubernetes. Therefore, it is usually good to err on the side of having too many labels rather than too few. You might have a label for the general application, the logical service it is being provided to, the application version, or any other number of aspects that you might want to query on at some point in time.

So, for instance, on the Pod template in your Deployment, you can add extra labels that are not being used by a selector property on either the Deployment or the Service. These can be used for your own searching purposes when using kubectl.

For instance, let's say you are running several web applications, each with their own database. You might use a label called `instance-kind` to say whether a Pod is a `web` or `database` Pod. But you might have another label called `app-name` to say which app it is for. Then, you can query your Pods either by which app they belong to or which kind of work it is running (or both).

9.6 Summary

In this chapter, we learned the following:

- Kubernetes uses YAML as the file format of choice for configuring clusters.

- Configuring using YAML files allows for version-controlling the state of the cluster and for configuring new, identical clusters quickly and easily.

- Most configuration files include `apiVersion`, `kind`, `metadata`, and `spec` keys, with the contents of the `spec` key varying by resource.

- When configurations are stored in YAML files, they can be applied using `kubectl apply -f FILE.yaml`.

- When applying configurations, Kubernetes uses the name of the object to know whether it should create a new object or update an existing one.

- Multiple related Kubernetes object definitions can be gathered together in a single YAML file with each configuration separated by `---` on a line by itself.

- Configuration files can be organized into directories, and the `kubectl apply` command can be applied to an entire directory at once.

- Kubernetes objects can be deleted by name or by label. You can also direct Kubernetes to delete all objects within a given file using the `-f` flag.

CHAPTER 10

A Full Kubernetes Cloud Example

Now that we know the basics of how Kubernetes works and have worked with a simple test app, we will now look at how a full application is put together. The application will be a simple message board.

This application will have four major components:

- A database (PostgreSQL)
- Backend servers for the Message Board API
- A caching server (Memcache)
- An HTML/JavaScript front end

These components will all be simple in order to focus our attention on the structure of the cluster. We will use Ruby Sinatra for the server and basic HTML/JavaScript for the front end in order to make the implementation as straightforward as possible.

The Message Board API will have two endpoints:

> **GET /api/messages/list** Return all messages posted to the message board.

> **POST /api/messages/create** Create a new message.

© Jonathan Bartlett 2023
J. Bartlett, *Cloud Native Applications with Docker and Kubernetes*,
https://doi.org/10.1007/978-1-4842-8876-4_10

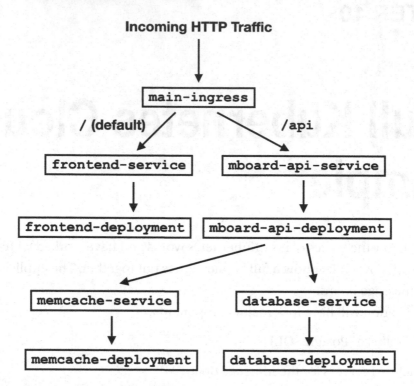

Incoming HTTP Traffic

Figure 10-1. *Basic Request Flow for Application*

The /api/messages/list endpoint will be cached for 15 seconds in the Memcache server, but the ultimate source of truth will be in the database. The front end will be a simple HTML file with some JavaScript pulled in. It will retrieve the messages upon loading through the Message Board API. When requested, it will also create a new message on the message board and then reload the message list.

Figure 10-1 shows how the Kubernetes application is structured. The incoming traffic hits the Ingress, which we call main-ingress in our cluster. Depending on the destination, the traffic gets routed to one of two destinations—either the Message Board API Service (mboard-api-service) or to our HTML/JavaScript front-end Service (frontend-service). Note that the diagram shows that the Services are backed by Deployments, but we left out the Pods themselves in order to simplify the diagram. The Message Board API Service itself makes use of two other services—the cache (memcache-service) and the database (database-service).

Our Kubernetes cluster definition will allow us to launch the entire application entirely from repeated invocations of the `kubectl apply` command on our different files. Additionally, since Kubernetes manages dependencies automatically, it doesn't even matter which order we deploy our YAML manifest files.[1]

10.1 The Application Code

Before we start looking at the Kubernetes deployment information, I wanted to do a quick walkthrough of the code itself. The API Service is a tiny app written in Ruby Sinatra, which was specifically chosen so that we could connect to a database, connect to a cache service, and implement two API endpoints with a minimum of code. The goal of this exercise is to demonstrate how *Kubernetes* works, not how to write a great application.

Figure 10-2 shows the main application code. It first loads the libraries it needs— `sinatra` (the application framework), `pg` (the database client library for PostgreSQL), and `dalli` (the caching client library for Memcache). It then defines a helper function `with_db` which connects to the database, performs a function (that will be provided), and then closes the database connection. By opening and closing a connection every time, the application is more resilient against database restarts.[2] The caching library is already sufficiently resilient against restarts and doesn't need extra code for it.

---

[1] Your application and services may *themselves* have ordering requirements that are outside of Kubernetes ability to determine. These can be handled in a number of ways. First, the application can be written so that the container itself will terminate until the dependency is met. Second, the application can be written to be resilient enough to give a worthwhile error and retry until the dependency is met. Finally, the application can be deployed as a Kubernetes StatefulSet where the dependencies are more explicitly managed. While the last one seems like it is a good idea, it is usually better for a Kubernetes Service to be able to be deployed and managed independent of its dependencies if possible.

[2] Most application frameworks handle database autoreconnection for you. However, those frameworks also take considerably more code to do simple apps like this one.

Note that the code depends on some environment variables to configure it. Specifically, PG_CONN_STR holds the PostgreSQL connection string, and CACHE_CONN_ STR holds the Memcache connection string. Kubernetes tries to make it so that the application does not need to know anything about Kubernetes. Instead, configuration information about the Kubernetes cluster is passed to the application using ordinary means such as environment variables or files.

When the server starts up, it creates the underlying table if it is not already there. It also makes a connection to the caching service. Two endpoints are then defined—a GET and a POST.

The GET endpoint has the database access wrapped in a cache request. The fetch command will check the cache, and, if the key is not present, it will perform the block of code and store the resulting value in the cache. If the key is present, it will just return what it finds. The value expires after 15 seconds. This value is just returned as a JSON-formatted array of the entire contents of the table.

```ruby
require "sinatra"
require "pg"
require "dalli"

# Convenience function for DB connections
def with_db(&block)
  conn = PG::Connection.new(ENV["PG_CONN_STR"])
  value = yield(conn)
  conn.close
  return value
end

# Create table if needed
with_db do |db|
  db.exec("CREATE TABLE IF NOT EXISTS messages (
    id SERIAL PRIMARY KEY, title text, message text)")
end

# Connect to memcache (autoreconnects automatically)
cache = Dalli::Client.new(ENV["CACHE_CONN_STR"])

get "/api/messages/list" do
  content_type 'application/json'
  data = cache.fetch("message-list", 15) do
    with_db do |db|
      db.exec("SELECT * FROM messages ORDER BY id").to_a.to_json
    end
  end
  return data
end

post "/api/messages/create" do
  content_type 'application/json'
  with_db do |db|
    db.exec(
      "INSERT INTO messages (title, message) VALUES ($1, $2)",
      [ params["title"], params["message"] ]
    )
  end
  cache.delete("message-list")
  return {"success": true}.to_json
end
```

Figure 10-2. *Main Application Code: server.rb*

```
source "https://rubygems.org"

gem "sinatra" # application
gem "pg" # database
gem "dalli" # memcache
gem "puma" # webserver
```

Figure 10-3. *Application Dependencies: Gemfile*

```
FROM --platform linux/amd64 ruby:3.1.2

COPY . .
RUN bundle install
CMD bundle exec ruby server.rb
EXPOSE 4567
```

Figure 10-4. *Docker Build Settings: Dockerfile*

The POST endpoint takes two POST parameters—title and message—which it stores in the database. After storing the data, it then invalidates the cache to make sure the next request retrieves fresh data. Finally, it returns a simple success message.

This application depends on two other files—the Gemfile (Figure 10-3) which describes the library dependencies (known in the Ruby language as gems) and the Dockerfile (Figure 10-4) which describes how to build the application into a Docker image.

If you have Ruby installed locally, you can run the code yourself simply by typing the following:

```
bundle install
bundle exec ruby server.rb
```

However, we are more concerned with building the container. Therefore, we can do that by doing the following:

```
docker build -t DOCKERREPO:TAG -f Dockerfile .
```

Here, DOCKERREPO is one of your Docker repositories, and TAG is the tag to use (probably latest). You will then need to push the image to your Docker repository in order for Kubernetes to find it. Kubernetes can work with any container registry, but the Docker Hub registry (hub.docker.com) is probably the easiest one to work with and is the one assumed in this book. For application code, you will want to be sure to push to a *private* Docker repository. Information about how to supply Kubernetes with the credentials to access this will be provided later in the chapter, as well as an alternative public repository if you just want to get started using a public Docker Hub image.

Now that we know what the code looks like, each of the next sections will describe how to create the Kubernetes objects that are required to deploy this application.

10.2 The Memcache Service

The first system we will look to deploy on our cluster is the Memcache system, simply because it is the most straightforward to configure and deploy. Docker Hub contains public containers for many common applications, and you can use these containers directly in your cluster. There are several available Memcache public container images, but we will use the "official" one, known simply as memcached.

Most standard container images offer configuration options which allow you to customize their behavior. These are usually available to be specified as environment variables or extra files in a volume mounted in the container or through command-line options that can be used by specifying them as part of the container command. In the case of the memcached image, we can specify a run command and run the memcached daemon with different arguments if we wanted. For our purposes, however, we only need the defaults.

Figure 10-5 shows the configuration of the service. It consists of a single manifest file with two YAML documents—the Deployment and the Service. For the Deployment, we only want one Pod running so that when we flush the cache we won't have stale data stuck in another server.[3] We want to use a Deployment even though we only have one Pod to manage, because the Deployment (and its generated ReplicaSet) manages keeping the Pod up and active, restarting it when it fails, and handling a graceful migration to new configurations when the configuration is changed. Additionally, we need a Service even though there is only one Pod (and therefore doesn't need to be load-balanced) because that is how other Pods will be able to locate the caching service.

---

[3] There are other ways to achieve this, but this was the simplest one.

```
apiVersion: apps/v1
kind: Deployment
metadata:
  name: memcache-deployment
spec:
  replicas: 1
  selector:
    matchLabels:
      component: memcache
  template:
    metadata:
      labels:
        component: memcache
    spec:
      containers:
        - name: memcache
          image: memcached:1.6
          ports:
            - containerPort: 11211
---
apiVersion: v1
kind: Service
metadata:
  name: memcache-service
spec:
  selector:
    component: memcache
  ports:
    - port: 11211
```

Figure 10-5. *The Memcache Service:* `memcache.yaml`

The configuration of the Deployment is fairly straightforward. It has a name, the number of replicas, the selector which tells it how to tell which Pods are under management, and a template which describes what the individual Pods will look like. Throughout this cluster, we are just using one label for all of our management: `component`. Remember, for the most part, labels are whatever you want them to be and have no special meaning in Kubernetes. We can call our label whatever we want and set the value to whatever we want. Here, we are setting the `component` label to be `memcache`.

The container's name is set to `memcache`, but the name really doesn't matter for single-container Pods. The `image` is the most important part, which sets the container image. We are using the `memcached` image, which is an "official" image so no user has to be specified here. The `ports` list the ports published by the container. This is actually just documentation and does not actually do anything in the container. It could be left off, but it is really useful to see which ports on a container we care about.

The Service definition is straightforward. The Pods for the Service are defined by the `selector`, and the `ports` listing tells what ports the Service should forward. In addition to the `port` key, a port definition can also have a `protocol` key so that other protocols like UDP or STCP are enabled (TCP is the default) and a `targetPort` key if the port on the Pod is different than the port being listened to. Personally, I don't like using `targetPort` if it is avoidable.

No `type` is specified, so it defaults to a ClusterIP service. This means that, when deployed, it will register a fixed internal IP address in the cluster where requests will be load-balanced across the participating Pods. This IP address will be available to the Pods by looking up the `memcache-service` name on the cluster, which is the name we gave to our Service.

☞ HEADLESS SERVICES

One interesting thing you can do with a ClusterIP service is to set the `clusterIP` key to None. This prevents the service from actually generating an internal load-balanced IP address inside the cluster and instead uses DNS to round-robin between the hosts. This is known as running a "headless" service. This isn't usually particularly faster (Kubernetes does some pretty advanced networking to make ClusterIP connections lightning fast and direct), but it does allow you to query the list of Pods that are included in a Service through DNS—a single DNS lookup will return all of the Pods that the Service is using. Some caching servers, for instance, can use this to auto-discover each other to maintain cache consistency across all instances.

10.3 The Database Service

Our cluster's database system will be run by a PostgreSQL database. Again, Docker has an official `postgres` image available. However, this time we require a little bit of configuration. The documentation for this image says that it requires that we set a password through the `POSTGRES_PASSWORD` environment variable. Additionally, we will want to change the directory where the data is stored for reasons that will be apparent later. This can be done by specifying the `PGDATA` environment variable.

Figure 10-6 shows the YAML configuration for the database. There are several interesting features which we will discuss:

- The data is being stored on a separate volume which will also be separately managed and survive reboots.

- The restart strategy for the Deployment is set to Recreate (the default is RollingUpdate).

- We are pulling the password from a Secret which will be separately managed (we will describe secrets in Section 10.6).

Let's talk about volumes first. With the Memcache service, if the application was restarted or redeployed on different Pods, we didn't really care if the whole thing was wiped out and rebuilt, because, ultimately, caches are all temporary. Likewise, for our actual Message Board API servers, we are storing no permanent state on the individual Pods. However, the whole point of a database is to have a persistent and reliable state which continues to exist even if the database dies or is restarted. Therefore, we will need some external storage which can be attached to this Pod.

The volumes section of the Pod template allows us to define storage. We are naming the volume database-data-volume, which only matters so that we can refer to it in the container's volumeMounts section. This is a persistentVolumeClaim, which means that the actual storage definition will be defined in another Kubernetes object. This will be called database-volume-claim. The access mode is set to ReadWriteOnce which means that it can be mounted and written to, but only by a single Pod at a time.[4]

---

[4] Other access modes are more specialized to specific volume types.

```yaml
apiVersion: apps/v1
kind: Deployment
metadata:
  name: database-deployment
spec:
  replicas: 1
  selector:
    matchLabels:
      component: database
  strategy:
    type: Recreate
  template:
    metadata:
      labels:
        component: database
    spec:
      containers:
        - name: postgres
          image: postgres:14
          env:
            - name: POSTGRES_PASSWORD
              valueFrom:
                secretKeyRef:
                  name: database-secret
                  key: password
                  optional: false
            - name: PGDATA
              value: /mnt/data/pgdata
          volumeMounts:
            - name: database-data-volume
              mountPath: /mnt/data
          ports:
            - containerPort: 5432
      volumes:
        - name: database-data-volume
          persistentVolumeClaim:
            claimName: database-volume-claim
---
apiVersion: v1
kind: Service
metadata:
  name: database-service
spec:
  selector:
    component: database
  ports:
    - port: 5432
```

Figure 10-6. *PostgreSQL Database Configuration:* `database.yaml`

```
apiVersion: v1
kind: PersistentVolumeClaim
metadata:
  name: database-volume-claim
spec:
  accessModes:
    - ReadWriteOnce
  resources:
    requests:
      storage: 10Gi
```

Figure 10-7. *Persistent Storage Definitions:* `storage.yaml`

The file (Figure 10-7) representing Persistent Volume Claims (PVCs) represents the volume in the abstract, and this gets tied either to a Persistent Volume (which represents preprovisioned storage) or to a Storage Class (which tells Kubernetes *how* to allocate new storage). In our case, we are not referencing either a specific Persistent Volume or a Storage Class, which means that Kubernetes will use its default Storage Class to allocate our volume. Different clouds will have different default Storage Classes, but most cloud providers have a default Storage Class that fits the most general usage patterns. You can find more information on storage in Appendix D.

Personally, I like to keep PVC definitions in a separate, environment-specific folder. In this case, I am putting `storage.yaml` in the `environments/production` folder. This allows me to, for instance, request less storage in local and staging clusters. I could even use different Storage Classes as well. Keeping cluster-specific configurations in a separate directory makes it easier to have multiple, slightly varying clusters.

☞ **EXPANDING FILE STORAGE SPACE**

If you need more storage space, the Linode's default Storage Class allows for volume expansion, meaning that the volume itself can be resized. For information on how to resize volumes, see Appendix D.2.

After creating the PVC, we referenced it in our volume list and mounted it in our container. We then pointed the PGDATA environment variable to the new volume. However, we actually pointed the PGDATA variable to a folder *under* the mount point of the volume. The reason for this is that PostgreSQL requires a fully empty directory to initialize the database for the first time, and Linux volumes typically have one or more files (such as the lost+found directory) at the mount point of the filesystem, which gives PostgreSQL fits. Therefore, by specifying a directory below the mount point, PostgreSQL can just create the folder and have it start empty.[5]

Since we are using persistent storage, this means that we can't replicate our instance or even restart it like normal. Therefore, we have to set replicas to 1 and set strategy to Recreate. Normally, a deployment, when doing an update, will try to start up new Pods before turning off old ones. However, if Kubernetes tried that, the volume would be in use when the new Pod booted up, so the new Pod could never deploy. Therefore, we are asking the Deployment to turn off the old Pod first when it needs to do an update.

☞ STATEFULSETS

If for some reason we wanted to replicate our instance (using replicated database slave servers), we would need to use a StatefulSet instead of a Deployment. StatefulSets allow for an ordering to the boot process, in order to allow the master to boot up before the slave servers. They also allow for PVC *templates* so that storage claims can be made for each deployed Pod. In a StatefulSet, each Pod gets a predictable name as part of the set so the Pods can find each other. If the StatefulSet is named myset, then the first Pod will be named myset-0, the second myset-1, and so forth. Additionally, each Pod will get a label with a key of statefulset.kubernetes.io/pod-name and the value set to the name of the Pod. This allows you to locate the individual Pod from a Service's selector.

For more about StatefulSets, see Appendix D.4.

10.4 The Front-End Service

The front-end service is managed by an Apache HTTP server. The configuration is shown in Figure 10-8. The basic structure of this configuration is that there is a Deployment which utilizes the standard httpd image to serve static files. However, before the main Pod launches, it first runs a container which checks out the code from a git repository into the right directory. Only after the code is copied over does it run the main container.

---

[5] If you're concerned, PostgreSQL is just fine after the first start with having an actual *database* directory there. It just gets confused if there are files in the directory and they aren't database files.

However, since the containers in the Pod have different container images, how do they communicate? They do this by both sharing a separate mounted volume. Here, since the size of the files will be small (websites are usually pretty tiny compared to databases), we are not provisioning our storage but merely using an empty directory on the host for our storage. Under the `volumes` key, there is a volume named `website-data`. Rather than referencing a PVC, it instead references an `emptyDir` with no additional options. This causes the Pod to create a volume out of an empty directory that can be shared among the containers within the Pod. This directory is considered ephemeral and will be deleted as soon as the Pod terminates.

The `template` for the Pod contains a section for `initContainers`. The single entry here is for a container (using the `bitnami/git` image) to clone the repository that holds the website code. In this case, the repository is a public repository so no credentials are needed. However, if you needed to clone a secure repository, `git` uses the `GITHUB_TOKEN` environment variable for token-based authentication. Setting that using a Secret would enable you to clone a private repository. The command to run is specified by the `command` and `args` keys.

One thing to note is that the initContainer mounts the volume on a different path than the main container. On the initContainer, the volume is mounted at `/tmp/code`, and, on the main container, it is mounted at `/usr/local/apache2/htdocs`. This was done simply to demonstrate that it can be done this way. Filesystems don't care where they are mounted. This is even true if they are mounted to multiple simultaneously running containers in the same Pod.

```
apiVersion: apps/v1
kind: Deployment
metadata:
  name: frontend-deployment
spec:
  replicas: 2
  selector:
    matchLabels:
      component: frontend
  template:
    metadata:
      labels:
        component: frontend
    spec:
      initContainers:
        - name: code-loader
          image: bitnami/git:2-debian-10
          command:
            - git
          args:
            - clone
            - https://github.com/johnnyb/k8s-example-frontend.git
            - /tmp/code/
          volumeMounts:
            - name: website-data
              mountPath: /tmp/code
      containers:
        - name: webserver
          image: httpd:2.4
          ports:
            - containerPort: 80
          volumeMounts:
            - name: website-data
              mountPath: /usr/local/apache2/htdocs
      volumes:
        - name: website-data
          emptyDir: {}
---
apiVersion: v1
kind: Service
metadata:
  name: frontend-service
spec:
  selector:
    component: frontend
  ports:
    - port: 80
```

Figure 10-8. *Front-End Service Configuration:* frontend.yaml

The front-end Deployment runs two replicas, which are then load-balanced by the Service using a basic ClusterIP service on port 80. I won't show the code for the front end in this book, but it is pretty straightforward. If you want to look at it, it is available at `https://github.com/johnnyb/k8s-example-frontend`.

10.5 The Message Board API Server

The code for the Message Board API was already given in Section 10.1. Here, it will be assumed that this was bundled and pushed to the private Docker Hub repository `johnnyb61820/k8s-example-api-private`. However, this depends on setting up authenticated access to Docker Hub. While I will show you *how* to do that, I'm not going to give you access to my account! Therefore, if you want to run this example yourself, you can do one of two things—either (a) you push it to your own private repository and set it up accordingly, or (b) you can change the repository to point to `johnnyb61820/k8s-example-api`, which is a public Docker Hub repository.

Figures 10-9 and 10-10 show the code for this Service. There are a few interesting components of this. The first thing to notice is that we are using a Secret to pull from a private Docker Hub repository. This is specified in the `imagePullSecrets` portion of our Pod template specification. We will cover more about Secrets in Section 10.6.

The second thing to notice is that we are pulling our environment variables from external configurations—either from Secrets or ConfigMaps (both of which will be covered in Section 10.6). This allows us to have different configurations in different clusters and environments. For instance, in our local development, we might just be running the database on our laptop and not on the cluster at all. Therefore, our ConfigMap might set the hostname to localhost instead of a service name. The environment variables built from a ConfigMap are PG_HOST and CACHE_HOST. The PG_PASS environment variable is built from a Secret.

To pull an environment variable from another source, the valueFrom key is used instead of the value key. Normally this is pointing to either a ConfigMap (using configMapKeyRef) or a Secret (using secretKeyRef), but it can also point to information about the Pod configuration itself (using fieldRef) or resource availability (using resourceFieldRef), but those are more rare. When pulling a value from a ConfigMap or a Secret, you need to specify the name of the configuration (remember, everything in Kubernetes has a name) as well as the key to pull the value from.[6]

---

[6] These can be set to be optional, but I would caution against that. It is good to be sure that the Kubernetes dependency manager can verify that everything is properly configured before deploying it. Thankfully, the optional key is set to false by default.

```
apiVersion: apps/v1
kind: Deployment
metadata:
  name: mboard-api-deployment
spec:
  replicas: 3
  selector:
    matchLabels:
      component: mboard-api
  template:
    metadata:
      labels:
        component: mboard-api
    spec:
      imagePullSecrets:
        - name: docker-token-secret
      containers:
        - name: mboard-api-container
          image: johnnyb61820/k8s-example-api-private:1.0.1
          ports:
            - containerPort: 4567
          env:
            - name: APP_ENV
              value: production
            - name: PG_HOST
              valueFrom:
                configMapKeyRef:
                  name: mboard-api-config
                  key: pg-host
            - name: PG_PASS
              valueFrom:
                secretKeyRef:
                  name: database-secret
                  key: password
            - name: PG_CONN_STR
              value: "host=$(PG_HOST) user=postgres password=$(PG_PASS)"
            - name: CACHE_HOST
              valueFrom:
                configMapKeyRef:
                  name: mboard-api-config
                  key: cache-host
            - name: CACHE_CONN_STR
              value: "$(CACHE_HOST):11211"
```

Figure 10-9. The Message Board API Service: mboard-api.yaml (Part 1)

```
---
apiVersion: v1
kind: Service
metadata:
  name: mboard-api-service
spec:
  selector:
    component: mboard-api
  ports:
    - port: 4567
```

Figure 10-10. *The Message Board API Service:* `mboard-api.yaml` *(Part 2)*

The next thing to notice is that the environment variable that gets passed into the container is *built* from other environment variables. Our container needs an entire PostgreSQL connection string, not just bits and pieces of one. Therefore, in this example we create the `PG_CONN_STR` and `CACHE_CONN_STR` environment variables out of previously defined environment variables. Setting the value of `CACHE_CONN_STR` to `"$(CACHE_HOST):11211"` causes the contents of `CACHE_HOST` to be included in this environment variable. Just be sure to define the composite environment variables *after* the components they are made from, or those components will be empty.

The final thing to note is that we are setting an environment variable called `APP_ENV` to `production`. This is a Sinatra-specific configuration which causes it to bind to all IP addresses on the host and not just `localhost`, so the port can be accessed by the Service.

The Service itself is straightforward, although the port it is listening on is 4567, which is the default port that Sinatra listens on. We could have set Sinatra to live on a more standard port, but in our case we will map it into a standard HTTP port in our Ingress (Section 10.7).

```
apiVersion: v1
kind: ConfigMap
metadata:
  name: mboard-api-config
data:
  pg-host: database-service
  cache-host: memcache-service
```

Figure 10-11. *The Main ConfigMap:* `mboard-api-config.yaml`

10.6 Configurations and Secrets

Pretty much every application has some amount of configuration to do, some of which involves sensitive information such as keys and passwords for external services. Configuration of well-known data is put into ConfigMaps, and sensitive data is put into Secrets. On the whole, they are not managed very differently. However, for multiuser environments, Kubernetes offers options to lock off certain cluster users from viewing secrets. Therefore, you could give a monitoring tool access to view cluster status without giving them access to the Secrets. Additionally, keeping sensitive data in Secrets is also required for some information (like `imagePullSecrets`).

The ConfigMap for our application is very straightforward and is shown in Figure 10-11. As you can see, the format is very straightforward. The ConfigMap is given a name, and then within that ConfigMap is a list of key/value pairs under the `data` key. Alternatively, if you need to store binary data in a ConfigMap, it can be specified using the `binaryData` key. The keys for those are still regular keys, but the values are base64-encoded binary data.

As mentioned, Secrets are managed almost identically to ConfigMaps, but with some important but subtle differences:

- The `data` key in a Secret defaults to being base64-encoded binary data. If you want regular string data, you need to use the `stringData` key.[7]

- Some secrets have very specific formats that must be followed, such as the Secret for accessing a container registry. Kubernetes will make sure that these Secrets have the correct keys and, to some extent, the correct formats for those key values.

- Kubernetes handles Secrets in a more secure fashion. It encrypts them when stored in physical media and maintains more controls over who can view/edit them. Additionally, `kubectl` won't show the Secret using the normal `get`/`describe` commands (see Appendix C.10 for information on how to view a Secret).

---

[7] This is done for two major reasons. The first is because even when someone is allowed to see a Secret, it is often best to at least keep the value obscured, and base64 does that. The second is that many secrets are in fact encryption keys, which are naturally binary data.

```
apiVersion: v1
kind: Secret
metadata:
  name: database-secret
stringData:
  password: mypass
```

Figure 10-12. *Database Secret:* `database-secret.yaml`

We have defined two secrets—one for the database service and one for pulling from our private Docker repository. The database service could have easily been a ConfigMap. Since the database is not accessible outside the cluster, the database password doesn't need high security. Nonetheless, it is probably a good habit to keep such information as a Secret. Figure 10-12 shows the database password as a secret. Note that, just like ConfigMaps, you can store more than one value in a Secret; we have just not done so here.

☞ EXPORTING CONFIGMAPS AND SECRETS AS FILES

Data inside a ConfigMap or Secret doesn't have to be short like ours, but having such ConfigMaps makes it easier to manage as they can be passed easily to containers through environment variables. However, larger values for Secrets and ConfigMaps can be passed to containers through volumes.

When defining volumes for a Pod, you can specify a `ConfigMap` key to make the volume simply make the keys available as files on the volume. By default, all keys will be available on the volume, but they can also be selected using the `items` array, where each desired ConfigMap entry is enumerated by the key field and the path that it should be stored on the volume is given by the `path` field. Using this mechanism, you can have a ConfigMap store larger values, such as entire properties files.

The example `volume` entry in the following creates a volume that has the `pg-host` variable stored in a file called `mypghost.txt`:

```
volumes:
  - name: myConfigVolume
    configMap:
    - name: mboard-api-config
      items:
        - key: pg-host
          path: mypghost.txt
```

If we left off the `items` array completely, it would show all keys in the volume using the key name as the filename. Secrets can be mounted the same way, using the key `secret` on the volume instead of `configMap` and the subkey `secretName` instead of `name`. The `items` array works equivalently.

```
apiVersion: v1
kind: Secret
metadata:
  name: docker-token-secret
type: kubernetes.io/dockerconfigjson
stringData:
  .dockerconfigjson: |
    {
      "auths": {
        "https://index.docker.io/v1/": {
          "auth":"am9obm55YjYxODIwOnlvdXRyaWVk"
        }
      }
    }
```

Figure 10-13. *Docker Hub Authentication Secret:* `docker-token-secret`

The secret for authenticating to our Docker registry is stored in a slightly different way. You can see this secret in Figure 10-13. In this Secret, we give it a `type`, which Kubernetes uses to validate the Secret. The type we use is `kubernetes.io/dockerconfigjson`. Note that the value in the YAML manifest file starts with a pipe symbol (`|`). This tells the YAML parser that this will be a multiline value. It then uses the indentation to know how long the value should be and strips off that indentation for the value itself. For Docker login secrets, the format is very straightforward. The key is .dockerconfigjson (don't forget the starting period), and the value is a JSON file describing authentication keys to different container registries.

The Secret shown is for the Docker Hub registry. For the Docker Hub registry, the key is just a Base64 encoding of USER:PASS where those are your username and password to Docker Hub, respectively.[8] Other container registries may have different ways of creating authentication tokens, but the format of the Secret is the same.

To create a token yourself, use the following command on Linux or Mac (or a Linux container), replacing USER and PASS with your own username and password. Note that the -n flag prevents a newline from being included in the data to be encoded.

```
echo -n USER:PASS | base64
```

Depending on the reason for the secret, I may put the secret either in its own top-level directory for my cluster configuration (secrets/), or, if they are environment-specific secrets, I put them in their respective environment directories.

10.7 Making an Ingress

So, the whole cluster is fully up and running, but the only problem is that it is inaccessible from the outside. While you *can* use a Service with a LoadBalancer to enable access to your services, the problem is that each service will wind up with its own LoadBalancer and therefore its own IP address, which also means you will need to configure a hostname and a TLS/SSL certificate for each one.

Instead, what we would like to do is to create a unified gateway to the world where we simply map in which services go to which URL paths. The gateway would then be the only location where we would need to worry about IP addresses, hostnames, and TLS/SSL certificates. Additionally, even if we break up our application into pieces that are developed and managed by different teams, to the outside world it looks like a single application. Finally, by putting everything on the same hostname, you eliminate a lot of headaches with web applications and CORS (the browser framework for giving permissions to JavaScript applications to make network requests).

For Kubernetes, such a gateway is known as an Ingress. Unfortunately, since Ingresses are very cloud-specific, Kubernetes requires that you specify an

---

[8] If you are concerned, I have put in a fake password for this auth token.

ingressClassName to tell it how the Ingress should be managed. However, there is an Ingress Class that you can install that uses nginx (an open source webserver) to run, known as ingress-nginx. While ingress-nginx isn't officially a standard part of Kubernetes, it is developed by the same group and is one of the more common ways of building an Ingress.

You can install this in three different ways:

1. You can directly apply the YAML configuration from a web URL. This is the easiest to do.

2. You can copy the web URL to your local Kubernetes configuration and apply it from there (this way it is part of your version-controlled cluster configuration).

3. You can install it using a Kubernetes package manager such as Helm.

For simplicity, we will opt for the first option. You can install this Ingress Class using the following command:[9]

```
kubectl apply -f https://bit.ly/ingress_nginx_1_2_0
```

This creates numerous objects in Kubernetes, including Pods and Services, but runs then in a different *namespace* so you don't see them normally. If you run kubectl get pods -A, you will see all Pods in all namespaces, and the -A flag can be applied to looking at other Kubernetes resources.

The configuration for the Ingress is shown in Figure 10-14. The ingressClassName tells the Ingress to use the installed nginx-ingress Ingress Class to run the Ingress. After applying the configuration (and waiting a few minutes for Kubernetes to finish setting it up), you should be able to find the IP address for your Ingress by doing the following:

```
kubectl describe ingress main-ingress
```

You can then pull up the service by going to http://THE.IP.ADDRESS.SHOWN/ on your browser. Congratulations—you have a running cluster!

---

[9] The full URL, which I have shortened here using Bitly, is https://raw.githubusercontent.com/kubernetes/ingress-nginx/controller-v1.2.0/deploy/static/provider/cloud/deploy.yaml.

The Ingress consists of a set of `rules` which tells the Ingress where different endpoints should go. The `path` key tells the incoming path, and the `backend` key tells which service/port to map it to. In addition to putting paths on the rules, you can also specify a hostname using the `host` key. This allows you to use the same ingress to service a variety of hostnames. The `defaultBackend` right under the `spec` (outside of the rules) services any request that isn't matched by a rule.

```
apiVersion: networking.k8s.io/v1
kind: Ingress
metadata:
  name: main-ingress
spec:
  ingressClassName: nginx
  defaultBackend:
    service:
      name: frontend-service
      port:
        number: 80
  rules:
    - http:
        paths:
          - path: /api/
            pathType: Prefix
            backend:
              service:
                name: mboard-api-service
                port:
                  number: 4567
```

Figure 10-14. *The Ingress Definition:* `ingress.yaml`

Here, our front-end HTML/JavaScript Service will be called for anything not otherwise matched by our rules. The one rule we have in place maps everything that starts with `/api/` to go to the `mboard-api-service` Service.

The Ingress is also where TLS/SSL configuration is done. Since that requires a specific hostname, I can't give a working example, but we will describe how it can be done. A `tls` section can be created under the `spec` key that is an array of TLS configurations. Each configuration will have a `hosts` key, which is a list of hostnames that this applies to, and a `secretName`, which contains the TLS/SSL key and certificate information. Figure 10-15 shows what such a secret looks like.

```
apiVersion: v1
kind: Secret
metadata:
  name: tls-example-secret
type: kubernetes.io/tls
data:
  tls.crt: BASE64ENCODEDCERT
  tls.key: BASE64ENCODEDKEY
```

Figure 10-15. *Example TLS Secret:* `tls-secret.yaml`

The corresponding TLS section would look like this:

```
tls:
  - hosts:
      - myhost.example.com
    secretName: tls-example-secret
```

Additionally, the `nginx-ingress` Ingress Class has a few additional requirements for TLS/SSL:[10]

- The `rules` section *also* needs to specify a matching `host` (this is on the *same level* as the `http` key).

- The `tls.crt` key in the Secret can contain multiple certificates, but they need to be in a specific order—leaf, then intermediate, and then root certificates.

The `nginx-ingress` Ingress Class can also manage automatically re-requesting certificates from Let's Encrypt or similar issuers, but setting that up is outside the scope of this book.

10.8 Final Thoughts

This was a long chapter, but I wanted to be able to walk you through a fully operational Kubernetes cluster setup all in one go, so you could see how all of the pieces fit together. You should now have a good feel for how Kubernetes works and the kind of thoughts

---

[10] More information about the TLS/SSL configuration for `nginx-ingress` can be found on their website at `https://kubernetes.github.io/ingress-nginx/user-guide/tls/`.

that go into planning a Kubernetes cluster. For your own clusters, you will probably want to create an account on Docker Hub or some other registry where you can store private container images.

In this chapter, I have put version tags on all of the images that we are pulling. This is a recommended practice, as it makes sure that you are fully aware (and in control of) of which version you are running at all times. However, note that, by the time you read this, these versions may be out of date and possibly have security issues. If you are using this for anything more than a test, please be sure to update the version numbers to the latest ones. Additionally, the version numbers I specified are major versions (and sometimes minor), not patch numbers. This is to make sure the version is still available at the time of writing. For a production cluster, it is generally preferable to be as specific as possible when specifying version numbers. You should probably also make your own mirror repositories for any public images you use to be sure that they remain available into the future and that the tags stay stable.[11]

Note that, in addition to this working on the Linode Kubernetes cluster, the configuration files in this chapter also work just fine locally using the Kubernetes cluster that is installed with Docker (you have to turn it on first). However, the resulting Ingress only gets a `localhost` IP address, while the Linode one gives you an IP address you can access from anywhere.

Also note that there is more than one way to structure such an app, and some of the architectural choices in this chapter are as much to demonstrate some of the Kubernetes features as anything. For instance, we chose to check out the HTML from a `git` repository using an `initContainer` rather than include it as part of a custom Docker container. Personally, I prefer to put all code into containers, so I know exactly what is being deployed and can easily roll back to a different version, but I wanted to show an example of how an `initContainer` was used and how they work together. My goal was to give you the broadest understanding of configuration choices in the simplest presentation possible.

If you had trouble with any of the steps in this chapter, Appendix F has some tips on troubleshooting Kubernetes issues.

---

[11] A mirror repository is a repository that you control which simply mirrors another repository. Other users may change the name or meaning of a repository or tag or remove it altogether. Having a mirror repository means that you have control of when these get created, updated, and deleted.

10.9 Summary

In this chapter, we learned the following:

- Applications are often built from a combination of standard and custom images.

- There are many different ways of configuring and deploying Pods onto the cluster, based on the needs of the service in question.

- Even if a service is made using a single Pod, it still needs a Deployment to manage the health of the Pod and a Service to allow other Pods to connect to it.

- External storage space can be easily provisioned to allow for space that survives the termination and recreation of Pods that use it.

- Environment variables, used to configure Pods, can be constructed from static strings, ConfigMaps, Secrets, Pod information, or previously defined environment variables.

- Kubernetes uses `imagePullSecrets` in order to authenticate with private container image repositories.

- The Ingress coordinates the different externally facing aspects of your application and provides a single point for TLS/SSL termination.

- Overall, most of the information about *how* Kubernetes works was in Chapter 8, but this chapter provided concrete details of how that information is specified and works together to create a real Kubernetes application.

CHAPTER 11

Going Further in Kubernetes

The goal of this book is not to be a complete reference but to get you up to speed quickly on how Kubernetes works so that you can easily make use of Kubernetes in your own organization. The foundation laid up to this point in the book should allow you to easily understand and apply other Kubernetes concepts using the standard Kubernetes reference material. In this chapter, we will present some additional Kubernetes ideas and features that may make sense for you to explore further for your own cluster but will not give them the same level of detail as before.

11.1 Cluster Namespaces

As your cluster gets bigger, it is important to keep parts of your cluster at least logically separated from each other. Namespaces allow you to group Kubernetes resources together.

Everything in Kubernetes occurs within a namespace. So far, we have just been using the default namespace, which simply has the name `default`. To create a new namespace, we can use a very simple YAML manifest like the one shown in Figure 11-1.

```
apiVersion: v1
kind: Namespace
metadata:
  name: my-namespace
```

Figure 11-1. Creating a Namespace: `namespace.yaml`

125

© Jonathan Bartlett 2023
J. Bartlett, *Cloud Native Applications with Docker and Kubernetes*,
https://doi.org/10.1007/978-1-4842-8876-4_11

This creates a namespace called `my-namespace`. Now, a Kubernetes object can be created within this namespace by specifying the `namespace` key in the object's `metadata`.

`kubectl` by default uses the `default` namespace. However, we can ask `kubectl` to show different namespaces by adding the `-n NAMESPACE` flag to any of the commands or `-A` to show objects from all namespaces.

All Service names get stored in CoreDNS as `SERVICE.NAMESPACE.svc.cluster.local`, and your Pod is set to search for hostnames first within `NAMESPACE.svc.cluster.local` for their own namespace and then within just `svc.cluster.local`. Therefore, inside a namespace, Pods will default to looking up bare Service names in their own namespace, and this will not look up a Service defined in another namespace. However, a Pod can access a Service name on *any* namespace by adding the namespace name to the DNS name they are looking for. So, if we are in a Pod that is in the `my-namespace` namespace but want to find the `database-service` Service that was defined in our `default` namespace, we can simply look in DNS for `database-service.default`.

We can also use an ExternalName Service to map a Service defined in another namespace into our own. As mentioned in Chapter 8, an ExternalName Service essentially defines a CNAME for our cluster so that Pods can reference outside services as if they were defined on the cluster. So, here, you can just do an ExternalName to the full cluster DNS name of the service (like `SERVICE.NAMESPACE.svc.cluster.local` as mentioned above).

Additionally, Kubernetes provides mechanisms to add resource restrictions and permissions to namespaces. You can specify that a cluster user only be given permissions to specific namespaces. Therefore, namespaces can be used for both logically separating pieces of a cluster and keeping the different parts controlled.

Deciding how to use namespaces depends on how your cluster is organized. For small clusters, just using the default namespace works perfectly fine. However, if you have a large application, sometimes larger components are easier to manage if they are considered separately and therefore can be put into their own namespace. Generally, keeping pieces of a single logical "unit" of your application in the same namespace generally makes the most sense. Additionally, externally managed components by systems such as Helm (see Section 11.2) are often placed in their own namespace as well in order to minimize the amount that the cluster administrator has to think about them.

11.2 Helm

While YAML manifest files are great for maintaining basic Kubernetes configurations, some people want more power. The problem with YAML files is that they are configuration files and therefore are not as powerful as actual code. While ConfigMaps offer a lot of flexibility, they can't do everything anyone might want. Additionally, adding external features to your cluster sometimes takes extra work. If a service requires a lot of configuration and coordination to get started, it might not be as easy as just specifying a container image to run.

Because of these issues, Helm was developed to be both a Kubernetes YAML templating engine and a package manager. Helm allows the definition of a complex service, known as a "Helm Chart," which can be easily installed and configured with a minimum of hassle.

For instance, while our database in Chapter 10 was simplified by having a single Pod running the whole database, most database setups include master servers, replica servers, and connection pools, all tied together. While this would take quite some doing to set up using normal Kubernetes YAML, with Helm Charts, one can simply say "I want a PostgreSQL database" and get the service up and running easily.

Installing Helm is straightforward but differs on each platform. It is a client-side tool, which means that it doesn't itself require any cluster resources to run. To install a service, you need only two steps: (1) install the repository that holds the Chart you want (if you haven't before), and (2) tell Helm to install the Chart. For the aforementioned database service, the commands are as follows:

```
helm repo add bitnami https://charts.bitnami.com/bitnami
helm install my-postgres-release bitnami/postgresql-ha \
   --set postgresql.replicaCount=3
```

This will create a whole slew of Kubernetes objects in your cluster. This creates Pods, Services, Secrets, ConfigMaps, PVCs, and other types of resources that are needed to get the database cluster running. You can identify the ones created by this command because they will all be using the label `app.kubernetes.io/instance` set to `my-postgres-release`. The actual connection point to your database will be through the service named `my-postgres-release-postgresql-ha-pgpool`. This will use PGPool to auto-switch between the master and replica databases depending on whether it is a read-only or a read-write transaction. If that Service name is too long for your liking, you can create an ExternalName Service to give you a shorter name.

However, the `helm install` command has the same drawbacks as all of the individual `kubectl` commands that we were trying to avoid by putting our cluster code in YAML manifest files. Essentially, we are losing the ability to hold the cluster state in a version-controlled file.

However, Helm offers an alternative. Instead of doing `helm install`, `helm template` will output a YAML file that consists of the Kubernetes changes it wants to make, and then you can keep it locally in your cluster's code repository and apply it with `kubectl apply` just like all of your other YAML manifest files. So, you could replace the `helm install` command above with the following command:

```
helm template my-postgres-release bitnami/postgresql-ha \
    --set postgresql.replicaCount=3 > database.yaml
kubectl apply -f database.yaml
```

This creates a file locally called `database.yaml` that stores the cluster configuration that `helm` generates then applies it like normal. In my opinion, this is a much better approach to Kubernetes cluster maintenance. It allows you to have full visibility into what is being installed on your cluster, make changes as needed, and keep it all in your version-controlled system.

In any case, Helm allows you to quickly add standardized services to your cluster. Here, we installed a database system. You might add a queueing system, an automation server, an S3-compatible object server, a WordPress server, or any of a number of other cloud services. You can even create your own Helm Charts.

For more information about Helm, see the website at `https://helm.sh`.

11.3 Capacity Management and Autoscaling

Autoscaling is the ability to add Pods to a Deployment in response to increased load or remove them in response to decreased load. In either case, the goal is to match cluster resources to what is actually required to handle the load. Personally, while I find autoscaling to be useful, it is actually a bit overrated. However, whether you do autoscaling or not, this section will also deal with other capacity management techniques that are generally important.

Generally, whether you have autoscaling enabled or not, you should know your cluster's capacity requirements. Then, whether you set your resources manually or through autoscaling doesn't make a lot of difference. Scaling a Deployment manually

just means changing the `replicas` value on its YAML manifest and then running
`kubectl apply`.

In order to do autoscaling, there are two things you need to scale—the number of
Pods and the number of Nodes. Scaling Pods is necessary, because, if you don't have
more Pods, you aren't actually using more cluster resources no matter how big your
cluster is. However, ultimately, those Pods have to run on Nodes. If you run out of Node
capacity, you are just out of capacity.

Autoscaling Pods is handled within Kubernetes using a HorizontalPodAutoscaler
object, while autoscaling Nodes is very cluster-specific. On Linode, you can autoscale
Nodes from the Linode Kubernetes administration panel by just clicking the "Autoscale
Pool" button by your Node pool, enabling the feature, and setting the minimum and
maximum number of Nodes that should be running in the Node Pool.

Autoscaling Pods requires four things:

1.   A running metrics server

2.   The `metrics.k8s.io` API to be installed on the cluster

3.   Resource limits set on the Pods

4.   A HorizontalPodAutoscaler to manage the actual act of scaling

First, we will look at running our metrics server. Thankfully, the metrics server *also*
provides the `metrics.k8s.io` API to our cluster, since it isn't installed by default in the Linode
cluster. The metrics server can be installed using Helm with the following commands:

```
helm repo add bitnami https://charts.bitnami.com/bitnami
helm install my-metrics-server bitnami/metrics-server \
  --set apiService.create=true \
  --set "extraArgs[0]=--kubelet-preferred-address-types=InternalIP" \
  --set "extraArgs[1]=--kubelet-insecure-tls"
```

Different parameters are needed for different clusters, but these work for Linode.
Setting `apiService.create=true` is what creates the API. The `extraArgs` settings tell the
metrics server how to connect to the cluster to get the information.

Next, you need to set usage limits on the Pods in order for them to measure how
close they come to those limits. This is done in the `resources/limits` section of a Pod
container template. You can add a `cpu` subkey which is the number of "virtual CPUs" that
counts as 100% usage (a virtual CPU is roughly equivalent to a single CPU core on the
Node that the Pod is running on).

The following is an example code snippet showing how to modify Figure 10-9 (our Message Board API Deployment) so that the main container in the Pod template can be set to have a CPU resource limit of 10% of a CPU:

```
containers:
- name: api-container
  image: johnnyb61820/k8s-example-api-private
  resources:
    limits:
      cpu: 0.1
```

Note that, with our setup, you *should not go anywhere near* having a CPU limit of 1. Think about it this way—the Pod has to be scheduled on a Node, and the Node has to do other things than just run the Pod. Therefore, if you have a single-CPU Node (like ours are), it can't possibly run a Pod which might use a full CPU's resource. Therefore, Kubernetes won't even try to schedule it.[1]

Finally, you will need to create a HorizontalPodAutoscaler object. These autoscalers will monitor utilization (defined by us in the preceding) on the individual Pods and determine if a workload (e.g., a Deployment or StatefulSet) needs to deploy more Pods. Figure 11-2 shows an example of an HorizontalPodAutoscaler that is set to autoscale a Deployment based on CPU utilization of its Pods, which triggers Pod scaling to target 50% usage.

---

[1] In fact, even if you have Node autoscaling turned on, it won't even try to boot new Nodes because it knows that none of them are large enough to run your Pods!

```
apiVersion: autoscaling/v2
kind: HorizontalPodAutoscaler
metadata:
  name: api-autoscaler
spec:
  scaleTargetRef:
    apiVersion: apps/v1
    kind: Deployment
    name: api-deployment
  minReplicas: 1
  maxReplicas: 10
  metrics:
  - type: Resource
    resource:
      name: cpu
      target:
        type: Utilization
        averageUtilization: 50
```

Figure 11-2. An Example Autoscaler: autoscale.yaml

The algorithm that the HorizontalPodAutoscaler uses is as follows:

$$dReplicas = ceil\left(\frac{cReplicas \times cMetricValue}{dMetricValue}\right). \qquad (11.1)$$

Here, "c" stands for "current" and "d" stands for "desired" on both the replicas and the metric value. So, let's imagine the following scenario: you have your CPU utilization set to 0.1, you are targeting 50% utilization (which would be 0.05 utilization), you currently have three replicas running, and their average utilization is 0.075. The replica count equation would be $ceil\left(\frac{3 \times 0.075}{0.05}\right) \rightarrow 5$. Therefore, the HorizontalPodAutoscaler would boot two additional replicas unless that goes beyond its maximum count. The algorithm itself runs every five minutes to prevent thrashing (continually booting and tearing down Pods).

If you have Node autoscaling on in your cluster, the cluster will even add or remove Nodes as well to accommodate your Pods.

11.4 DaemonSets

Typically, Pods are scheduled by Kubernetes itself to make the best use of cluster resources. However, sometimes you specifically want something to be running on *each* Node. Examples of this can include specialty Node monitoring tools, log collection tools, networking tools, or storage tools.

Another interesting example of a DaemonSet is for a caching service. In Figure 10-5, we configured a single instance of Memcache for the entire cluster. However, there are other ways of doing this. We could have configured Memcache as a sidecar container within the main Message Board API Pod, so that every such Pod has both the Message Board API and a caching server. However, a more interesting configuration is to have one caching server per *physical Node*. Turning the Memcache Deployment into a DaemonSet would do this.

To accomplish this, all you have to do is make three small modifications to the configuration in Figure 10-5:

1. On the `memcache-deployment`, change the `kind` from `Deployment` to `DaemonSet`.

2. Remove the `replicas` field.

3. In the `memcache-service`'s `spec`, add the field `internalTrafficPolicy` and set it to `Local`.

Since we haven't changed the name of the Service, if you run `kubectl apply` on the new configuration, it will all work automatically. Since the Memcache Service is a ClusterIP service, this doesn't change anything about how the Message Board API Pods communicate with the Memcache Service. The `internalTrafficPolicy` field tells Kubernetes to route requests to this service to only Pods running on the same node that it is being requested on. That implements the "magic" of the idea, but it is a little dangerous because it will drop traffic if it can't find an implementation of the Service on the local Node. That works since the workload is a DaemonSet; but just remember to remove the line or change it to `Cluster` if you ever go back to the workload being a Deployment.

Note that, since the new `kind` has changed, if you already had the previous deployment installed on your cluster, you will want to delete the old one since it is no longer applicable. Also note that having only one caching server meant that the cached data will never be inconsistent. Here, having multiple cache servers may mean that results don't necessarily show up until the cache expires (about 15 seconds).

11.5 Jobs

Almost every cloud has processes that run outside the normal request/response cycle. Transcoding videos, running a monthly billing cycle, and performing a mass data migration are all things that happen on a cluster, but don't fall into the traditional Deployment idea. These are normally handled with Jobs or CronJobs.

Jobs are different from other kinds of workloads we have considered because they are *supposed* to finish. However, Kubernetes needs to know if it was successful or not, so that it can know if it needs to rerun the Job or not. For this, Kubernetes uses the exit status code of your Pod. If it returns a zero status code, it is considered successfully completed. Any other status code is considered a failure. On a failure, depending on what your `restartPolicy` is, Kubernetes will either rerun your Pod (if it is set to `OnFailure`) or just report that the Pod died (if it is set to `Never`). You can also specify a `backoffLimit` if you want to prevent failed code from restarting forever.

A simple job consists of just a name and a Pod template. Figure 11-3 shows a job that runs a dice-rolling image. If you `kubectl apply` this YAML manifest file, it will create a job, run the Pod, and then keep the non-running Pod around until the Job is deleted so you can check logs. Note that you will need to delete and recreate the job if you want to run it again.

```
apiVersion: batch/v1
kind: Job
metadata:
  name: roll-dice
spec:
  template:
    spec:
      restartPolicy: OnFailure
      containers:
        - name: main
          image: johnnyb61820/roll-dice
```

Figure 11-3. *Simple Job Example:* `simple-job.yaml`

If a Job requires that multiple copies of the same Pod be booted (i.e., to work through a job queue in parallel), you can set a `parallelism` key under the top-level `spec` to the number of copies you desire. The Job will be considered "complete" when all Pods have exited with at least one of them exiting with a success status code. Instead of running in parallel, you can also specify a job to run multiple times consecutively by using `completions` instead of `parallelism`. This simply specifies the number of times you want the job to complete successfully.

To run a job regularly on a schedule, you should use a CronJob. If you're not familiar with it, "Cron" is the scheduling service for Unix-based systems, and that is where this workload gets its name. Essentially, a CronJob will create Jobs continually. Just like Deployments will create a number of Pods based on a template, the CronJob will, according to schedule, create new jobs according to a template.

Figure 11-4 shows the code for a simple CronJob. It has several new keys (only the first two are required):

- `schedule`, which tells it when to run

- `jobTemplate`, which is the template for creating new Job objects

- `concurrencyPolicy` (set to either `Allow` or `Forbid`), which tells it whether or not it can run if the previously launched Job is still running

- `successfulJobsHistoryLimit` and `failedJobsHistoryLimit`, which tell Kubernetes how many old (completed or failed) Jobs it should keep around before it starts cleaning them up (deleting them) automatically[2]

---

[2] If not set, these default to 3 and 1, respectively. Setting them to 0 means that the jobs are never cleaned up.

```
apiVersion: batch/v1
kind: CronJob
metadata:
  name: roll-dice-often
spec:
  schedule: "* * * * *"
  concurrencyPolicy: Forbid
  successfulJobsHistoryLimit: 5
  failedJobsHistoryLimit: 5
  jobTemplate:
    spec:
      template:
        spec:
          restartPolicy: OnFailure
          containers:
            - name: main
              image: johnnyb61820/roll-dice
```

Figure 11-4. Simple CronJob Example: `simple-cron-job.yaml`

The contents of the `jobTemplate` match what is expected for a Job, as you can see by comparing it to Figure 11-3. The format of the `schedule` field is a little strange if you aren't familiar with the Unix Cron system. Essentially, there are five fields: minute (0–59), hour (0–23), day-of-month (1–31), month (1–12), and day-of-week (0–6, Sunday–Saturday). You specify whether or not the job should be *allowed* to run on each of these. Since we specified * for each value, that means it runs every minute (i.e., it is allowed to run on all minutes of all hours of all days of the month of every month on every day of the week). So, if I wanted something to run every hour on the hour, I would specify it at "0 * * * *". Essentially, I'm only giving it permission to run on minute zero, but everything else can happen anytime. If I wanted something to run at 2:45 PM on Wednesdays, I would specify it as "45 2 * * 3".

Note that there are some occasions where the scheduler might schedule a job more than once. You should write your code so that it allows for this possibility.

11.6 Cluster Security

Entire books have been written on Kubernetes security, and we won't attempt to replicate them here in a short section. However, it is important to have a basic understanding of how Kubernetes security works. At the core of Kubernetes security is the Role, which defines a set of permissions within the Kubernetes network. This focus on Roles is frequently referred to as RBAC, or "Role-Based Access Control."

A ClusterRole consists of a name for the role and a list of rules telling Kubernetes what parts of the cluster the ClusterRole grants access to. Each rule contains (a) an array of API groups that this rule relates to (`apiGroups`), (b) a list of Kubernetes resources to grant permission to (`resourceNames`), (c) a list of actions that the user can perform with these resources (`verbs`), and sometimes (d) a list of specifically named objects within the resource that the user has access to (`resourceNames`).

If you think about our YAML objects, they all have an `apiVersion` that has a format of `GROUP/VERSION`. The `GROUP` in that syntax is the API group. The group should be specified as `""` if it is the core API group (the one that just has `v1`). The resources should simply be named as all-lowercase plural strings representing the resource, such as `services`, `configmaps`, `deployments`, or `ResourceAll` for everything. Finally, the actions, known as *verbs*, are the operations that can be performed on the resource. Common actions are `get`, `list`, `create`, `update`, `patch`, `watch`, `delete`, and `deletecollection`. The verb `VerbAll` represents all actions. A separate object type, the Role, is exactly like a ClusterRole but exists within a specific namespace.[3]

A ClusterRoleBinding (or a RoleBinding if it is in a namespace) assigns a ClusterRole/Role to a list of "subjects." A `subject` can be thought of as a user-like object. A subject has a `kind` field which can be set to `ServiceAccount`, `User`, or `Group`. It also has a `name` field which tells which account to refer to (this is case-sensitive). For ServiceAccounts, this also has a `namespace` which says which namespace the ServiceAccount is defined in.

Kubernetes "users" can be divided into two basic types: ServiceAccounts (which are managed within Kubernetes) and Users (which are managed by third parties). Usually, cluster administrators are authenticated by third-party plug-ins, which grant the user a TLS certificate which names their username on the system and the groups they are involved in. This allows Kubernetes administrators to use their own company logins when logging in to the cluster. Kubernetes has a standard authentication plug-in which allows for authentication using OpenID Connect, or custom plug-ins can be built for connecting with other third-party authentication services. After authenticating,

---

[3] This is a separate type of object because Kubernetes only allows namespaced or non-namespaced objects. Therefore, despite their similarities, the architecture of Kubernetes requires that Roles and ClusterRoles be different types of resources.

the user will then receive a certificate stating their username and group memberships. Kubernetes will then simply trust the user and group names on a properly signed certificate. Therefore, User and Group objects are not managed within Kubernetes. ClusterRoleBindings and RoleBindings simply refer to them by name, exactly as they will appear on the certificate.

A Service Account is used by Kubernetes to enable applications to access the Kubernetes API. Essentially, it allows an application running on a Pod to identify itself back to the Kubernetes system. ServiceAccounts are maintained in YAML manifest files just like all other Kubernetes objects. ServiceAccounts by themselves are basically just names.

Figure 11-5 shows a ServiceAccount that has a role which allows it to list pods and services.

```
apiVersion: v1
kind: ServiceAccount
metadata:
  name: my-service-account
---
apiVersion: rbac.authorization.k8s.io/v1
kind: ClusterRole
metadata:
  name: list-services-pods
rules:
  - apiGroups: [""]
    resources: ["services", "pods"]
    verbs: ["list", "get"]
---
apiVersion: rbac.authorization.k8s.io/v1
kind: ClusterRoleBinding
metadata:
  name: list-services-pods-binding
subjects:
  - kind: ServiceAccount
    name: my-service-account
    namespace: default
roleRef:
  kind: ClusterRole
  name: list-services-pods
  apiGroup: rbac.authorization.k8s.io
```

Figure 11-5. *Example Service Account Configuration:* `my-service-account.yaml`

ServiceAccounts can be assigned to Pods by simply adding the field
`serviceAccountName` to the Pod or Pod Template spec, referencing the created
ServiceAccount. When the Pod runs under the ServiceAccount, Kubernetes creates a
directory on the pod, `/run/secrets/kubernetes.io/serviceaccount`, which contains
three files for accessing the Kubernetes API: `token` (the token the Pod should use
to authenticate itself to Kubernetes), `namespace` (the default namespace the service
account should be using), and `ca.crt` (the certificate our Pod should use to verify
Kubernetes).

I'm not going to give a full tutorial on using the Kubernetes API, but, if you apply this
service account to the `mboard-api-deployment` Pod Template spec, you can log in to the
pod (see Appendix C.2) and perform the following commands to list information about
the Kubernetes API.[4]

```
SVC_ACCT_PATH=/run/secrets/kubernetes.io/serviceaccount
TOKEN=$(cat ${SVC_ACCT_PATH}/token)
CERT_PATH=${SVC_ACCT_PATH}/ca.crt
curl --cacert $CERT_PATH -H "Authorization: Bearer ${TOKEN}" \
    https://kubernetes.default/api
```

The first part of the `curl` command should be a part of every request, as it performs
the two-way authentication between the Pod and the Kubernetes API. There are two
basic structures for the URL to hit—one for the core API resources (those without a
group name in their `apiVersion`) and those for the rest. The core API resources can be
accessed at the following URL (all on one line):

```
https://kubernetes.default/api/APIVERSION/namespaces/NAMESPACE/
    RESOURCE/NAME
```

So, to get information about our `mboard-api-service` Service, since Services is part
of the core API, we would access the following URL (all on one line):

```
https://kubernetes.default/api/v1/namespaces/default/
    services/mboard-api-service
```

If you aren't specifying a specific named object in the resource, you can leave `NAME`
off. Use the word `default` to use the default namespace. For API resources that are

---

[4]For more details on the Kubernetes API, you can refer to the documentation available at
`https://bit.ly/kubernetes-api`.

defined within a group, you can access them through the following URL structure (all on one line):

```
https://kubernetes.default/apis/APIGROUP/APIVERSION/namespaces/
  NAMESPACE/RESOURCE/NAME
```

Finally, there are two situations in which you can leave off the `namespaces/` `NAMESPACE` part of the URL—when listing all objects from all namespaces (in which case the `NAME` is left off as well) and when accessing resources that *cannot* have a namespace, such as Nodes.

11.7 Customizing Kubernetes

This subject is pretty far outside the scope of this book, but I did want to point out that Kubernetes has the ability to be extended. There are two main ways to extend Kubernetes, and they can be used by themselves or combined:

- Adding controllers
- Adding new resource types

A controller is essentially a Pod which runs in a service account which performs custom actions based on what it finds when accessing the Kubernetes API. Controllers essentially run in a loop, checking the Kubernetes API for cluster configuration, and ensuring that the desired state of the cluster matches what the controller wants based on what the controller is programmed to do.

Many Kubernetes objects we have already seen are managed by controllers. When you issue a Deployment, there is a controller that is watching the Deployment's resources. When a change to the Deployment is made, the controller then checks to see what ReplicaSet changes it needs to make to get the cluster in line.

To imagine what a controller would look like, let's say we wanted a feature that ensured a maximum lifetime of a Pod. This feature could be enabled by a label on the pod, such as `podMaximumLifespan`, and set to the number of seconds we wanted the Pod to live. Then, the controller would simply run in an infinite loop, each time querying for a list of Pods. Each time through it would check each Pod and see if it had the `podMaximumLifespan` label. If it did, it would compare the age of the Pod to the lifespan specified, and, if it was too old, it would terminate the Pod. This sort of behavior can be deployed as a Pod through a regular Deployment with a ServiceAccount specified.

This can be made even more interesting by the addition of new resources. Adding a resource essentially means adding a new type of YAML manifest file that can be saved into the cluster. This is made by adding a CustomResourceDefinition to the cluster. Adding a CustomResourceDefinition automatically creates new endpoints in the Kubernetes API for accessing these resources.

By themselves, adding a resource does nothing except create a bucket to put YAML data in. What makes it more interesting is when a controller is reading the newly created API endpoints and performing behaviors based on these new resource types. As an example, you could create a resource type of MessageQueue, which created and configured a message queueing service in the cluster. The details would be handled by the controller, and the cluster administrator would just define what it is they wanted. The controller would continually monitor the API for changes and then bring the cluster into conformance with the new request. It would also look to see if the cluster itself has drifted away from the desired configuration (i.e., if Pods are terminating unexpectedly) and attempt to heal the cluster back to the state specified by its configuration. To make these operations more efficient, the Kubernetes API has a `watch` action which you can hit to only receive data for changes in cluster configuration. When a controller is combined with a CustomResourceDefinition, it is oftentimes termed as an "operator."

Additionally, Kubernetes also added the idea of a "mutating admission controller," which allows you to modify parts of specifications that are added to Kubernetes. This allows you to, for instance, automatically add container sidecars to Pod definitions. For instance, if you wanted to automatically add a logging container to all Pods, you could use such a controller for taking all incoming Pod definitions and modifying them to add the logging container automatically.

11.8 Additional Information

The appendixes to this book have a lot of additional information about Kubernetes that did not fit well in the main flow of the book. You are encouraged to read through the appendixes to learn more about more specialized areas of Kubernetes.

11.9 Summary

In this chapter, we learned the following:

- Cluster resources can be grouped together into namespaces, which can be used both for organization and for some amount of security separation.

- Helm offers a way of creating YAML specifications from templates and installing them into your cluster.

- Pod resource usage can be constrained by setting resource limits.

- If a Pod's resource usage is constrained, the number of Pods launched by a ReplicaSet can be modified using a HorizontalPodAutoscaler, but this requires some additional setup on the Kubernetes cluster.

- If your cluster provider supports it, the number of Nodes in your cluster can also be autoscaled as well.

- DaemonSets can be used to enforce running a single Pod on each Node, which can be used to provide a Node-local caching mechanism.

- Jobs can be used to run one-off container instances that run until completion.

- CronJobs are jobs that are created from a template on a scheduled basis.

- Security can be provided to a cluster through Roles and RoleBindings.

- Pods can be given access to the Kubernetes API through ServiceAccounts, which creates a certificate and token which can be used for API access.

- The Kubernetes API is available on the cluster through the `kubernetes.default` service.

- Kubernetes can be customized by providing controllers (Pods that modify the cluster state based on the Kubernetes API) and/or CustomResourceDefinitions (essentially custom Kubernetes resources).

- The appendixes contain additional information about various aspects of Kubernetes that could be helpful to you.

PART III

Architecting for the Cloud

CHAPTER 12

A Cloud Architecture Introduction

Now that you know how to put a Kubernetes cluster together and what most of the major components of Kubernetes look like, in this part of the book, we are going to back up and look at what the cloud looks like from a higher level. This part of the book has less of an emphasis on Kubernetes itself and more of an emphasis on the overall design of the cluster. Since you now know what the Kubernetes components look like and how to put them together, I'm going to expect that you can apply that information in order to translate these architectural ideas into specific Kubernetes YAML manifests to apply to your cluster.

12.1 What Is Cloud Architecture?

As mentioned in Chapter 9, infrastructure as code (IaC) provides for a lot of advantages. One of those is that it is very easy for someone who knows Kubernetes to look at your cluster's configuration and understand what the cluster is doing. However, before you actually write the YAML manifests for the first resource, it is good to take some time and *plan* what you want your cluster to look like from a conceptual perspective.

Depending on what level of detail you are operationally responsible for, cloud architecture plans usually have two basic types of components:

1. Diagrams of the cloud components and their relationships to each other

2. Documents describing policies that should be followed when building applications

145

© Jonathan Bartlett 2023
J. Bartlett, *Cloud Native Applications with Docker and Kubernetes*,
https://doi.org/10.1007/978-1-4842-8876-4_12

These plans help a team understand both the conditions under which their code will be running and how to work together as a team. We refer to this planning (and the generated plan) as the *cloud architecture*.

The fact is, every cloud has an architecture because humans think about things before we do them, even if only briefly. Even if you are a solo developer, you have an architecture—a way that you think things will work in your system—in mind. Taking the time to put it on paper is an important step even if it is only for your own clarity about what you will be doing.

Even if you are the solo developer on your project, isn't your goal for your project to be wildly successful? At some point, you will need to involve other people. It is at this point where having a documented architecture will have an exponential payoff. New developers will very quickly be able to understand both what they are doing and how they can successfully work within the existing framework. The application as a whole will benefit because the architecture will ensure and enforce consistency between the old and new code.

12.2 Architectural Diagrams

An architectural diagram is a picture which represents some important aspect of how the cluster is laid out or how data flows within the cluster. Taking the effort to create a diagram of your proposed and/or actual cloud architecture has several advantages.

First of all, it provides both you and others with diagrams that can be used for other people to better understand the cloud's architecture. Most people understand diagrams much better than text or code. Showing someone a diagram communicates numerous ideas quickly, even if they aren't themselves programmers or cloud architects. Having diagrams of what your cloud looks like conceptually helps people of all disciplines and skill levels better understand what you are trying to accomplish.

Think, for instance, if your manager wants to know why cloud costs are so high. You can use a diagram to show them why you have allocated your chosen resources. Now think about a new programmer coming on board. Rather than making them dig through your YAML manifests to understand the cloud setup, the programmer can just look at the diagram and have a decent big picture overview. This can prevent numerous mistakes by the programmer. Perhaps, for instance, the programmer thought that every Pod was sharing a global cache rather than accessing a Node-specific one. Looking at an architectural diagram can clear that up quickly.

Second, taking the time and effort to plan out an architecture helps you think of alternatives. After a while, most cloud architects can think of a basic architectural plan to accomplish a goal rather quickly, and it is tempting to skip the actual architecture step. However, by explicitly visualizing the plan ahead-of-time, it is much easier to think of ways that the plan can be improved. Visual representations engage your mind in a different way than textual representations. Therefore, having the architecture drawn up will help you think about your architecture in new ways.

Having an architectural plan also facilitates receiving feedback. Frankly, most programmers don't want to read your YAML manifest files, no matter how much time you spent getting them just right. However, if you show them a good diagram of the system, they may be able to give you feedback on how the architecture may or may not work with the application. Perhaps there is something that is more stateful than you realized. Perhaps a system at the core of your cloud is actually more unreliable than you realized. Perhaps there is just something obvious that you missed that someone can help you with if you just showed them a diagram of what you were planning on doing.

Architectural diagrams can also make parts of your architecture more explicit which are only present implicitly. What triggers a process to start and stop, and what are the decision points along the way? With distributed systems, sometimes this isn't always clear just reading code because the actual flow is often split between system (and therefore code) boundaries. Therefore, it can only be made visible by creating diagrams, as it is not implicitly visible within the code. Making a diagram will help people better see how the different aspects of your system are affected by different events and provide a more holistic view of how the data flows.

Finally, having an architectural plan helps immensely when planning or discussing changes to the architecture. It is much easier when talking with someone about changes to show those changes by drawing boxes and lines compared to having to talk about them and hope someone is following along. Showing the old diagram and new diagram side-by-side helps people understand what changes are coming and helps communicate why they are important.

12.3 Application Policies

Every application that is beyond toy-level has multiple pieces that have to work together. This cooperation between pieces can either be ad hoc, where every point of interaction generates a new decision or protocol, or well-crafted, where the decisions are made ahead-of-time and every point of interaction follows a predictable pattern.

It is true that in the early stages of development, many applications get by just fine with ad hoc cooperation. This is especially true for solo or pair developers, because the communication between them is so efficient. However, as more people get added to a project, the more lines of communication are required.

Think about it like this. For n people, the number of lines of communication between them is $\dfrac{n^2 - n}{2}$, a number that grows *faster* than the number of people. For one person, there are no lines of communication. For two people, there is one line of communication. For three people, there are three lines of communication. For four people, there are six lines of communication.

Ad hoc interactions between components usually involve having to communicate these interactions to the whole team. However, having *policies* that govern how the code interacts with the system as a whole means that programmers don't have to do this. As teams become bigger, this is a huge time saver. When using ad hoc interactions, teams get stuck trying to communicate ideas and changes and even trying to solve the same problem repeatedly. A good set of policies will minimize (but probably not eliminate entirely) the number of ad hoc interactions between system components and therefore minimize the amount they need to be communicated, negotiated, or even designed (since the policy will likely dictate the design to some extent).

What types of policies you will need is somewhat dictated by the application you are working on. The most effective teams I've seen had policies that were geared toward the specifics of the application that they were working in. Nonetheless, let me provide you a set of common policies and why having such policies are helpful.

> **authentication protocol**: Obviously, we don't want each part of the application to implement its own authentication protocol. Therefore, one has to be decided upon. This also involves details such as protocols for passing authentication details between systems, access revoking, etc.

authorization control: How do we decide whether or not a particular user is authorized to view a piece of data or perform a function? Having a clear role or permission system and knowing what those roles/permissions mean are very important.

common message formats: Every system usually has some structures that are common to all (or nearly all) applications within the system. Having a common definition of what these structures should look like is important for the cluster. At minimum, standards for identifiers and keys should be established, such as whether to use sequential increasing numbers, UUIDs, etc.

common subsystems: Many applications wind up having subsystems that are built more than once. In one cluster group I was involved with, there were three separate implementations of a file-handling service that all did basically the same thing. The groups simply hadn't talked to each other enough to know that they were each independently solving the same problem.

sources of truth: Each piece of data on a cluster should have a "source of truth"—essentially, which application or endpoint is ultimately responsible for that data. Oftentimes data gets passed down the ladder, and it is good to know where the "official" version of that record is. This is important so that you know both where to go to get refreshed data as well as where to put updates. It also helps you more clearly identify dependencies within the system.

error message protocol: Having a common error message format in your network protocols helps programmers to simplify their error-handling and can help them provide a more uniform experience to the user. Knowing what error responses will look like prevents bugs that arise from ad hoc error formats.

logging format: Having a common logging format can help the team trace problems in the system and can help programmers involved in different parts of a project track down bugs. It can also help for generating reporting on problems.

coding style: Having a coding style guide helps make code written by more than one person more readable and eliminates many conflicts by simply having the choices premade. However, overly strict adherence to a style guide can also cause team conflicts.

response time: Having a response time policy helps developers know when they need to switch their network interactions from direct request-response to something more like opening up a process that then can receive status checks until it is done.

pagination: Do requests receive all of the data at once, or is the data broken up into pages which can be requested one page at a time? How are those pages controlled?

Which of those policies your team needs is very dependent on the team itself. As you build your system, other policies may become clearly needed. In any case, my hope is that this list will inspire you to think about policies that your team may need. Because the list of possible policies is so wide-ranging, this part of the book will only focus on a few of them which are more commonly needed and have an outsized impact on your cloud architecture.

12.4 Summary

In this chapter, we learned the following:

- Cloud architecture consists of developing a set of logical plans, including diagrams and policies, which outline the general framework that your cluster will implement.

- Taking the time to formalize your architecture, even on small projects, will pay off as the projects grow and become more successful. Having architectural documents to show new developers helps bring them up to speed quickly on the project.

- Cloud architecture can be implemented by Kubernetes code, but should not just be considered a graphical form of YAML files.

- Good cloud architecture diagrams will include necessary and relevant details for understanding and decision-making but avoid irrelevant ones.

- Cloud architecture diagrams can make implicit flows more explicit and understandable, showing a unified flow of data and processes across system boundaries.

- Cloud architecture also incorporates policies which govern the interaction of different systems. Establishing clear policies makes it easier for multiple teams and multiple developers to interact without causing coordination problems.

CHAPTER 13

Basic Cloud Architectures

In this chapter, I want to walk through several common examples of cloud architecture. The goal is to present you with a starting point for building your own architecture. For basic applications, most cloud architectures are pretty similar to each other, so don't worry if you wind up using one of these essentially unchanged. That's actually pretty typical for smaller applications. However, as you grow, you will find certain aspects of your architecture or your application giving you trouble, which should trigger you to think about redesigning your cloud architecture to address those pain points.

You should note that in this part of the book, I'm not really doing much that is Kubernetes-specific. Cloud architecture tends to be largely independent of the implementation. Many visualization resources (icon sets, etc.) are very cloud-specific, but my goal here is to simply convey the *idea* more than the implementation. You should choose the visualization that best communicates to your coworkers what you are trying to accomplish. It's not a problem to use Kubernetes-specific icons (the Kubernetes project provides an icon set if you want), but I typically choose not to, because my goal is not to simply have a visual representation of my YAML manifests but to instead have a representation of the ideas that sit behind those manifests.

13.1 A Basic Load-Balanced Architecture

The Message Board API we built in Part is a basic load balanced architecture. In such an architecture, there are three essential parts and one optional part:

- The load balancer
- The application server
- The database
- The caching server (optional)

153

© Jonathan Bartlett 2023
J. Bartlett, *Cloud Native Applications with Docker and Kubernetes*,
https://doi.org/10.1007/978-1-4842-8876-4_13

Let's start by considering what the Message Board API looks like in the absence of caching. Figure 13-1 shows what this looks like. In this diagram, the arrows show the direction of request initiation. The Internet requests data from the load balancer, which passes the request to one of the replicated services, who in turn initiate requests to the database for data.

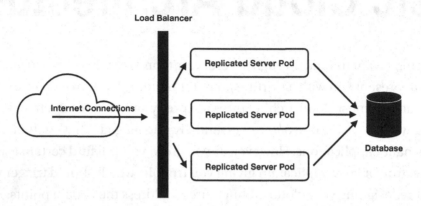

Figure 13-1. *A Simple Replicated Service*

You can see how much clarity a simple diagram like this adds to the understandability of a cluster configuration. Also note how simplistic it is, making use of only the most basic shapes. This is important for a simple reason—having diagrams is much better than not, and if you try to make every diagram a piece of art, it won't be very likely to be maintained or even drawn up in the first place.

Additionally, you don't want viewers to be bogged down in the details. The goal is to help them wrap their minds around the process, so the simpler the diagram, the better. Note also that we aren't capturing every Kubernetes object in our diagram—only the important ones. The database itself consists of *both* a Pod and a service, but, since the database isn't replicated, the Pod and the Service act basically like a single unit from the perspective of the developer.

Remember, the goal isn't to just replicate the YAML, but the goal is to communicate important and relevant information about the structure of the cluster to others.

13.2 Adding Caching to the Architecture

Now let's look at several different alternatives for adding caching, representing the different caching mechanisms we have discussed throughout the book (specifically in Chapters 10 and 11). Figure 13-2 shows the configuration we started with, where all of the Pods shared a single, monolithic cache. It shows the requests going *through* the cache, representing the fact that, ultimately, the requests are going to the database, but the cache is acting as an intermediary.

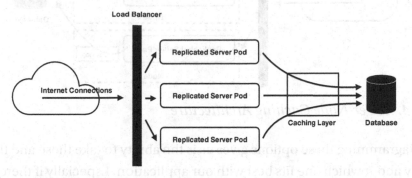

Figure 13-2. *A Single Monolithic Caching Architecture*

Another caching architecture we discussed was adding on a cache as a sidecar to each Pod. Figure 13-3 shows what this looks like. Here, we can see that each Pod has a cache off to its side, representing the sidecar configuration.

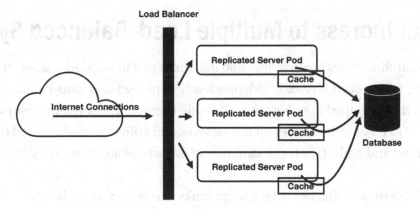

Figure 13-3. *A Per-Pod Caching Architecture*

Finally, Figure 13-4 shows what it looks like if we have the caches running as a DaemonSet with the cache routed only on the local Node. Here, since the caching is Node-specific, we added the concept of a Node to the diagram. It isn't that our other situations didn't have Nodes, but it's that the Nodes weren't especially important to the architecture.

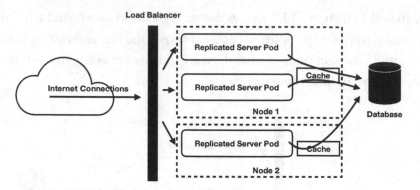

Figure 13-4. *A Per-Node Caching Architecture*

What diagramming these options gives us is the ability to take these and think more clearly about which one fits best with our application. Especially if there are other people involved, having diagrams of the possibilities facilitates discussion of the relevant details. The thing to keep in mind is that what counts as "relevant" is highly informed by experience. Try to think through the different possibilities and include in your drawings all of the components that make a difference to the outcomes.

13.3 An Ingress to Multiple Load-Balanced Systems

Many cloud architectures are just repeated instances of a basic load-balanced architecture, where each service is independently deployed and load-balanced. These services are then grouped together under a single Ingress, where the Ingress provides a common HTTPS termination for all the services and splits the traffic based on the requested host and path. This is the structure of our whole application that we built in Chapter 11.

Figure 13-5 shows what our total system looks like. Again, note that even though the cache and database are technically behind a load-balanced ClusterIP service, we are not showing that because, from the programmer's perspective, they are operating as a single unit.

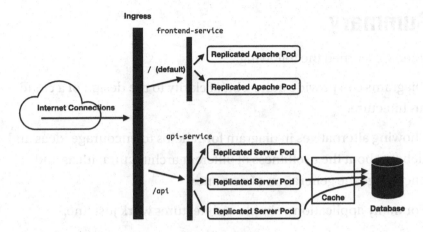

Figure 13-5. *The Cluster Ingress and Destinations*

The important thing that each of these diagrams is representing is as follows:

- The important aspects of the physical cloud organization

- The important aspects of the logical cloud organization

- The direction that the request is flowing

While there are many other aspects of a cloud architecture that may need to be diagrammed, getting the important aspects of the physical and logical structure of your cloud as well as how the data moves in the system is necessary and helpful for pretty much every application.

Additionally, several cloud providers have available what are known as *reference architectures*, which are architectural documents that specify typical architectures that address typical workloads. Google Cloud provides a searchable database of reference architectures at https://cloud.google.com/architecture. Many other cloud providers have reference architectures available, too. These can often provide good starting points of different architecture needs.

13.4 Summary

In this chapter, we learned the following:

- Diagrams can provide quite a bit of clarity to the design of a cloud architecture.

- Showing alternatives in diagram form helps to encourage ideas and debate about the usefulness of different architectural ideas and encourage the generation of new ones.

- For many applications, simple architectures work just fine.

- Many applications consist of simply an Ingress providing access to several services implementing a basic load-balanced architecture backed by a database and possibly a cache.

- Simpler diagrams are better as they are easier to maintain, more likely to be created in the first place, and force you to think about which details of the architecture are important to communicate.

- Many cloud providers provide reference architectures to give you starting points for architecting for various workloads and needs.

CHAPTER 14

A Basic Microservice Architecture

Most applications these days are moving to a microservice architecture. A microservice is a style of architecting that focuses on splitting applications into separately managed components. This chapter will detail what that means and what policies that implies to an application using this architecture. As a cloud administrator, your job is to customize these policies so that they work better with your team and your application, communicate them to the team, and enforce their adherence.

14.1 What Is a Microservice Architecture?

Microservice architecture is a way of thinking about applications in a way that both takes advantage of new technologies that are available for building applications and takes into account the way that real teams work on applications. Essentially, the goal is to split the application into smaller, *independently managed*, largely decoupled components. Because the components are smaller, this allows teams to be smaller. Because the components are decoupled, teams waste less time coordinating with each other.

Most microservice architectures include the following features:

1. Strict front-end/back-end separation. The front end is usually a static HTML/JavaScript app that interacts with an API rather than an integrated part of the server-side application using HTML forms for postback.

2. The back end is broken up into "services," which are small units of cohesive functionality.

159

J. Bartlett, *Cloud Native Applications with Docker and Kubernetes*, https://doi.org/10.1007/978-1-4842-8876-4_14

3. Each service uses a separate codebase, usually with a different developer or team managing each codebase.

4. Each service can be separately developed, built, tested, and deployed. There is no monolithic release for the application as a whole, just for the individual services.

5. Fundamental non-backward-compatible changes to the endpoints are usually managed by versioning the endpoints paths.

6. Services share a common authentication and authorization mechanism, usually using HTTP Bearer tokens (using the `Authorization: Bearer YOURTOKEN` header).

7. Service-to-service communication is generally done through a message queue when possible (see Chapter 11), though occasionally services will call each other directly (usually passing on the received security credentials for authentication).

8. Microservices generally each have their own database or at least their own tables in that database.

The rest of this chapter will go into more detail on several of these issues.

14.2 Authentication and Authorization

Authentication and authorization is one of the key cornerstones of a microservice architecture. Authentication to a microservice is usually done by passing in a securely generated token, known as a Bearer token. This is usually done through the HTTP `Authorization` header, whose value is then `Bearer TOKEN`. Sometimes the token can also be passed as a GET parameter or in the HTTP request body as well.

When a service that receives a token from the user calls another service, they can pass on the token they received from the user and thus invoke the downstream service as if it were the user making the request. Alternatively, if a higher permission set is needed, the service can create its own administrator-level token and issue the downstream request as itself.

There are generally two styles of token management—centralized and decentralized. In the centralized model, there is a service that has the responsibilities of creating the tokens in response to a valid login request, validating tokens from microservices, and giving additional authentication and authorization information to microservices upon request. Essentially, for each request, a microservice will make a call to the authentication microservice, which will check the validity of the received token, and get back information about who that token belongs to and what permissions, groups, and/or roles they are involved in. This obviously produces a strong dependency on the authentication service and means that if the authentication service is down, pretty much all of the services in the application are down. Some mitigation can be done by caching the results of these requests, though such caching should be pretty short in duration in case the token gets revoked or the user's permissions change.

I greatly prefer the decentralized model. In this model, the token itself contains within it all of the basic details of authentication, user identity, user groups, roles, and permissions and verifies those details with a cryptographic signature from the authentication server. This allows microservices to validate the identity of the person presenting the token without having to actually talk to the authentication service. The fact that the authentication server signed the token means that it was generated by the server.

A JWT is a JSON-based token which contains this type of signed authentication details. A JWT payload generally contains the following standard(-ish) fields:

> **iss**: This is the issuer of the token.
>
> **sub**: This is the subject of the token (i.e., the user's user identifier).
>
> **aud**: This is a list of "audiences" (recipients) the JWT is intended for. A JWT is supposed to be rejected if the service does not recognize any audience in the list.
>
> **exp**: This is the expiration time of the JWT, expressed as seconds from the epoch (can be a decimal).
>
> **iat**: This is when the JWT was issued, again as seconds from the epoch.

Most JWTs also include numerous custom fields used by a microservice. One of the cloud architect's job is to identify which fields belong in such a token. Essentially, the goal of additional fields is to reduce dependencies and callbacks to the authentication and identity services. Typical custom fields would include the user's name, email address, groups, roles, and permissions the user has.

The main challenge of JWTs is the fact that, since the authentication server is never accessed, it is difficult to revoke a JWT. The most straightforward way to mitigate against this is to give JWTs relatively short expiration times and require clients to obtain a new JWT relatively frequently, usually using a separate token, known as a *refresh token*. Refresh tokens are typically long-lived, since their only purpose is obtaining a new JWT. If a user's privileges are changed or revoked, this is reflected when they use the refresh token to obtain a new JWT. Using this mechanism, microservices are completely independent of the authentication service. The onus is on the client to make sure their JWT is properly refreshed.

In Kubernetes, issuer information, the issuer certificate, and audience information can be supplied to services via ConfigMaps.

14.3 Choosing Where to Cut the Application

One of the big architectural decisions when building a microservice architecture is how to identify what belongs together in a microservice and what can be separated out into a different microservice. Identifying the right place to "cut" an application into pieces is a bit of an art form. However, the general rule is to think about how different ways of cutting the application will create dependencies between microservices. The best way to cut the application into microservices is the one that allows each microservice to operate with the fewest dependencies on other services.

This decision is coupled with other decisions about the architecture. A good understanding of the possibilities that message queueing (Chapter 15) allows for will help inform the decision. Deciding on standard message formats will also inform the decision. Generally, a good way to think about it is this—can I adequately test the microservice without having to have the other microservices running? Or, at most, with a simplistic mock of any necessary service? If I can't test my microservices independently, then I haven't done a good job at making the cut.

14.4 URL Path Layout

Generally, in Kubernetes, microservices get fused together into a single application and API structure via an Ingress. However, for this to work, you need to decide on how URL paths will be laid out in the Ingress. Here, I will give what I believe are best practices for API paths.

First of all, I like to group all of the microservices into a top-level path, such as /api. This allows for me to run front-end apps (and even possibly the website) on the same domain under their own path (such as /apps) without worrying about any interference. This allows the API to be easily used by the front end and website. Since they are on the same server, you eliminate both CORS issues and some configuration issues. It also gives front-end and website developers a single path to avoid when making their changes. Without a single top-level path for your API, you would have to continually coordinate with the front-end and web teams to make sure that new paths you introduce are not conflicting with theirs.

Second, I like to give each service a single path namespace under /api. So, for instance, the authentication service might be in /api/authentication. This allows for easy deployment and integration with Kubernetes. Since each application has its own path, this works well with Kubernetes Ingress objects.

Third, I like to version all of my services. So, the second version of my authentication API would be available in /api/authentication/v2. This yields a number of benefits. Since the API is versioned, I can introduce new, breaking changes by simply incrementing the version number. Old software can use the old versions. Also, I can use logs/metrics on the usage of old APIs to see when they are out-of-use and can be retired (or see who needs to be updated to call the new version of the service). This structure also allows me (or the team) to decide whether to deploy a version as a separate service or just as a new path within the existing service. For instance, v3 might be such a radical rewrite that it is really its own separate code base, programmed, managed, and deployed independently of the other versions. By using the /api/SERVICE/VERSION layout, I can actually deploy the versions themselves as separate services with separate paths in the Ingress. Alternatively, if it is a minor revision, I can run both v2 and v3 from the same service. This path layout gives a huge amount of flexibility for such deployment decisions.

Finally, the rest of the path depends on your service and your cloud architecture. I personally prefer using REST-style endpoints. However, a good case can be made that identifiers should be part of the query string and not the URL path, as that makes a better separation between locating the endpoint and passing parameter data. In any case, the path structure after /api/SERVICE/VERSION is going to be heavily dependent on the service itself.

14.5 Quickly Transitioning to a Microservice Architecture

Oftentimes, the starting point for architecting is not a blue-sky initial project, but moving an existing large application into a microservice idea. Oftentimes these are on non-cluster-based servers as well. Therefore, the goal is usually to modernize the architecture—move from a traditional server-based monolithic application into a cloud-based microservices framework.

There are three things that greatly increase the success of such endeavors:

1. Don't try to do it all at once.

2. Maintain backward compatibility.

3. Start with something easy (bonus points if it results in a big win).

Your first goal is to get a stable foundation which allows you more freedom to deploy your microservices. Therefore, a good starting move is to simply create one component—an Ingress which forwards all traffic to the existing service. Having an Ingress in front means that you now have control over where endpoints go. Therefore, you can easily replace existing endpoints with new microservices or create new endpoints for your microservices. This is an easy step that lays the foundation for future steps and maintains full backward compatibility. You don't even need to bring your existing application into the cloud to make this work.

Figure 14-1 shows what this can look like. Here, you can see that the Ingress is pointing the path `/api/yourfirstservice/v1` to the first microservice in our architecture. The default path (for all other request paths) is being routed to the legacy monolithic service. Putting an Ingress in front of the monolithic service makes it easier to manage the transition, as it puts access to the monolithic service under the control of the microservice architecture.

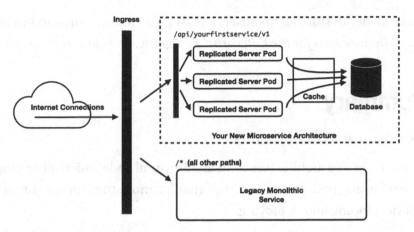

Figure 14-1. *Using an Ingress for Transitioning to a Microservice Architecture*

Your second goal should be to pick one or two starting microservices to replace existing endpoints as a pilot program. These don't even have to necessarily match what the future microservice architecture will look like. The goal here is to (a) prove (both to management and to yourself) that pieces of the application *can* be managed as microservices and (b) provide a template/framework for moving the rest of the application.

The most important consideration here is success—you want to have a successful pilot launch that you can build on. However, if possible, it's also good for either your first or second deployment to yield an explicit business success, so you can better demonstrate the value of the approach. One possibility is finding a buggy endpoint and replacing it with a less buggy microservice. Alternatively, you might find something that would specifically benefit from the fact that microservices are separately scaled. For instance, many clusters have certain endpoints that eat up long-lived connections, such as file upload processes. Moving these to a microservice means that a bunch of people uploading files won't negatively impact the main service, as they are scaled independently.

Again, the *most* important thing for your initial deployment is simply a successful deployment. Showing business value upfront is good, but I am at least personally convinced that microservice architectures are generally the most valuable for businesses in the long run even if there isn't short-term value. The value of the microservice architecture comes from its flexibility, ease of management, and ability to make development teams more effective. As applications get bigger, simply having a monolithic application incurs complexity costs in terms of testing, debugging, onboarding new developers, and the increased requirement for communication between developers.

For a more in-depth study of microservices, see Kasun Indrasiri and Prabath Siriwardena's *Microservices for the Enterprise: Designing, Developing, and Deploying.*

14.6 Summary

In this chapter, we learned the following:

- A microservice architecture is an architectural style which allows for breaking an application down into smaller, more manageable units for developing and deploying.

- Ideally, microservices minimize communication, dependencies, and coupling between components so that they can be independently built, tested, managed, and deployed without causing bad interactions with other microservices.

- A microservice architecture relies heavily on common authentication and authorization protocols, ideally decoupling the microservices from the authentication service uses token technologies such as JWTs.

- Choosing how to cut the application into microservices is one of the most important architectural decisions in microservice architectures.

- The path layout for microservices in an Ingress should also be carefully considered. The recommendation here is to use the general structure of `/api/SERVICE/VERSION` for versioned API endpoints.

- When beginning with an initial monolithic system, the first task should be to get the monolithic system under an Ingress, which will allow for easier transition of individual URL paths onto microservice endpoints.

CHAPTER 15

Enterprise Message Queues

A message queue is a special service that handles message passing between services in your cluster. Using message queueing in your cloud architecture enables a whole host of benefits, including the following:

- Increased resiliency to failures
- Decreased coupling between services
- Lower request latencies
- Higher-level management of service-to-service data flows

Essentially, the foundational goal of a message queue is to enable reliable delivery to unreliable services. Directly calling a service through HTTP is like making a phone call. If the service is down, they won't pick up the phone, and you'll need to figure out what to do then. A message queue is like sending them a letter. Your only task is to get the letter into your outgoing mailbox. From that point, it is the post office's job to deliver the letter. I don't have to worry about when the recipient is home at any particular time or even if they left for vacation for several months. If the recipient isn't home, the message will be waiting for them in the mailbox when they get there.

The reliability and availability of the message queue *itself* is critically important to a successful microservice implementation. Most microservices are architected so that the reliability and the availability of the message queue is assumed. Otherwise, if the microservice had to account for the message queue not being there, there wouldn't be much reason to have it in the first place, since one of the primary goals is to handle the case where the recipient is temporarily unavailable.

© Jonathan Bartlett 2023
J. Bartlett, *Cloud Native Applications with Docker and Kubernetes*,
https://doi.org/10.1007/978-1-4842-8876-4_15

15.1 Basic Message Queue Components and Terminology

While there are a lot of different details that can go into message queueing, this section will focus on the most important ones and those that tend to be available for almost any message queueing platform. Every queueing platform tends to use terminology slightly differently, but hopefully this will give you a good starting point for understanding.

To begin with, the core of every messaging platform is the *message broker*. This is essentially the "post office" of the system. The broker handles receiving, storing, and delivering of messages. The message itself is known as the *payload*. In addition to the main payload, sometimes additional metadata is sent with the payload as well. Sending a message is often referred to as *publishing*.

Message brokers organize message delivery using *channels* (also called *queues*). A channel is a predefined and configured line of communication. When you post or read messages, you always specify the channel that you are sending to or reading from. While there are innumerable ways to configure a channel, there are usually three basic modes that a channel can be in:

> **work queue:** In this configuration, every message that is sent is read exactly once. Usually, there is a defined service who is listening to this queue to perform a task.

> **publish/subscribe:** In this configuration (often abbreviated as "pub/sub"), a channel has multiple receivers. Each receiver subscribes to a channel (often referred to as a "topic"), and every message published to the channel is then replicated and delivered to every subscriber.

> **Streaming:** This configuration is very similar to publish/subscribe, except that the messages are permanently archived. This allows new subscribers to either start from the current message or start from the very first message ever sent, depending on the need.

For each of these modes, additional configurations can be made about the reliability of delivery and the durability of the message. How long can a message stay on the queue without being read before it is considered to be undeliverable? If a message is missed, how problematic is it? Do we need to be sure each message is written to disk before telling the publisher of the message that it is sent, or can we do memory-only queues for fast speed? Is double delivery of a message a problem? How problematic is it for messages to be delivered out of order? These are the sorts of questions which govern the configuration of queues.

Oftentimes, if a message can't be delivered (either because no one is reading it or because they are erroring out before confirming that it has been processed), it gets sent to what is known as a *dead-letter queue* (abbreviated as a *DLQ*). This allows system administrators to be notified when there are permanent failures in the messaging system and to inspect the messages to determine what went wrong. Then, since the message is sitting in the DLQ, it can be replayed back to the main queue when the appropriate fixes have been made or be permanently deleted if the message itself is the problem.

Let's now look at the three main channel modes and what they offer.

15.2 Working with Work Queues

The work queue is the simplest form of message queueing. Essentially, this allows messages to be sent asynchronously to systems which are either slow, offline, or frequently down. Basically, it allows the senders and receiver to work at their own paces, and the message broker manages the imbalance.

For example, let's say that you have a single Pod that transcodes video. People can upload video to your system at any time, but the transcoder may not be available at that time (it may be transcoding someone else's video). Therefore, you could create a work queue. The service that receives the video would store it somewhere and then simply post a message to the work queue through the message broker. For the receiving service—that is the end of the matter—it has done its job. Then, whenever the transcoder is available, it will ask the message broker for the next message. In some message brokers, the message is marked as "in-progress" until the worker has verified that it has completed the task so that the message can be redelivered if the task fails at some point.

Another usage of this paradigm is delivery to a system that may be unavailable. More and more, the functionality of your system depends on the functionality of *other people's* systems. The more dependencies there are, the more likely it is that *some* system is down at any given point. If delivery is managed through a message broker, this becomes much less of a headache, because the message broker itself manages working with the unavailable system.

As an example, at one company I worked at, we used a third-party emailing program that would sometimes go down for five minutes at a time. Originally, we had it set up so that the programs that needed to send email would directly contact the third-party program through its API. However, this meant that developers only had three choices if the API failed—they could fail the whole request, they could ignore the error and never deliver the email, or they could implement really complicated retry logic themselves.[1] Switching to a work queue solved these issues.

The applications would post the message to the work queue. Since the message broker is part of our internal system, it is simply assumed to be operational.[2] Then, we had a process that would read a message from the queue (marking the message as "in process") and attempt delivery. If delivery succeeded, we would tell the queue that it succeeded. However, if it failed, we just let the message time out, and the message broker would attempt delivery later. If there were more than 30 failed attempts, the message would be moved to the dead-letter queue, and an admin would be notified that there was an *actual* problem, not just an intermittent one. Working in this way transformed the system from an unreliable point of failure that was endlessly problematic to a very reliable system that never gave us any problems.

Now, so far, we have been treating the recipient of the work queue as if it were a single process. Generally, there is a single *logical* process reading from the work queue, but there might be multiple workers. If you think about our video transcoding example, what would happen if we wanted to add another transcoding Pod? Now, there are two *workers* for our work queue. With a work queue, typically if one worker receives a message, it is then unavailable to the other worker unless that task fails. Thus, a message is delivered a single time to a service, but there may be multiple Pods that each could be the recipient. This is often referred to as the *competing consumer* messaging pattern.

---

[1] Just to be clear, writing your own retry logic is generally a bad idea because not only is it a giant waste of time, but it is also really hard to get correct. It also adds an entire layer of needless complexity and does so repeatedly for every time you need it. While you could write a library to do this, if you did it right, well, you would have just reimplemented a message broker!

[2] If you have retry logic for your message broker, you are doing it wrong. Think about it this way—are you also going to have retry logic if your retry logic fails? Ultimately, you have to depend on something, and the message broker (perhaps along with minimal retry logic in the message broker's API library) is usually made to be the piece that never fails, or, if it does, you might as well fail the whole request. And, if the message broker fails, you *should* fail the whole request for sure.

15.3 Decoupling Systems with Publish/Subscribe

Another important paradigm is the publish/subscribe or pub/sub paradigm. In this paradigm, important application events are "published" to the message broker. Then, a set of processes which have "subscribed" to the channel are then delivered the message. The application doesn't actually know (or likely even care) who receives the message. This allows for a powerful paradigm for integrating multiple systems which act together and also lets teams operate largely independently of each other even when working with the same requests.

Let's start with the simple case of publishing a web article. We can imagine a publish/subscribe mechanism here. In this imaginary scenario, the web publishing system has exactly two jobs—manage the publication of your article, and then notify a pub/sub channel about the event. The goal is to keep the publishing system doing one task (and doing it well)—managing publication of the article. You might have other things going on, but you can have them all work independently by subscribing to the channel and listening for events.

After publishing your article, you might have all sorts of things happen:

- You could post your link to search engines to make sure they know about the new content.

- You could send an email to people subscribed to your blog to let them know about the post.

- You could trigger a text-to-speech processor to make an audio recording of your post that readers can listen to.

- You could add a process to do machine translations of your post into a number of languages.

The possibilities are endless. Each of these can be a separate subscriber to the channel. Then, they can each be developed independently and do not require any coordination to accomplish. The only thing required is a pub/sub channel where relevant messages are published and subscribers who process those messages.

The architecture for such a messaging system is shown in Figure 15-1. You can see the message coming into the appropriate channel on the message broker and then being replicated out to each of the subscribing services. The sender does not have to even know who is subscribed, because the subscribing, replicating, delivering, and monitoring are managed by the broker.

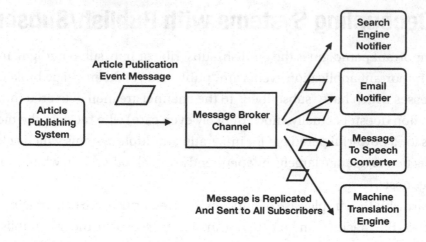

Figure 15-1. *A Simple Publish/Subscribe Architecture*

This helps not only your development team (because the different tasks can be easily coded and integrated independently), but it also improves the tasks *themselves*, because they can all work asynchronously. If the text-to-speech processor is down, no problem! It isn't slowing anyone else down; it just means that the audio file won't be available for a little while. If the email system is down, again, no problem! As soon as it's back up, messages will start sending again.

Not only is publish/subscribe decoupling the tasks and teams, but it is decoupling the processes themselves so that problems in one don't interfere with another.

Let me share with you a real-world publish/subscribe mechanism I developed for a team. Essentially, we had an agreed-upon message format for general events that customers in the system perform. Each message was a JSON-encoded value which had the fields userId, eventType, and productId (as well as others, but these are enough to paint the picture). So, if the user purchased a product, the purchasing system would publish a message that said something like the following:

```
{
    "userId":"id123",
    "eventType":"purchase",
    "productId":"prod456"
}
```

The purchasing system's *only* jobs were to finish the purchase and then notify everyone else by sending this message to the channel. The subscribers to the channel, however, had a whole host of other jobs. We had subscribers which did the following:

- Store the event in our customer relations system.

- Post the event in the email marketing system to trigger post-purchase emails.

- Record the purchase in our registration system for warranty servicing purposes.

- Send the purchase event to our retailer loyalty program in case there was a retailer who needed credit for the sale.

- Send the event to the analytics service for business intelligence.

In large enterprises, you wind up with a lot of different systems to interact with which do not share the same databases. Therefore, having a publish/subscribe mechanism means that you can easily write integrations which share data at the appropriate time and in the appropriate ways. Since the message broker, not the application, is handling repeating the message to each subscriber, we can also add subscribers without modifying any of the code in the purchase system. If we need another post-purchase service, we can just add it to the list of subscribers. The team that is focused on the purchasing system can now *just* focus on the purchasing system. All of the add-ons can be added by other teams on their own schedules according to their own priorities and don't even necessarily need to clear it with the purchasing team.

15.4 Event Bus Architecture

Note that, in some architectures, the same channel is used for a variety of different message types from a variety of different publishers. This is known as an *event bus* architecture. If you think about the "customer event" message I just described, you can see that the eventType could actually be all sorts of things, not just a purchase. If the user uses the product, that could be published on the channel. If the user transfers the product to a different owner, that could be published on the channel. When the user creates their account, that can be published as well. If the user calls the company, that can also be a publishable event.

All of these different systems can be creating messages with a well-defined, agreed-upon basic format and publishing them to the same channel. Then, you can have systems which are subscribed to the channel but only care about certain messages. They can read and ignore the ones they don't care about and then process the ones they do care about.

For instance, the customer relations system probably wants to know *everything* about a customer, even if it doesn't have a specific action to perform. That way, if a customer service representative is on the phone with them, they can see everything that has happened. On the other hand, the retailer loyalty program probably doesn't care about phone calls that the user makes to the company, so they will probably ignore those messages.

Figure 15-2 gives a general view of what this looks like. On the top of the diagram are the publishers, whose messages all go into the same channel on the message broker. Then, on the bottom, the messages get replicated and distributed to each logical subscriber. In theory, a system could be both a publisher and a subscriber, but their roles in each of these cases are probably distinct.

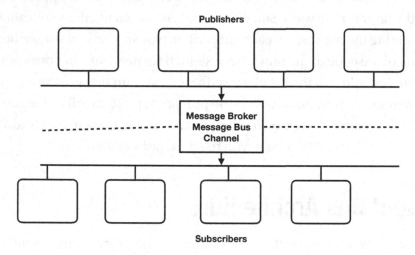

Figure 15-2. *A Message Bus Architecture*

In all, event bus architectures allow a high degree of flexibility by creating general but flexible standards around messaging within your organization. The *technology* isn't any different from ordinary publish/subscribe—you would usually use the same type of channels on the message broker for both. However, the generality of the mechanism allows for a lot of flexibility in how the various groups in the organization are able to coordinate their efforts.

15.5 Message Streaming for Permanent Replayability

An outgrowth of publish/subscribe is known as *message streaming*. In ordinary publish/ subscribe (and in work queues), once a message is fully processed (all of the subscribers have reported that they have processed it), the message disappears. However, there are some occasions when it would be really nice to be able to get back old messages.

A message streaming channel is one where the messages never disappear. At any time, a subscriber can request old messages or request that the message broker start replaying messages from any point in time. A new subscriber can either start at the current end of the feed, or they can start all the way at the beginning of the feed and get all of the messages that were ever sent to the channel.

There are a lot of problems that this solves, but one of them is the "startup" problem. Usually, when you have a new subscriber to the queue, they may need your past history. For instance, if our organization changes to a new customer relations management system, they would probably like to get all of the back data for customer interactions. In traditional systems, this is usually handled by a one-time, special import. However, managing the cutover point is often difficult. Which specific records did I miss while I was trying to do a data dump of old records? Which ones got sent twice?

Instead, with a streaming system, you can just say, "replay everything from the beginning of time." Then, the new customer relations management system would have the same data as if it were the primary system the whole time.[3] There is no messy loading step—it is all the same process.

Some streaming systems specialize in large quantities of data, especially for analytics. Applications send every conceivable metric to the stream, and the stream has specialized processors which convert the mass of data into usable analytics.

15.6 Two-Way Messaging

So far, the messaging that we have discussed is one-way messaging. This is because one-way messaging provides the most power to the most people for the least amount of additional work. Additionally, one-way messaging provides the most amount of

---

[3] However, you do have to be careful to not trigger real-world actions (like emails) when doing these sorts of loads.

decoupling between systems, allowing teams maximum independence, so it is usually preferred when possible. However, I would be remiss if I did not mention two-way messaging at least a little bit, because it does have its usefulness.

While some message brokers specifically support two-way channels, you can really do two-way messaging by simply having multiple one-way channels, with some sort of descriptor used to identify the interaction so that the process receiving a response knows *which* message is being responded to. Alternatively (and somewhat equivalently), on some platforms, you can do two-way messaging by opening up a dedicated channel for the response and simply including the response channel name in the initial message.

However, there are many additional two-way messaging patterns that can be adopted. We won't go into detail here, but some examples include the following:

> **request/reply**: This is the two-way pattern we have just covered.

> **status indication**: In this pattern, the initial recipient continually updates the sender as to the status of the progress. Imagine, for instance, transcoding video. The original process may want to know how far along the process is, so the recipient provides not just a single "yes, we're done" response but continually tells the initiating process how far along it is.

> **scatter/gather**: This is similar to publish/subscribe, but where each recipient sends information back to the originator of the message, usually with a timeout so that the originator knows when to stop receiving messages. An example of this is if you were going to get shipping quotes from multiple shippers. You would send a request to a publish/subscribe channel, and each subscriber would then respond back to the response channel. After the timeout, the original sender would have a complete list of quotes available and would not even have to know about the different services individually.

> **first responder**: This is similar to scatter/gather, but the original sender only waits for the first response back. The others are ignored.

In all, two-way messaging is much more difficult to coordinate and debug, so, unless it is required by the application, it is best to try to avoid it. Nonetheless, when required, knowing common ways they are put together is important.

15.7 The Job of the Cloud Architect

So what roles specifically fall on the cloud architect?

First of all, the architect needs to define the main locations where the application will use message queues. The architect needs to think about the application as a whole and think about which components can be better served by breaking them into independent pieces. The questions the architect should ask are as follows:

- Where is the application talking to external systems?

- Where is the application talking to unreliable systems?

- Which parts of the process are intrinsic to the action, and which ones are add-ons?

- Which parts of the process require immediate work, and which can be done later?

- Which parts of the process require more intensive resources or time to complete?

- Which parts of the process are teams regularly having to coordinate on?

- What are the main "events" which happen within your system that other systems might want to know about?

- What information would be generally interesting across multiple teams?

Then, the architect will break up the application into pieces which communicate using a message broker. The architect decides the messaging pattern used and what the messages will look like. If an event bus architecture is chosen, the architect defines a general message format that will be used.

With the messaging channels, patterns, and formats chosen, the architect is now in a good place to decide which message broker to use. This will be based not only on support for the chosen messaging patterns but also on the relative importance of reliability, security, speed, observability (the ability to see into the queueing system to diagnose problems), ease of management, and ease of development. For most cases, I think ease of management and ease of development are both underappreciated. Some message queueing systems (such as Kafka) are notoriously difficult to set up and manage, but they offer massive scaling benefits if they are set up properly. However, a message bus isn't helpful if the message bus itself winds up being the source of problems and frustration. Larger organizations may be able to have an entire team built around making sure the message bus works well, but for most organizations, the important thing is that the message bus just works without having to care for it.

☞ A NOTE ON MESSAGE SIZES

There are essentially two basic message sizes—thin messages and fat messages. Thin messages contain only the most minimal information that other processes need in order to get started. That is, the message contains only basic message data and keys to other relevant data stores. If the receiving process wants more data, they can look it up themselves in the appropriate data store.

Alternatively, a fat message contains most information that most processes will likely need about all relevant data objects. The goal of a fat message is to minimize the amount of additional network and database traffic that adding processes will likely trigger. Having fat messages means that the receiving processes can focus on *processing*, not *retrieval*, which itself causes systems to be more coupled to each other than you might desire.

Deciding on whether you want to use thin or fat messages is another important architectural decision. Thin messages put the least constraints and load on the sender, while fat messages put the least constraints and load on the receiver.

Interestingly, the decision is not always a technical one. I have often found that, especially when using a message bus architecture, if I want to encourage people to post to a message bus, thin messages increase adoption from within my team. Essentially, the fewer tasks someone has to do to send a message, the more likely it is they will adopt that data flow. Then, once everyone is sending on the bus, people recognize it as sufficiently interesting and useful to also read from it.

While there are more options than just the extremes of fat/thin, I find that thinking in these terms helps me to decide just how much data I want in my message.

15.8 Getting Started with Message Queueing

There are so many message brokers available, and each of them has a whole host of configuration options. For the purposes of this chapter, we will focus on broQue, since it is the most straightforward to get working.[4] You probably would want to configure it much more than we are here, but it is enough to demonstrate the point. Other message brokers that are worth looking into include Dapr, RabbitMQ, KubeMQ, Kafka, and a multitude of others.

To install a barebones configuration of broQue, you only need to issue the following command:[5]

```
kubectl apply -f https://bit.ly/broque_simple_install
```

This creates a service named broque that is listening for HTTP connections on port 80. It also creates a PVC for storage, so restarting the Pod won't lose your data. The default install of broQue does not set up any authentication, so you can easily send and receive using unauthenticated API calls. Therefore, to demonstrate how it works, we will simply deploy a Pod that will give us HTTP access to the broQue system:

```
kubectl run my-kmq-shell --rm -it --image johnnyb61820/network-toolkit
```

We will be doing a publish/subscribe set of requests. We will have a channel named mychannel and subscriptions named mysub1 and mysub2. Feel free to add more subscriptions as you wish.

By default in broQue, nothing needs to be done to create a channel. Looking at a channel, subscribing to a channel, or posting a message to a channel will all auto-create the channel for you. Therefore, let's start by posting a message to the channel:

```
curl -X POST http://broque/v1/channels/mychannel/messages \
  -dmessage=Hello
```

This returns back the message header information, which includes the message reference, which is how the message is identified on the system.

---

[4] In full disclosure, broQue is my own personal project, built for the express purpose of being easy to get started using. As of the time of this writing, it is mostly useful for experimental and demonstration purposes but will hopefully grow into fully operable message broker.

[5] For more complete installation instructions, see the repository README at https://github.com/johnnyb/broque.

Reading from a named subscription will auto-create it. We can create a subscription and read from that channel with the following command:

```
curl http://broque/v1/channels/mychannel/subscriptions/mysub1/messages
```

This should return an empty array of messages, because we started the subscription *after* we posted the message. When a subscription is created, it starts at the current location in the message stream. However, we can reset a subscription back to the beginning of the queue by issuing the following command:

```
curl -X PUT http://broque/v1/channels/mychannel/subscriptions/mysub1/reset
```

Now, run the command to check messages again, and you will get the message back. Run it again, and you will get nothing back, since all the messages have been read. However, if you wait 30 seconds and query it again, you will see the message again. The reason is because when a message is read, the system does not know if you successfully processed the message, so it gives you some time (30 seconds by default) to process the message, and, if it didn't hear back from you, it assumes that the processing failed.

To mark the message as having been processed successfully, we can mark it as "complete" by taking the message_reference field (which we will refer to as MSGREF) and perform the following (all on one line):

```
curl -X PUT http://broque/v1/channels/mychannel/subscriptions/
    mysub1/messages/MSGREF/complete
```

If you don't want to perform this second step, you can tack on ?autocomplete=true to the command to retrieve messages. However, using this added completion step gives a lot of automatic failure management, as it will autodetect failures by recognizing when a message has not yet been completed.

To add another subscription to the channel, simply run the command again with a new subscription name:

```
curl http://broque/v1/channels/mychannel/subscriptions/mysub2/messages
```

Again, this will return an empty array, because it starts at the end of the channel. Now, post another message to the channel:

```
curl -X POST http://broque/v1/channels/mychannel/messages \
    -dmessage=AnotherMessage
```

Now, when you query each channel, the message should be available in both of them. You will need to run the `complete` step for *each* subscription.

How this would work in an application is that you would have an agreed-upon channel name to communicate. The sender(s) would post messages to the channel (probably in JSON format). The receivers would then run in a loop where they asked the system for new messages, processed each message, and marked the message as complete if the processing was successful (or did nothing if it was not).

Some pseudo-code for such a process would look something like this:

1. Retrieve a list of messages from the queue.

2. For each message in the list

   (a) Perform the task.

   (b) If the task failed, skip the message.

   (c) If the task succeeded, mark the message as complete.

3. Perform a short delay.

4. Go to step 1.

Depending on the message broker, you may or may not have to worry about two simultaneous readers picking up a message simultaneously. Some brokers will never deliver a message to more than one recipient simultaneously, while others have looser guarantees.

As you can see, message queueing provides a very simple and elegant mechanism for achieving a number of results simultaneously, including making systems more manageable, more decoupled, and more scalable. For a more in-depth look at message queueing, see Hugo Filipe Oliveira Rocha's *Practical Event-Driven Microservices Architecture: Building Sustainable and Highly Scalable Event-Driven Microservices*.

15.9 Summary

In this chapter, we learned the following:

- Message queueing allows for decoupling different components of your application.

- Message queueing automatically handles imbalances between the reliabilities and availabilities of different systems.

- Message queues can make unreliable systems act reliably and, using dead-letter queues (DLQs), can notify system administrators of permanent failures and then allow for diagnosis and retrying of the messages.

- Message queueing consists of a message broker, which is the system that handles the messaging, a set of channels which receive and distribute messages, and clients which contact the message broker to send and receive messages on a channel.

- A work queue is a channel where requests are placed and a single receiver takes the request and processes it asynchronously.

- A publish/subscribe channel is a channel where requests are placed by a single sender but can be processed by any process that is subscribing to the channel. The sending process does not need to change any of its code in order to support more receivers.

- A streaming channel is like a publish/subscribe channel except that the messages never disappear but can be replayed at any time from any position in the stream.

- A message bus is a publish/subscribe channel that can also be written to by multiple senders, using a shared general message architecture. Recipients may not be interested in the full range of messages received but can filter those that they care about.

- Two-way messaging can also be implemented with message queues, though they remove some of the architectural benefits of message queues in general by increasing coupling between the sender and the receiver.

- The cloud architect's job is to identify which systems would benefit from being decoupled using a message queue, what kind of channel should be used, and the format of the messages used on the channel.

CHAPTER 16

Architecting Data Stores

The term *data store* is a generalization of the idea of a database. Relational databases, hierarchical databases, key/value stores, and even filesystems are all examples of data stores. In Kubernetes and other cloud-oriented systems, data stores are treated in a very special way.

The goal, in general, is to make the applications themselves contain as little persistent state as possible in order to allow them to be maximally scalable. However, for a system to be useful, the data has to go *somewhere*. That location is known as a data store. However, since data stores, unlike most of the rest of the cluster, specialize in storing state, there are a lot of special considerations that go into architecting them.

The questions that have to be answered include things like what data is being stored, which system needs to access it, how often do these systems need to access it, how does the data need to be queried, and how long does it need to last. Questions like these guide the selection of data stores and their architecture.

16.1 Types of Data Stores

The traditional go-to data store for most enterprises has historically been relational (SQL) databases. While I still recommend these as the official data store of record for most types of data (and the best all-around data store), other types of data storage have arisen in recent years that are worth incorporating into various aspects of a cloud infrastructure.

The term *NoSQL* has become popular recently as a catch-all for any sort of non-relational database. However, I think that, as a term, it yields more heat than light. There is almost no unifying principle behind NoSQL databases except that they aren't relational, so treating them as a unified entity under the banner of NoSQL is less than helpful. Instead, it is more helpful to talk about the different types of data stores that are available and how they are useful.

© Jonathan Bartlett 2023
J. Bartlett, *Cloud Native Applications with Docker and Kubernetes*,
https://doi.org/10.1007/978-1-4842-8876-4_16

16.1.1 Relational Databases

The primary type of database structure used by enterprises of every size is the relational database, and for good reason. Relational databases are built around a solid theoretical foundation developed in the 1970s developed by researcher E. F. Codd. He conceived of the idea of a relational database where data is stored in tables with fixed columns. The database tables are intended to be *normalized* so that data only resides in one place in the database, and it can be readily queried and updated from a definable location. Essentially, every record has a primary key column (usually an integer or a UUID) identifying it, and its relationship to other records is expressed via recording the primary key to a column in the other records (known as foreign keys).

In a relational database, the logical and physical structure of the database are separated. The tables in a database are defined according to the way the real-life entities interact. The tables are queried by essentially ad hoc combinations of joins and filters on the tables. However, these combinations are sped up through the implementation of indexes which allow fast lookups by various columns. Modern relational databases will take a programmer's query and decide the best physical course of action based on the indexes available. The same query may have two radically different physical interpretations based on which columns are indexed. Thus, the role of programmer (how the data is structured and what I want to query) and database administrator (how the database is stored and accessed physically) are separable roles.

Is your query load dominated by full-text query searches? Add an index for it! How about continually joins between two specific tables. Add an index to make it faster! Indexes are not the only way that database administrators can alter the physical storage of records, but it is the most common way and also the way that is least database-specific.

Relational databases also generally have very good transactional support. This means that updates to a database can be grouped together so that they are *all* triggered or none of them are. This means that no process that queries the database will receive halfway-updated data. Additionally, most relational databases will not commit their transactions until the data has been physically written to the disk in a way that can be recovered upon a crash. This means that, once the transaction has succeeded, the programmer can have full faith that the record will not be wiped away because the machine crashed or some other similar problem occurred.

These abilities and guarantees oftentimes make relational databases somewhat slower than other types of data stores. However, keep in mind that the power and utility of these features caused such databases to rise to power in a time when the speed costs were even more pronounced than they are today. Sometimes the "newer" data stores are actually reincarnations of previously outdated data store technology wrapped in a new name. That doesn't mean that they don't have their place, but relational databases are the standard enterprise data store for good reason.

My personal preference for a database system is PostgreSQL, as it can natively handle more data scenarios seamlessly than any other database I've encountered. In PostgreSQL, individual columns of a single record can hold up to a gigabyte of data, and rows can still be sorted by columns of that size! Basically, it can handle with ease any amount of data you want to throw at a PostgreSQL database. Additionally, a number of other types of database technology can be incorporated into a PostgreSQL database, as I will show in later sections.

16.1.2 Key/Value Stores

The most common supplement to a relational database is a key/value store, commonly used for caching. In Chapter 10, our application implemented a caching layer using a key/value store known as Memcache. Redis is another popular alternative that is slightly slower and more complex but adds a lot more configuration and clustering options, including the ability to work as a distributed caching system.

In the configurations we have discussed in Chapter 13, the caches were basically independent of each other. That's essentially a design constraint with Memcache. However, with Redis, the different caches can be synchronized. Updating or invalidating a cache key can be made to propagate throughout all of the Redis nodes.

Key/value stores are usually extremely fast, but they are also limited in a number of ways. Since they are key/value, they can essentially only be queried based off of their keys. You can't give arbitrary queries for different pieces of data—the key is either there or it isn't. Additionally, most key/value stores are ephemeral—they are built to expire their contents. Memcache, being memory-only, loses all data when it is restarted. Redis has the ability to write data to disk so that all of your cached data isn't flushed on a restart, but it still doesn't have all of the guarantees of a relational database.

The main thing to keep in mind is to make sure you know the conditions under which your cache is good or bad and how to expire entries that are no longer relevant.

16.1.3 Document Databases

The rise of so much JSON data has led to databases which specialize in this kind of data, known as *document databases*. Document databases are usually focused on arbitrary JSON documents and allow for querying the database either by key or by some arbitrary field in the JSON document.

Usually, the design requirements leading to a document database are the following:

- JSON-structured documents, usually with a flexible structure

- A few common fields that the documents are queried by

- A key to identify the document (this can be either in the document itself or assigned outside of the document)

- The need for very fast lookups

The most popular document database today is probably MongoDB. MongoDB is fast and scalable, where each node can be written to. It has a specialized query language for searching the database, and indexes can be created for any path in the JSON document. It is sufficiently fast that, when I first used it, I forgot to add an index on the field I was searching with, but didn't notice for several years. Even then, it wasn't a speed issue, even with hundreds of thousands of records.

16.1.4 Full-Text Databases

Some databases specialize in full-text search. Full-text search differs from normal wildcard searching in that it generally supports matching words, phrases, and even different spellings of words within text. Think of it as incorporating the flexibility of a Google search into your database.

Full-text databases can also conglomerate multiple fields of a record into a single unit to do full-text searching on. For instance, if part of the text was in the title, and part of the text was in a document, a full-text search engine will search both of those simultaneously. Such engines also have excerpting abilities, so they can show you which part of the text matches for better display for the users.

Popular full-text searching database includes Solr, Sphinx, Lucene, and ElasticSearch.

16.1.5 Object/File Stores

Amazon's S3 introduced the world to object storage. Essentially, this creates an unlimited disk space accessible to all members of the cluster and possibly even the public. Since Amazon's introduction, a number of services have been established that have essentially mimicked the interface or features that Amazon's S3 provides, such as Linode, Google, and Azure.

Object stores are essentially permanent, disk-based key/value stores for large amounts of data, intended to act as a filesystem. The keys essentially look like a filename (including directories), and the value is the file data and metadata (such as the content type).

Object stores often provide a number of services that are helpful. Because writing to and reading from large files (especially over slow connections) can use up your web server's resources, many of these services provide mechanisms for clients to securely read and write data using pre-authenticated tokens separately from the main web server. Since object stores are not traditional filesystems, they are not limited the way most filesystems are to being mounted by only one server but can be utilized by every server in the cluster.

16.1.6 Specialized Persistent Stores

Some stores are just, well, special. These are usually highly specialized services (such as the message queues discussed in Chapter 15) that have very specific storage needs. Since these are each individually very different services, it is difficult to give any general principles about them, except to say that you should always think about whether the complexity of managing the store outweighs the gains you will generate by using them.

16.2 Implementing Stores Using a Relational Database

While high-speed specialty versions of each of these stores can be found and implemented, it is amazing how much of them can be implemented using relational database technology, especially with PostgreSQL. I have found that PostgreSQL is both the easiest to manage database and the most flexible. It simply always works the way I expect and doesn't give me problems. And, it turns out, most of the other types of databases can be easily implemented on PostgreSQL with just a few lines of table definitions.

16.2.1 Document Databases

Interestingly, most of the features of a document database can be replicated using PostgreSQL using the jsonb column type. The following PostgreSQL table definition replicates the most commonly used features of a document database:

```
CREATE TABLE document_db_table(
    id uuid PRIMARY KEY default gen_random_uuid(),
    document jsonb
);
CREATE INDEX ON document_db_table USING GIN(document jsonb_path_ops);
```

This will create a table that can not only hold JSON data but allow indexed querying of it. To insert and query a record, all you need to do is the following:

```
INSERT INTO document_db_table (document)
    values ('{"mykey1":"myval1","mykey2":"myval2"}');
SELECT document FROM document_db_table
    WHERE document @> '{"mykey1":"myval1"}';
```

The @> operator tells PostgreSQL to do a query based on a partial document match. Other JSON query operators are also available. If you need an identifier for the document, that is contained in the id field as a UUID.

So, while document databases do perform some specialized functions that you may need, PostgreSQL gives you the vast majority of the features from within the framework of a standard relational database.

16.2.2 Full-Text Search

Again, PostgreSQL takes care of most of your needs for full-text search using their TSEARCH system (this was formerly a separate module but is now integrated into their core database). The PostgreSQL TSEARCH system has a few new datatypes (we will look at two) and a few new operators (we will look at one). The tsvector is a custom datatype that is the result of taking a string (which can be as large as needed) and converting it into a workable format for searching. On the flip side, a `tsquery` is the result of taking a query string and converting it into a format for searching. The source for the `tsquery` can either be PostgreSQL's custom search language or a plaintext freeform query. Finally, the `@@` operator is able to perform a search on a `tsvector` using the `tsquery`.

Let's have a table which contains a document with a title, text, and keywords:

```
CREATE TABLE mydoctable(
    id uuid PRIMARY KEY default gen_random_uuid(),
    name text,
    document text,
    keywords text
);
```

Now, let's think about at how we might do a full-text query of this table from a user-entered query. First, we would want to concatenate the `name`, `document`, and `keywords` fields (with spaces between them). Then, we would want to convert it to a `tsvector` for searching. Finally, we would want to convert the user's query into a `tsquery` and match it using `@@` to our `tsvector`.

This is accomplished with the following simple query:

```
SELECT * FROM mydoctable WHERE to_tsvector(
    'english',
    name || ' ' || document || ' ' || keywords
) @@ phraseto_tsquery(
    'english',
    'this is my search query'
);
```

The 'english' parameter is to specify English language conventions for searching.

The problem with this query is that the search will be slow because the searched string isn't indexed. Since we are searching on the converted value of the combined fields, the index needs to be on that as well. You would create an index for that like the following:

```
CREATE INDEX ON mydoctable USING GIN(
    to_tsvector(
        'english',
        name || ' ' || document || ' ' || keywords
```

```
    )
);
```

Now you have an indexed full-text search!

PostgreSQL full-text searches support a number of other features (such as excerpting and sorting), so this just touches the tip of the iceberg. Additionally, PostgreSQL also supports other types of indexed fuzzy text searching such as regular expression searching, trigram searching (similarity-based), Levenshtein distance searching (another similarity-based algorithm), and phonetic searching (searching based on word sounds).

So, while there are reasons to use a full-text engine, I would always look and see if your relational database can handle your needs first.

16.2.3 Object/File Stores

If you need to use the features for out-of-band storing and writing features that are provided by most object/file store mechanisms, then using a specialized service for that may indeed be appropriate. Additionally, with extremely large files (over a gigabyte) such as videos, again, you may need to use an object/file store. However, for simply storing files, PostgreSQL again comes to your aid.

PostgreSQL can store large amounts of binary data straightforwardly in their bytea field type. Unlike many databases, PostgreSQL is perfectly happy with extremely large text or binary fields. An individual field size within a record can be as large as a gigabyte, and a single record can be over a terabyte! So, with normal circumstances, you are not overrunning PostgreSQL's limits.[1]

So, a general object/file store-like table might look like the following:

```
CREATE TABLE files (
    id uuid PRIMARY KEY default gen_random_uuid(),
    filepath text,
    created_at timestamp default 'now',
    content_type text,
    data bytea
);
```

---

[1] Even though many larger file sizes are within PostgreSQL's technical specifications, dealing with larger file sizes can cause performance problems.

```
CREATE UNIQUE INDEX ON files(filepath);
```

Alternatively, if you are worried that your ORM (or developers) will do a `select` * and not realize how much data they will get back, you can store the data itself in a separate table.

16.2.4 Key/Value Stores

The key/value store, operating as a cache, is the one component I usually keep outside of the relational database. The entire point of the key/value store as a cache is not that it gives you additional functionality (key/value pairs are trivial in SQL) but rather that it gives you additional speed and scalability along explicit search paths.

Key/value stores are, in most cases, essentially workarounds for limitations of relational databases. In practice, I've found that the combination of using relational databases for "official" storage and key/value stores for high-speed caches works really well in a very wide range of situations.

16.3 Database Topologies

When scaling your database beyond a single Pod, the question of database topology comes into play. Database topology deals with how the different database Pods relate to each other.

There are three standard database topologies:

Standalone: A standalone database runs in a single Pod and doesn't really require any special management.

Master/replica: A master/replica topology (sometimes referred to as master/slave) essentially has a main read/write database (the master) which is the official record of all transactions. These get copied to other databases which are read-only. The master can maintain consistency (since it manages all writes) but the replica provides additional scalability for reads. Master/replica systems can also be configured in a "high availability" mode so that if the master goes down, one of the replicas becomes the master.

Multimaster: In a multimaster topology, data is replicated, but writes can occur on any database instance. This provides maximum scalability (since you don't have a write bottleneck) but usually costs some amount of data consistency guarantees which then have to be either provided by or accounted for by the application instead of being automatically handled by the database.

Regional: A regional topology works similarly to either a master/ replica or a multimaster topology, but only parts of the data are replicated. An example of this might be a branch office of an organization. Their local database doesn't need *all* of the data, just the relevant parts for their organization. Likewise, many people push the database all the way to handheld devices and treat each device as a tiny regional database that is then synchronized with the master server. This allows the application on the device to treat the database as a local store and then leave the database to properly synchronize itself with the master database(s).

By default, PostgreSQL runs well in stand-alone or master/replica mode. However, additional tools can be added so that it also works in multimaster mode. The PGPool system is a proxy that sits in front of multiple PostgreSQL instances and separates reads to individual instances and copies writes into all instances, creating (with some limitations) a multimaster configuration. For Kubernetes, the `bitnami/postgresql-ha` Helm chart mentioned in Chapter 11 runs in a multimaster configuration using PGPool.[2]

If you can cleanly separate out your reads and writes, the master/replica gives the most power while maintaining all of the data semantics of a stand-alone server. It essentially requires that you have two separate database connections—a read-only connection and a read-write connection—and only use the read-write connection when needed. Additionally, if the write does not need to occur immediately, you can achieve even more scalability by deferring the write to a message queue (see Chapter 15). Then, the load on the master is irrelevant, as the speed of queue delivery can be modified to accommodate the master server, and writes can be delayed until the master has more available processing power.

---

[2] A more integrated (but proprietary) system is EnterpriseDB's BDR (bidirectional replication) system.

16.4 Database Partitioning

Some situations benefit from *database partitioning*. This is where data is physically split up and stored in different database servers which are either never synchronized or only partially synchronized. This sort of situation can provide maximum scalability when parts of your data don't need to interact with one another.

As an example, let's say that you have your data organized by customer, but no two customers' data will *ever* interact directly. For this, you could actually partition your cluster into multiple, identical clusters, where each cluster only contains a subset of customer data. The login system may contain a map of which cluster each customer belongs to so that, after logging in, they simply are redirected to their own cluster. This provides an extreme amount of scalability, as the cluster doesn't need to share anything, except perhaps which customer belongs on which cluster.

Another option would be to separate out customers regionally and have regional data centers which are physically close to the customer to provide them with lower latency connections. One could even do both, having multiple clusters in each region.

Another way to split out data is known as *sharding*. In database sharding, data is physically distributed to different database systems based on key. For instance, keys 1 through 1000000 may go to one database, and keys 1000001 to 2000000 may go to another database. This has a lot of the benefits of multimaster databases but allows for even more throughput because writes to the database don't have to be replicated. However, when sharding, you lose a lot of the benefits of relational databases, as queries now have to take into account the database topology. Some of this can be mitigated either at the database level (if the database has native support for sharding), at the proxy level (some proxies support sharding), or at the library level (libraries are available to split requests according to shard). In all cases, sharding is complex to set up and manage and should be avoided unless you know that you are planning sufficient scale that it will be needed.

16.5 Using UUIDs for Primary Keys

You might have noticed in my examples that I am using UUIDs (universally unique identifiers) for primary keys. I am a big proponent of architecting database tables to use UUIDs for primary keys and wanted to take a moment and share with you why I think this is a good idea. In short, UUIDs provide a mechanism for generating unique keys on your database that don't require synchronization while also making them unpredictable from the outside.

If you're not familiar with them, a UUID is basically a randomly generated 16-byte (128 bit) value, usually presented as a hex string (usually formatted as HHHHHHHH-HHHH-HHHH-HHHH-HHHHHHHHHHHH). Because the value is so large, there is essentially no chance that two randomly generated UUIDs will ever be identical. While collisions are not *impossible*, you would need to generate 2.7 *quintillion* UUIDs before you had a greater than 50% probability of having *even one* duplicate.[3] Of all possible problems in your cluster or application, this is the least likely one to run into.

Because UUIDs are randomly generated, they are very helpful with scalability. If your database is distributed (multimaster or partitioned), if you are using consecutive integers for IDs, then the systems have to coordinate in order to not accidentally give duplicate IDs. With UUIDs, no coordination is needed—we know the identifiers are unique.

Likewise, there are often times when you need to copy bits of data from staging to production. Without UUIDs, you have to remap all of the primary keys and foreign keys to new values that make sense in the new database. Using UUIDs, you know that all of the keys will maintain their uniqueness when moved from one server to the other. This also means that data imported from external sources, if they are also using UUIDs, can be done so without having to modify keys.

Additionally, UUIDs provide a measure of security. Again, because they are randomly generated and contain so many bits, no one can guess a UUID. While this doesn't provide strong guarantees (you still shouldn't automatically trust a UUID sent from outside the system without validating it), it does mitigate against many kinds of attacks that are based on predicting identifiers.

Another value of a UUID is the ability to identify a unique row not only in your table but in the *whole database*. Because UUIDs are *universally* unique, that means that having a UUID alone gives you sufficient information to identify a row. However, that doesn't necessarily mean there is sufficient information to *find* your row. If you don't have information about which table the UUID is from, you would wind up having to search all of them to find the right row. Still, there are some database patterns that are helped by having a UUID that can refer to any row in the database.

---

[3] There are different UUIDs with different types of guarantees. I'm generally referring to type four UUIDs (randomly generated), which are the most prevalent kind these days.

There are two primary drawbacks to UUIDs. The first is that they are in fact long and difficult to communicate manually. If you have a customer reading a URL to you over the phone, the chances that they will miscommunicate a UUID is pretty high. If they are embedded in URLs, they make for longer and less pretty URLs. Finally, they offer no contextual information at all. A sequence number at least gives you a clue about when the identifier was generated. Properly generated UUIDs contain no contextual clues at all.

The other drawback is that, in extremely insert-heavy loads with extremely large datasets, the randomness of UUIDs can affect index performance and cause transaction slowdowns. This can be almost entirely mitigated by using special index-friendly UUID generating functions (specifically `uuid_time_nextval`). Those aren't installed by default on PostgreSQL but can be found at `github.com/tvondra/sequential-uuids`. Note that this compromises a small amount on the randomness of the UUIDs but, if they are needed, is well worth the trade-off.

16.6 Thinking About Sources of Truth

The one other thing I want to mention related to data stores is that, for any value stored, you should recognize exactly one location as being the "official" location for that data, known as the *source of truth*. This location may be in the database, or it may be in a third-party system. You may have copies of this data floating around in any number of data stores. However, in all cases, you should know where the data's *official* location is. This helps all systems recognize which primary system must always be kept up-to-date and which direction data should flow in when refreshing other caches in other locations.

My database professor, Dale Hanchey, used to say, "a man with one watch knows what time it is, but a man with two watches isn't sure." The idea is that if you have more than one official source of truth for a piece of data, reconciling them becomes difficult. Knowing which location is the primary and which are secondary makes reconciling data differences straightforward.

16.7 Summary

In this chapter, we learned the following:

- Modern applications require a number of different types of data stores based on the type of data and access patterns needed.

- Data stores require special attention in Kubernetes clusters because they are stateful components.

- Relational databases are the foundation stone for data stores in most enterprises.

- Key/value stores are usually used for ephemeral caches in many applications.

- Document databases specialize in storing and querying ad hoc JSON documents.

- Full-text databases specialize in providing textual searches across multiple fields in an intuitive way and also providing excerpts related to search results.

- Object/file stores store large files and provide out-of-band mechanisms for reading and writing the files in the system, so the webserver does not have to maintain long-lived connections for this task.

- Many of these different types of data stores can be at least rudimentally implemented on relational databases.

- Databases support a variety of topologies which allow them to be scaled, such as master/replica, multimaster, and regional.

- Database partitioning allows for data to be divided between completely separated database systems but makes managing that data more complicated.

- Using UUIDs as primary keys yields many advantages for databases, including making identifiers where are unguessable, globally unique, and integratable across systems.

- When building applications using multiple data stores (or third parties), it is important to keep in mind which location is considered the official source of truth for each data item.

CHAPTER 17

Extended Cloud Topologies

In this chapter, we will cover extended cloud topologies. The topology of a cloud is the general interconnectedness of physical and logical components of a cloud.

In a typical Kubernetes configuration, the topology is a relatively simple or "flat" topology. There is a series of Nodes which are presumably all sitting in the same data center. These Nodes are connected together internally with a Pod network, utilizing a set of "internal" IP addresses that are only routable to Pods that are inside the network, but any Pod within the network can reach any other Pod by knowing the Pod's IP address.

The primary topological concern in such a cluster is which Pods are scheduled to which Nodes. We discussed a few topological concerns in such a simple configuration in Chapters 11 and 13, such as the question of where to put caching servers and how they should be arranged on the cluster. In this chapter, we will go over some additional topological configurations and how they are handled both architecturally and within Kubernetes.

17.1 Terminology

To begin with, we need to get comfortable with some terminology regarding cloud topologies. While terminology can vary, you will find several terms that pop up consistently regarding cloud topology.

First up are *availability zones* (sometimes just called "zones"). Many data centers are divided into availability zones. Each availability zone within a data center is topologically "close" to the other availability zones in the same data center, but each availability zone has independent power and networking. In theory, the idea is that, since power and data are independently supplied to each availability zone, a disaster in one zone won't

© Jonathan Bartlett 2023
J. Bartlett, *Cloud Native Applications with Docker and Kubernetes*,
https://doi.org/10.1007/978-1-4842-8876-4_17

spill over into the others. A construction worker with a backhoe might accidentally take out the incoming data feed for one availability zone but probably not more than one. Since the Nodes within an availability zone are topologically close, there is no problem with them sharing resources such as load balancers, caching servers, etc. The Nodes in two availability zones in the same datacenter can be treated as if they are right there on the same network. Note that even though multiple availability zones are supposed to be isolated from each other sufficiently so that problems in one don't affect the other, in practice this isolation does not work quite as well as advertised, even among the biggest and most popular cloud services.

Going wider are *regions*. A region is essentially a separated datacenter. These datacenters might be in the next town or in the next continent. Whatever they are, they are physically separated, and access to resources in a different region requires going across the public Internet.

Going even wider is the *inner edge*. The inner edge is essentially the part of the network that is closer to your users, but outside of where you directly control. An example inner edge service is a Content Delivery Network (CDN), such as Akamai or StackPath (and some cloud services offer their own CDNs as well). Here, an external service provides content delivery to users. You don't have to worry about getting your content close to the user, as the CDN will direct the user to a server that is physically close to them and replicate the data to them from there. So, for instance, you could host your images in a CDN, and you would direct traffic to those images through the CDN instead of through your own network. Then, the CDN would make sure that when the user accesses that data that it is accessed through a server that is physically close to the user.[1]

At the furthest reach is the *outer edge*. This is usually what is happening on a user's own device. Working with the outer edge usually involves things like offloading processing to the user's own device, caching data or images on the user's device, preloading data onto the user's device, or sometimes even having the user's device participate in activities for the server or another user.

Cloud topology can include interactions at each of these levels.

---

[1] While CDNs are usually considered inner edge systems, not all of them actually sit closer to the user than your own datacenter. Nonetheless, architecturally, you can consider them to be on the inner edge because they function that way—outside of your network, but not on the customer's devices. Whether or not the CDN has architected *themselves* to be close to your user's computer is something you should check out with the CDN if that is important to your architecture.

17.2 How Kubernetes Handles Extended Topologies

Historically, Kubernetes has generally favored a "flat" topology, where the only topological concern was handled at the Node level. To implement a more topology-aware cluster, one either needed to be very clever at how one provisioned and labeled Nodes, or you had to provide completely separate Kubernetes clusters for each topological unit. This was usually done by creating completely separate clusters and then using ExternalName Services to refer to endpoints in the other cluster.

More recently, however, Kubernetes has instituted somewhat standardized conventions for labeling Nodes based on their topologies. Cloud providers are not required to follow these conventions or even to have all of these different topological levels. Linode, for instance, only provides Nodes and Node groups (still within the same availability zone) for topologies.

The standard topological levels that the Kubernetes conventions recognize are Node, availability zone, and region.[2] Each of these has standardized labels on the Node that reflect information which can be used to schedule Pods and route traffic in a topology-aware manner. The standard labels are kubernetes.io/hostname for the name of the Node itself, topology.kubernetes.io/zone for the availability zone, and topology.kubernetes.io/region for the region.

Essentially, each Node gets labeled with these labels set to the values that correspond with the given topology. These topology-related labels are collectively known as *topology keys*. Topology keys make it so that scheduling Pods and routing network traffic can occur in a way that is more topology-aware.

To begin with, you can define Pods (and PersistentVolumes and PersistentVolumeClaims) to have a nodeAffinity. This means that you can define a set of labels that a Node should have in order for a Pod to be scheduled on it (either required or preferred). Additionally, you can schedule a Pod to be near (or not near) other Pods with a specific configuration that are in the same topological area. So, for instance, if you wanted to spread Deployment replicas into different availability zones in a region, you could mark the Pods to have an affinity to Nodes in a specific region but an anti-affinity (not want to be scheduled into the same Node as) with Pods that have the same labels

---

[2] Some work has been done to extend Kubernetes to the inner edge, known as the KubeEdge project. However, this project is still in its early stages. However, if you are interested, more can be found at https://kubeedge.io/.

that are in the same zone. Therefore, Pods will be preferentially scheduled into different zones within that region. The intricacies of all of the Pod scheduling options are outside of the scope of this book, but a few more details can be found in Appendix E.

Then, when routing traffic, oftentimes it is good to keep traffic local. You can *force* the traffic of a Service to only go to the same Node (but be dropped otherwise) by setting a Service's `internalTrafficPolicy` to `Local` (see Chapter 11). However, that method is a little too heavy—it would be nice to simply prefer certain configurations, and not force them. Kubernetes is currently working on a variety of options for using topology keys for preferentially routing traffic based on network topology, but the specification is in quite a bit of flux at the time of writing and is not well-supported. For cloud providers that support it, the current best practice is to add the following annotation to simply enable topology-aware routing for a Service:

```
metadata:
  annotations:
    service.kubernetes.io/topology-aware-hints: auto
```

If your cloud does not support the feature, it will ignore the annotation, but, if it does, it will preferentially guide traffic to the Service to Pods that are on Nodes whose topology keys mark them as more "local" than other Pods.

If you require more control over your traffic, several topology-oriented add-ons are available to help you achieve higher levels of control. While outside of the scope of the book, Linkerd, Istio, and Envoy all can add such features (and more) to your Kubernetes cluster.

However, even with the advent of topology keys, sometimes the best management strategy is to simply use multiple, separately managed, flat clusters, which communicate with each other through public or private endpoints. In the future, Kubernetes is looking to add in the concept of a *supercluster*, which entails multiple, connected clusters, but that work is still in-progress. You can presently use Linkerd (and other similar tools) to create a supercluster, but it is not natively a part of Kubernetes yet.

17.3 Considerations for Multiregion Deployments

While having multiple regions sounds nice in theory, in practice it brings a lot of additional headaches. Perhaps the benefits outweigh the problems, but it is good to know what the problems are to begin with.

First of all, remember that traffic between regions usually travels across the public Internet. Therefore, all communication between regions needs to be scrutinized in several ways:

- Traffic between regions is *slow*, so you need to try to make sure that data is moved *before* it is needed.

- Traffic between regions is *expensive*, so you need to make sure that you don't transmit more than you need to.

- Traffic between regions is *potentially intermittent*, so you need to make sure that each region can operate if temporary connection problems arise.

- Traffic between regions is *publicly viewable*, so you need to be sure to encrypt your connection in some way, either through a VPN, an encrypted proxy, or by using secure protocols.

- If you are connecting to an endpoint or service in another region, and not using a VPN or proxy, then you need to be aware that the endpoint is reachable by the entire Internet, and be sure that it is either appropriately firewalled or sufficiently secured that this is okay.

However, multiple regions can also bring advantages that make them worth the scrutiny. First of all, regions usually are very separate from each other. It is rare that outages affect more than one region without simply affecting the Internet as a whole. Second, using multiple regions can allow you to bring your services so that they are physically closer to your users. Within the United States, this is not a huge issue. However, as the distances increase, many localities can only get reliably fast responses from datacenters that are physically close to them. Therefore, having multiple regions allows the cluster to more adequately serve their user base in other locations in the world.

You can initially place a user in a region using services such as GeoIP and GeoDNS. GeoIP can query IP addresses to find their likely location of origin. GeoDNS can put different DNS configurations in different geographic areas, so that a given domain name will resolve differently in different areas. Both of these technologies can be used to drive users to the appropriate region.

For users which can be located in entirely separated clusters, you can sometimes let the user specify where they want to go simply by registering different domain names. For instance, your United States-based cluster might be accessed as example.com, while your Australian cluster might be accessed as example.com.au. This allows for relative simplicity in management and puts the users in charge of where they want to go.

Honestly, most organizations do not need multiregion cluster configurations. For those that do, recognize that, with pretty much any setup, multiregion configurations exponentially increase the amount of planning and management that are involved with cloud maintenance and engineering. Usually, the best option for multiregion clusters is to have clusters which themselves operate independently but occasionally synchronize basic data (such as customer lists) back-and-forth.

17.4 Summary

In this chapter, we learned the following:

- Topology refers to the physical organization of the cloud at the network level.

- By default, Kubernetes is generally designed around a "flat" topology where Nodes are the only important topological idea.

- Other levels of topology include availability zones ("nearby" networks that operate with independent power and data), regions (separate data centers that have to be accessed across the Internet), the inner edge (separate entities such as CDNs which operate networks outside your control, near the user, but not on the user's own devices), and the outer edge (the user's own devices).

- Kubernetes networks can support topology keys, which are labels attached to Nodes that specify which availability zone and region they are a part of.

- Pods can use Node affinities and anti-affinities to specify how they should be distributed on the network.

- Newer Kubernetes versions can use topology keys to more effectively route requests to Services to a topologically close Pod.

- Sometimes network topology is realized by making multiple, independent Kubernetes clusters in different regions which communicate with each other.

- Multiregion deployments have many drawbacks which should be evaluated compared to the benefits.

- Some new technologies such as GeoIP and GeoDNS can be used to help direct users to a datacenter that is topologically closer to them and thus reduce latency for the user.

CHAPTER 18

Architecture Values

This book has focused primarily on the mechanics of putting clusters together. However, in this chapter, I want to take a step back and think about several values (sometimes called "qualities") that cloud architects usually hold when analyzing implementation options. I call these "values" because these are not directly related to the function of the tasks of the cluster themselves but about more on the meta-aspects of cloud architecture.

Many of these values are relatively unimportant when your architecture is small or you don't have many users. However, as the functionality, complexity, and popularity of your application grow, so does the importance of each of these values. I can't tell you at any given stage which of these are going to be important to your application. However, if you keep in mind the concepts, you will be better equipped to recognize when you are in need of being more proactive in each of these areas and may decide to add additional tooling and/or internal procedures and policies around them.

This chapter may seem to just be a list of lists. To some extent, that's correct. My primary goal is to give you lists of things you should be thinking about as you move forward and to give you familiarity with terms that other people use in conjunction with cloud systems. You don't need to take all of these values fully into account when you start out but rather pick the ones most important to your application's needs. As you grow, this chapter will give you the vocabulary you need to think about and describe the values you need to grow into.

18.1 Scalability

The most obvious value is scalability. Scalability is different than performance. Performance is about "how fast" something runs. Scalability is about to what degree will adding hardware (e.g., Pods and/or Nodes) improve the throughput of the system.

© Jonathan Bartlett 2023
J. Bartlett, *Cloud Native Applications with Docker and Kubernetes*,
https://doi.org/10.1007/978-1-4842-8876-4_18

For instance, if doubling the number of Pods doubles the potential throughput of the system, your architecture is perfectly scalable. This is also known as linear scalability, because if you plot the number of real resources and available throughput on a graph, it forms a perfect line. However, if doubling the number of Pods only increases the throughput by 10%, your architecture is not very scalable. In some really bad cases, adding Pods actually *decreases* the throughput.

The cloud architect rarely has much control over performance (except to ask the developers to do it better) but usually has a lot of control over scalability. The architecture itself usually defines how scalable the system is. Thankfully, for most basic applications, scalability is available almost automatically in cloud architectures. If you have a replicated service, usually scaling the number of replicated Pods increases throughput almost linearly until the limits imposed by your database system.

Therefore, the most important things to keep in mind when architecting for scalability are the situations which lead to unscalable systems and actively avoiding them. Some of these include the following:

- Avoid storing state in your services. When making an application scalable, making the requests as stateless as possible makes it easier to scale by adding additional hardware.

- Avoid two-way message queues. The goal of having message queues is so that you *don't* have to wait on another service before moving forward.

- Avoid direct interdependencies between services. Try to move as many interdependencies between services into message queues.

- Identify potential bottlenecks. Ultimately, every application has bottlenecks where scalability breaks down. Knowing where they are enables you to be proactive about mitigating them. Two common bottlenecks are your database service (everyone uses the database to store and retrieve state) and your authentication service (if you're not using JWTs, many requests have to ping back to this service to verify tokens).

For the most part, bottlenecks in cloud applications can be avoided through the use of message queues, proper caching, and smart usage of database resources.

18.2 Observability

Because cloud architectures have so many different pieces, it is important that an organization be able to see and manage what is happening on the cluster on an operational level. This is known as *observability*. Observability includes things like logging, metrics, and status readouts from your cluster. Are you able to see problems when they happen? Are you able to see what a system is doing in order to know if it is causing problems? Are you able to understand how the system is behaving in real time?

Think about message queueing from Chapter 15. From an observability standpoint, we might want to know things like how many messages are outstanding on each channel, what is the throughput on each channel, which channels are not being delivered, and which channels are erroring out. If a message winds up in the dead-letter queue, is that easy to find out? Can we see the failing messages?

Take standard logging. The first level of observability would be to write important information to a log. A second level might be to have a standard format that the team knows about. A third level might be to package all of the logs up from each Pod and ship them to a standard location. A fourth level might be to add a query and analysis tool such as ElasticSearch on the logs so that anyone on the team can search the combined logs quickly and find patterns, such as "what time did the 500 errors start increasing?"

Some programming languages have observability tools that allow you to measure how much time is spent in each function in production situations. This allows developers to proactively look at where their code needs additional help.

18.3 Traceability

If you've noticed, the trend in cluster architectures is to break the application up into pieces. This helps in a number of ways but hurts in one important one—traceability. Traceability is the ability to follow a request through the system across all of the different services.

Debugging live problems can sometimes be difficult in a distributed system because you can only follow the request in the main, front-end system. If you have a service that calls a service, it is sometimes hard to tie the downstream error with the upstream request. Finding out where something went wrong and what request it was associated with can take some effort. Traceability refers to the ease with which this can be done.

Some cloud architects enable traceability by creating "trace identifiers" at the initiation of a request and adding that to every message that gets passed through the system. Others simply encourage increased logging so that it is clear when each request is made, where it went, and who picked it up.

The W3C has a recommended format for trace headers that are passed via HTTP. The recommended format is (using all lowercase hexadecimal digits) VV-TTTTTTTTTTTTTTTTTTTTTTTTTTTTTTTT-PPPPPPPPPPPPPPPP-FF and should be placed in the `traceparent` HTTP header. The meanings of these fields are as follows:

> **V**: This is the version identifier (for this specification version, it is always set to 00).
>
> **T**: This is a globally unique, 32-character ID for the trace itself. This can be generated as a UUID without the dashes. If received from a request, it should be passed forward, because it indicates the call is part of another trace.
>
> **P**: This known as the "trace parent," and it is the ID of the request within the processing system.
>
> **F**: These are the "flags" for the request, and it is a bit array. Currently, only one flag is supported, the rightmost bit, which is set to 1 if the parent has recorded sampling information about the request already. This can be used by the receiver to know if it, too, needs to record additional data about the request in order to be tied together with the parent call.

If using this system, if an application receives a `traceparent` header, it should keep the trace ID but modify the trace parent to represent itself when making further requests.

Additionally, another field called `tracestate` consists of additional key/value pairs that are added by each system along the way. These `key=value` pairs are vendor-dependent, but they have some basic formatting and processing rules. For the format, each pair is comma-separated without spaces. The keys contain lowercase letters, numbers, and a few symbols (hyphen, underscore, asterisk, and forward slash). The values are up to 256 bytes long and contain any *printable* (no spaces) ASCII character that is not an equal sign or a comma. For the processing, each system can add new keys for downstream requests by appending them to the *left* of the list. It shouldn't repeat any keys, but, if it needs to modify a `key=value` pair, it can remove the old one and add the new one to the left.

While the standard for tracing via HTTP is officially defined,[1] there is also a growing list of other protocols which use these same fields for downstream requests, usually focused on message queueing protocols. While there are a number of software tools that support reading traces, the one I have personally used is Elastic APM.

18.4 Testability

Testability is the ease with which tests can be created and applications can be verified to be performing within specification. The microservice architectures covered in this book make your systems more amenable to testing, because the outline of what each component of the application does is smaller and more well-defined. As a value, testability means not only making sure there are tests for your code but architecting your application so that testing is easier.

Some basic types of tests include the following:

Unit Tests: A unit test usually tests a very small piece of the application, such as a single class.

Integration Tests: An integration test usually tests a larger swath of the system, such as the entire request cycle for a specific endpoint. Additionally, integration tests often contain sequences of requests for making sure that request sequences work properly.

Functional Tests: A functional test tests the software *and* its dependencies. In a cloud architecture, this usually means running the test against a fully operational cloud cluster.

My recommendation is to focus your efforts on integration tests. If you properly test the endpoints, then your units are more or less tested "for free." However, if there are specific issues you want to test for in a class or function, or certain complicated processes or situations that you want to be sure get handled correctly, there are often occasions where unit tests are the best tool.

Tests can be helpful not only for verifying your code but also during development itself. Oftentimes the test tools are much easier to quickly see the effects of your most recent change than trying to invoke the requests yourself.

---

[1] The official W3C recommendation is at www.w3.org/TR/trace-context/.

I also recommend that every application has continually running functional tests. These don't have to be extensive but should run the application through a basic request process to make sure that all of the components are up and responding appropriately. In cloud architectures, there are so many systems being deployed independently, and usually so many people working on them that it is important to be able to say, "yes, at the present time, requests are being processed appropriately through the system." I've seen a number of people try to forego continuous functional testing, thinking that, if they have done a functional test in the test system, there is no need to do ongoing tests in the production system. This usually doesn't end well.

Even in perfectly tested configurations, most cloud applications have some reliance on third-party services which may go down at some point. Continually testing production using functional tests will let you know about problems earlier rather than later.

While every language has its own testing framework, probably the most common functional testing system (as of the time of this writing) is Postman, though many others are also available. If there is one aspect of your cloud application which should be operated independently of your cloud, it is the functional testing operation. You want your functional testing to be up even when your whole cloud is down so that it can be sure to still be able to tell you when you have problems.

18.5 Predictability

One thing that you never want as a cloud administrator is a *surprise*. You want to know how your cluster will respond to all sorts of circumstances. What happens when load increases? What happens if a server goes offline?

Thankfully, using Kubernetes itself adds to system predictability quite a bit. Because Kubernetes is written to self-manage and self-heal to some extent, it means that, for a large number of cases, Kubernetes will maintain predictability. If a Pod or even a Node crashes, Kubernetes knows what to do to get your cluster back to a known-good state.

There are also additional settings you can apply to your Pod specifications to add to predictability. Pod specifications support a number of options for resource limits and guarantees. Setting those will be sure that both you and Kubernetes are clear as to how much headroom is available within your Nodes and cluster and will schedule Pods accordingly.

However, the cluster architecture itself can also lend itself to predictability. Using message queues (Chapter 15), for instance, helps to isolate systems from each other. This means that a problem in one system will have minimal effects on other systems. You can control not only the communication channels but the speed at which messages are consumed.

Predictability means that, even in adverse circumstances, you have control over how your cluster responds.

Another component of predictability is related to costs. Whatever cloud provider you use, you should be sure that you are familiar with how they charge for their services. You should know what the cost impacts are of increased traffic and usage of the application. One of the reasons I like Linode is that their pricing model is very straightforward. On other cloud providers, you need to come up with some pretty advanced modeling to really know how much you are going to pay. Just be sure that you are able to adequately estimate cost impacts of various circumstances and even new features.

18.6 Repeatability

Repeatability is the ability to recreate your cluster at-will. This is important for a number of reasons. For almost every application, you want to be able to make a testing cluster, and you want it to very closely resemble your main cluster. This requires repeatability. Additionally, many applications, as they become more popular, need to be deployed on-site for certain users or have customized deployments for others. Being able to repeat a deployment aids in this. Finally, we don't like to think about it, but there are disaster scenarios where we need to rebuild the cluster from scratch and from backups.

Kubernetes itself aids in repeatability. Since your code is built into container images, and your manifest files contain the definition of how these should be deployed, just by using Kubernetes, you already have a very repeatable cluster configuration. However, you should also be *practiced* at repeating the cluster. Do your manifest files actually represent the cluster as it exists? You should periodically recreate a test version of your cluster from manifest files just to be sure.

Repeatability applies to more than just the cluster itself, though. When developing software, you don't want your build process to be based on whatever your last developer's personal machine configuration was. You want to know that you can rebuild your code at any time, and you know what sort of configurations are required to match exactly what is on the server right now.

This is one of the things that sparked the current interest in continuous development and continuous integration (CI/CD) tools. BitBucket, GitHub, and a number of other vendors and open source tools are available which help you define build pipelines that can be used to automate building your software at any point. Because the build process is offloaded to an external service which has to be configured, you are directly in charge of that configuration. Since it builds on a third-party server, you know that the build configuration is not based on any developer's personal development environment. Using tools such as these creates a repeatable development environment so that you can be confident that as new developers join the team, the build process will be consistent.

While there are a number of ways to configure CI/CD processes, my personal preference is to have builds triggered by specially formatted tags (such as `release--X.X.X`), which build, test, and package the code into a final container image, which is then transmitted to my repository, ready to be used when specified by the Kubernetes manifest. That way, there are no manual processes that apply to the code from the time it is checked in to the time it is pulled by the testing cluster. Additionally, using Kubernetes and container images means that the image for the testing cluster is identical to the image that actually gets deployed into production.

18.7 Integrity and Security

Integrity means that the system only allows valid actions to be performed on it. The most obvious part of integrity is security, where you are preventing bad actors from intentionally doing things which compromise system integrity. However, you also have to watch out for unintentional breaches of integrity. Simple things like how the system handles invalid requests or bad data affect system integrity.

Honestly, most security issues are inseparable from other integrity issues. Security issues arise because a programmer or architect did not take integrity seriously enough and another programmer found a way to exploit this fact. While there are a lot of important things you can do to protect your system's security, they are all bound up with your system operating correctly.

There are basically two levels of security to consider—cluster security and program security. Cluster security is about making sure that the cluster is off-limits to bad actors and that each user on the system only has access to what they need to do their job. Program security is about making sure the application code only allows valid operations to occur by people who have the authorization to do so.

Within an application, the simplest way to ensure security is to (a) know which values are trusted and untrusted and (b) validate all untrusted values. Many application developers (especially newer ones) don't have a sufficient understanding of what values can be trusted, so some training may be needed. Some things to check are as follows:

- All references to database identifiers coming from a request should be verified that the user has appropriate access to those resources.

- The browser itself is an untrusted source. Always assume that any code on the browser can be modified and any request from the browser can be manually altered before sending. This includes not only parameters but also request headers.

- The format of any field whose format is important to the integrity of the system should be checked.

From a cloud architect's standpoint, some things to keep in mind are as follows:

- Minimize external access points. Internal systems such as databases and caches should not be available to the Internet at large. Additionally, endpoints which are for internal use only should not be accessible from the outside.

- Use the principle of least privilege. This means that no process should have more privileges than it needs to accomplish its tasks. This can be further enhanced by firewalling cluster components from each other which do not need to access each other. This also includes only giving cluster users the privileges they need to do their jobs.

- Always use separate accounts for access. It is a bad idea to have shared group accounts, since, when team members change, you will need to revoke their access, and that is hard to do with shared group accounts. This is true both for internal systems and external systems, though it is not always avoidable for external systems.

- Don't confuse obfuscation with security. Having a hard-to-guess endpoint isn't the same as having a secure endpoint. Remember, your attacker may be a former employee.

- Always know who or what you are trusting. Some architects mandate a zero-trust policy where there is no "inside" the network, but, at minimum, you should have an awareness of what pieces you are trusting.

One way of specifically addressing security concerns is known as *threat modeling*. Here, developers or architects gather around and look at different types of threats and how they might impact the system. Common types of threats to examine include the following:

Impersonation: This is where an attacker fakes an internal or external system. Your application thinks it is talking to the "real" system, but really it is talking to an attacker.

Spoofing: This is where an attacker fakes requests in order to make the service think the attacker has more privilege than it really does. Usually this occurs when an application trusts a value that it can't verify. For instance, an attacker could take a request for something that the attacker does have access to but modify the request so that it refers to entities the attacker doesn't have access to.

Tampering: This is where an attacker steals or modifies data in order to trick the system. An example would be getting bad data written to a cache in one request which is then read by another request to get elevated privileges.

Repudiation: This is where an attacker can prevent their actions from being recorded in logs or other data stores.

Information Disclosure: This is where an attacker gets the system to provide more data than it should. For instance, if order numbers are sequential, someone might be able to guess an order number and get information about the user. Alternatively, error messages may include more information about the system than they should.

Denial of Service: This is where an attacker is able to overwhelm the application, usually using a minimum of resources on their end. It usually isn't possible from an application level to defend against a denial-of-service which simply consists of overwhelming traffic, but you can defend against abusers sending large numbers of requests for resource-intensive endpoints.

Elevation of Privilege: This is where an attacker finds a way to use a lower-privileged account to gain privileges reserved for higher-level accounts. An example would be if an email system had a templating language for mass emails, but the templating language ran in the context of the administrator of the email system, not the user who purchased the system, thus potentially allowing the user to execute administration privileges.

For the Kubernetes cluster itself, Kubernetes has a lot of additional options that we have not covered in this book for improving security, including NetworkPolicy objects which limit Pod-to-Pod communication, user and service account management, encryption at rest, various types of authentication plug-ins, and encrypting Pod-to-Pod network traffic when running Kubernetes on untrusted networks.

18.8 Summary

In this chapter, we learned the following:

- Architectural values are ideas to keep in mind when building architectures.

- At small scales, architectural values are not always needed.

- As an application grows, so do the number of architectural values needed to keep the application under control.

- Additionally, as cloud administrators gain more experience, the more they understand the value of the architectural values.

- Scalability is the ability for an application to perform better when more resources are added.

- Observability is the ability to know the state of the cloud and application at any time.

- Traceability is the ability to trace a single request through different systems.

- Testability is the ability to test your application, both before it is deployed (using unit and integration tests) and after (using functional tests).

- Predictability is the ability to know how your cluster will respond to changes, stresses, and challenges, as well as knowing how these will affect the costs of your solution.

- Repeatability is the ability to redeploy your cluster from scratch or to build your application from scratch.

- Integrity is the ability of the system to prevent users from performing invalid operations on the application or the cluster as a whole.

CHAPTER 19

Conclusion

In this book, we have looked at how containers have revolutionized the way that we think about and deploy software services, we have looked at how Kubernetes operates as a cloud operating system enabling us to orchestrate our containers into a unified cloud application, and we have looked at many cloud architecture patterns and considerations to help you analyze and design the perfect cloud architecture for your application.

I don't expect you to be able to put everything in this book into practice all at once. I would advise you to start with just a few ideas that are relevant to your application and learn to do them well. Then, later, come back to this book for more ideas. You will find that there are parts of this book that you skimmed over because you didn't think them important that are now reflected by your present reality. I've found that message queueing, in particular, is something that newer architects (and smaller applications) don't see the need for, but the utility of them quickly becomes apparent as complexity grows, external dependencies are added, or bottlenecks appear.

In any case, it is my hope that this book grows with you and helps you continually level up your cloud architecting abilities. Everyone has to start somewhere, and I hope that this book has provided a great starting point for you in understanding, designing, and building cloud architectures for your organization.

© Jonathan Bartlett 2023
J. Bartlett, *Cloud Native Applications with Docker and Kubernetes*,
https://doi.org/10.1007/978-1-4842-8876-4_19

APPENDIX A

Navigating the Linux Command-Line Shell

In the Kubernetes world, you are rarely doing full system administration tasks. However, knowing the basics of how to navigate around Linux using a command shell (also called a terminal or the command line) will help you immensely both for building container images and troubleshooting running containers. While this certainly isn't a full introduction to the command shell, it will hopefully give you a place to start.

A.1 General Command Format

Linux commands usually follow the same basic format, based largely after human communication. The command is listed first because that is the name of the program which runs the command. Most commands take one or more *arguments* which can be considered similar to direct objects of a sentence. Additionally, many commands take options (also called flags, modifiers, or parameters) which modify the behavior of the command. These are very similar to adverbs. Options are usually given by prefixing them with a dash. For instance, to change the "list directory" command (ls) to show a long-form listing, you add the -l option to the command. Thus, the command to show the long-form listing is ls -l.

Sometimes options themselves take arguments. However, if they don't, you can oftentimes stack them. For instance, ls can also show hidden files with -a. You *can* do both options with ls -l -a, but you can also squeeze them together with ls -la. Many commands have both long options and short options, with the longer version of the

© Jonathan Bartlett 2023
J. Bartlett, *Cloud Native Applications with Docker and Kubernetes*,
https://doi.org/10.1007/978-1-4842-8876-4

option usually preceded by two dashes. For instance, instead of doing `ls -a`, you could instead type `ls --all`. If you don't know how to invoke a command, most commands have a help screen that you can invoke by doing `MYCOMMAND -h` or `MYCOMMAND --help`.

While each command has its own quirks and abilities, this general command format is common to most commands in Linux.

A.2 Package Management Commands

We will start by looking at how to install additional packages. Most container images are fairly minimal, so you'll need to install even some of the basic commands to do much of anything worthwhile. In fact, a large part of writing a `Dockerfile` is installing necessary utilities.

Each package manager usually has commands to do the following:

1. Update the metadata (the list of packages and versions available).

2. Upgrade the existing packages (i.e., install security updates).

3. Search for packages by search term.

4. Install packages (including all dependencies).

5. Uninstall packages.

6. Clear metadata.

However, the particular package management commands you use to do those operations is dependent on which Linux distribution you are running. However, the tools are all extremely similar, so learning one will get you a long way toward learning the others.

Additionally, the names of packages in each system will differ, as well as what comes installed by default. While the various installation commands for a variety of Linux distributions are available in the following, going forward we will use the `debian` official image as the standard. For any command in this appendix not installed by default in the official `debian` image, we will provide the name of the Debian package you will need to install to use the command.

A.2.1 Debian Package Management

Debian-based distributions (which include the popular Ubuntu distribution) use the `apt` package management system. Their package management tools include the following:

1. Update the metadata: `apt update`

2. Upgrade the existing packages: `apt upgrade`

3. Search for packages: `apt search SEARCHTERM`

4. Install packages: `apt install -y PACKAGENAME`

5. Uninstall packages: `apt remove -y PACKAGENAME`

6. Clear metadata: `apt clean`

For most container images, in order to use any of the `apt` commands, you need to start by issuing `apt update`. Lots of older documentation uses the older name of the command, `apt-get`.

A.2.2 Alpine Package Management

The Alpine Linux distribution was covered in Chapter 4. This distribution uses the `apk` package manager. Several important `apk` commands include the following:

1. Update the metadata: `apk update`.

2. Upgrade the existing packages: `apk upgrade`.

3. Search for packages: `apk search SEARCHTERM`.

4. Install packages: `apk add PACKAGENAME`.

5. Uninstall packages: `apk del PACKAGENAME`.

6. Clear metadata: Running each command with the `--no-cache` flag purges the cache after each command.

A.2.3 CentOS/Fedora/RHEL Package Management

The last one we will look at is the `microdnf` package manager,[1] used in Red Hat- and CentOS-based container images. Several important `microdnf` commands include the following:

1. Update the metadata: `microdnf makecache`.

2. Upgrade the existing packages: `microdnf upgrade`.

3. Search for packages: `microdnf repoquery SEARCHTERM`.

4. Install packages: `microdnf install -y PACKAGENAME`.

5. Uninstall packages: `microdnf remove -y PACKAGENAME`.

6. Clear metadata: `microdnf clean all`.

A.3 Basic Linux File Commands

ls This command lists all of the files in your current directory. Using the `-a` switch will show all files, including special and hidden files (files starting with a .), and the `-l` switch will show additional information about the files. You can also specify a specific directory to list at the end of the command.

cd This changes your current directory. If the argument starts with a /, then it is an *absolute* path starting from the root of the filesystem hierarchy. If the argument starts with a ~, it is a path that starts from your home directory. Otherwise, it is a *relative* path starting from your current directory. The special directory .. represents the parent directory, and the special directory . represents the current directory. Therefore, to get to the parent directory of your current directory, just do `cd ..`.

---

[1] The actual distribution package management tool is called `dnf`. The main difference is that `dnf` supports Python plug-ins and has a Python dependency (which would make the container larger), while `microdnf` is just based on C code. For those who used Red Hat-based distributions in the past, `dnf` is the successor to `yum`.

pwd This prints out your current directory. It stands for "print working directory."

cat This command simply spits out a given file to the screen.

head This command gives you the first few lines of a file. `head -n NUM FILENAME` will give you the first NUM lines of the FILENAME file.

tail This command gives you the last few lines of a file. `tail -n NUM FILENAME` gives you the last NUM lines of the file FILENAME.

mkdir This creates a new directory within your current directory (or anywhere at all if you give it an absolute path starting with / or ~).

rm Removes a given file. If you want to remove a whole directory tree (the directory and all of the files/directories in it), add the `-r` switch. Just be careful!

nano (in nano) This is a simple text editor that comes with many Linux distributions. Common commands to use within nano are control-o which saves (outputs) the file, control-x which quits, and control-w which searches.

vim (in vim) The vim application (or its older brother, vi) is an editor that you will find on nearly *any* Linux-like system. It is very powerful, but please read a tutorial on it before attempting to use it. Its primary benefits are that its keyboard interface is based on where your hands naturally sit on the keyboard and that its small footprint and longstanding heritage mean that you will never be on a Linux or UNIX machine that doesn't have it installed.

A.4 System Diagnostic Commands

If a container isn't running properly, and rebooting it isn't fixing the problem, it may be time to run diagnostics on the container itself. If you can get a shell into a running container (see Appendix C.2), the following commands can help you to get a better idea about what is going on in the container. However, you may have to install some of these commands before using them, depending on the container image you are using.[2]

> **ps (in procps)** This command gives you information about processes running on the system. This has numerous options that can give you almost any piece of information you want to know. However, my favorite way of calling it is `ps -afxww` which gives you a list of all of the processes currently running displayed as a tree so you know which process spawned which other process.
>
> **free (in procps)** This gives a short rundown of the current memory usage on the system. `free -h` gives the most readable output.
>
> **top (in procps)** This command gives you information about which processes are using the most system resources. Use `q` to leave `top`.
>
> **kill** This command delivers signals to processes by their PID. The default signal it gives is `SIGTERM`, but it can also deliver other signals. The command format is `kill -SIGNAL PID`, where `SIGNAL` is either the name or number of the UNIX signal to send, and `PID` is the process ID of the process to give the signal to (see the `ps` command to see how to get the process ID). The most standard signals are `SIGTERM` (request but don't force a process to exit) and `SIGKILL` (force a process to exit immediately with no cleanup). However, many processes implement other behavior for other signals. For instance, a `SIGHUP` signal sent to a Java process will cause it to dump a stack trace of all threads to its log (and then continue on).

---

[2] If you do add packages to modify your Pod, you should probably terminate it after you finish your commands and let Kubernetes boot up another one. The reason for this is that now this one particular Pod is different from the others, so it is best to remove it so that you don't have one sitting out there that is different.

lsof (in lsof) This lists every open file in your container and what process has it open.

strace (in strace) This command allows you to list all of the system calls (places where a process calls out to the operating system) that a process is making. If a process is stuck or doing something weird and you don't know what or why, this is a good frontline tool for diagnosis. You run it as strace -p PID_OF_PROCESS. Note that some container runtimes don't give users sufficient permissions to run strace or need specific configurations in order to do so.

screen (in screen) This is a convenience utility that allows you to run multiple shell sessions from the same command-line window. However, more importantly, it lets you disconnect from a shell process (control-a then d), log off, and then log in later and reconnect to that shell session with screen -r. This allows you to run long-running commands from a shell session without having to maintain connectivity.

A.5 Network Diagnostic Commands

Similar to the previous section, you may often have to diagnose network issues. The commands below, if installed, will enable you to diagnose network problems from within a Pod.

ping (in inetutils-ping) This command requests a simple aliveness check from the given host or IP address. This can be used to verify connectivity between Pods by pinging the IP address of one Pod from another. Note that you cannot ping a Service. You can also do this to check connectivity to outside hosts, though many firewalls will block such requests.

traceroute (in inetutils-traceroute) This command is used to trace the route that packets are transmitted to a given host or IP address. This can be used to see *how* packets are getting from one location to another. Again, this can be used for Pods but not for Services. Additionally, running traceroute to an outside host can show how traffic is routed to those hosts, but again many firewalls will block such requests.

telnet (in inetutils-telnet) Telnet used to be the way that you accessed machines remotely, before encryption became a necessity. Now it is often used to make direct connections with remote servers for testing. For instance, to talk to a webserver directly, you can type in `telnet REMOTE.MACHINE.NAME 80`, and it will connect you directly to port 80 on the remote machine. Remember that `telnet` will display information directly to your screen, so be careful if sensitive data may be returned.

openssl (in openssl) This command is similar to `telnet`, but, instead of doing a bare TCP connection, this will open up an SSL/TLS connection. The `openssl` command will handle the encryption, decryption, and certificate handling and simply present to you the decrypted channel. This command has a lot of options, but the basic way to use it is to say `openssl s_client -connect HOST:PORT`.

nslookup (in dnsutils) This command allows you to easily look up DNS information on a host. Running `nslookup HOSTNAME` will return all A records for that host (usually only one, unless you are running a headless service). `nslookup` is tied in to Kubernetes CoreDNS.

dig (in dnsutils) This command looks up DNS information on a host, but does not use Kubernetes CoreDNS by default, so it doesn't return Kubernetes records.

ss (in iproute2) This command gives information about open sockets on your machine. The two commands to focus on here are `ss -plnt` for looking at listening TCP connections and `ss -plnu` for looking at listening UDP connections.

tcpdump (in tcpdump) This can be used to dump all network traffic in and out of the Pod.

A.6 Application-Level Diagnostic Commands

Many commands run at a higher level than bare operating system or networking. There are commands for doing HTTP connections, database connections, etc. Several of these commands include the following:

curl (in curl) This command does pretty much any type of HTTP request you might want to perform. The basic usage is `curl http://example.com/path/name`. This downloads the document at the given URL and prints it to the screen.

ab (in apache2-utils) This is the ApacheBench command which is used for performing HTTP benchmarks. It works almost identically to the `curl` command above, except that you can give it a `-n NUM` flag for the number of connections and the `-c CONN` flag for the number of simultaneous connections. This is used to simulate traffic load on a resource. It prints out result statistics.

psql (in postgresql-client) This command gives you access to the PostgreSQL interactive SQL prompt. The `-U PGUSER` option indicates which PostgreSQL user you will access the database as, the `-h HOSTNAME` option says what host you want to connect to, and the command argument will be which database to connect to.

mysql in (mysql-client) This command gives you access to the MySQL (or MariaDB) interactive SQL prompt. It has the same basic usage as `psql`.

A.7 Permission-Based Commands

Normally, containers run as a "virtual root" user. This means that, from the container's internal perspective, the container thinks it is running as root, but, from the Node's perspective, the container is not running with any particularly privileged user. This means that most permission-oriented commands are irrelevant for most containers. However, this isn't always the case. These commands will help you manage file permissions when permissions matter.

chown This changes the user and group ownership of a file. If you do chown fred FILENAME, then fred becomes the owner of the file. If you do chown fred:stonemasons FILENAME, then fred becomes the owner and the group stonemasons becomes the group owner of the file. You can add the -R option to change the ownership of a directory and all of the file/directories underneath it.

chgrp This is like chown, but just for group ownership.

chmod This changes the permissions on a file. Each file has separate permissions for the user owner (u), the group owner (g), and everybody else (o). The basic set of permissions are read (r), write (w), and execute (x). To add execute permission to the owner of a file, you would type chmod u+x FILENAME. To add read permission to everybody on a file, you would type chmod a+r FILENAME, where a refers to all users (u, g, and o). To remove group write permission on a directory and every file/directory under it, you would do chmod -R g-w FILENAME.

su This command stands for "switch user." Without any arguments, this switches the user to the root user. You usually want to add the -l option, which means to act as if you logged in with this user, which will take you to the user's home directory and run other login tasks. If you give it an argument, it will be the name of the user you want to switch to. You must enter that user's password in order to switch users.

sudo This command lets you temporarily run a command as another user (normally as root). The configuration of this command is beyond the scope of this book, but man sudo should give you good information.

A.8 Basic Linux Filesystem Directories

One important part of knowing where to find things is to know where Linux likes to put things. This section is a brief introduction to the standard structure of the Linux filesystem. Container images don't follow these conventions as closely because a lot of these ideas are to help server administrators, and containers aren't servers in the traditional sense. Nonetheless, knowing what is generally expected in a Linux filesystem will help you navigate around it better.

/ This is the root of the filesystem tree. Every file and directory is contained somewhere in here.

/boot This directory holds basic files for booting up (like the Linux kernel). You should usually stay out of this directory. This is normally absent in containers.

/dev In Linux, devices are represented as files, and they live here. These are usually absent in containers.

/etc This directory contains most of the configuration files for the computer.

/proc This directory contains a directory for every running process on the computer describing its state (the name of the directory is the process ID of the process). The /proc filesystem also has other files to represent operating system status information.

/tmp This directory is used to store temporary files.

/var This directory holds *var*iable files—files that are tied to programs and are intended to change during the operation of a program. For instance, your database is usually stored in a subdirectory of /var because it is changing and it is managed by the database software instead of by the user.

/var/log This directory holds most of the log files for the system.

/var/spool This directory is mostly used for transient data within a system, such as current mail for a mail server, jobs for a print service, etc.

/usr This directory is a mostly read-only directory used to store programs used by the machine in the course of its operation. This contains the following:

/usr/bin The files in this directory are the programs (i.e., *bin*aries) that are normally used on the server by users and other programs. Also note that there is a directory /bin which has the programs that are necessary for proper bootup.

/usr/sbin The files in this directory are the system programs (e.g., daemons and system tools) that are available for use on this machine. Also note that there is a directory /sbin which has the system programs that are necessary for proper bootup.

/usr/lib The files that live here are the system *lib*raries that support the applications. There is often a /usr/lib64 directory for 64-bit libraries. Also note that there is a directory /lib which has the libraries that are necessary for proper bootup.

/usr/local This directory has almost an identical structure to /usr, but the programs installed here are usually compiled by the system administrator. Unlike /opt (where each program gets an entire directory to themselves), the programs installed here all share the same bin, lib, and sbin directories.

/home This directory holds the home directory of each user on the machine except root. This is usually absent in containers because there are usually no users except the container's virtual root user.

/root This is root's home directory.

/opt This is a directory that often has custom-installed applications. In /opt, each program usually has its own directory.

APPENDIX B

Installing Applications

One of the goals of this book is to minimize the amount of installation that is required to get up and running. For the majority of this book, you only need two programs installed: Docker and kubectl. And, as it so happens, current versions of Docker actually include kubectl as well. Additionally, Docker itself provides you access to innumerable pieces of software that no longer require explicit installation. You simply run the software as a container image, and, if you don't already have it, Docker will go out and fetch it for you. Since the containers run essentially independently of your main operating system, this works without having to actually install the application on your system.

If you are on a Mac, I highly recommend installing Homebrew, which is a development package manager for Mac. It is available online from brew.sh. To install a package with Homebrew, you just do brew install PACKAGENAME.

If you are on Windows, I recommend that you use Chocolatey for a development package manager. It is available online from chocolatey.org. To install a package with Chocolatey, you just do choco install PACKAGENAME.

On Linux, package management depends on the distribution. The three most popular are Debian (which uses the apt command for package management), Red Hat or CentOS (which uses the dnf command for package management), or Alpine (which uses the apk command). This appendix will focus on Debian. Package names may differ on other distributions. Also, be sure to run apt update and apt upgrade before running other commands.

B.1 Installing Docker

The installation process varies by operating system, but installing Docker is fairly straightforward. However, you must be running a 64-bit operating system on a 64-bit processor (both of which are common today) in order to run Docker.

231

© Jonathan Bartlett 2023
J. Bartlett, *Cloud Native Applications with Docker and Kubernetes*,
https://doi.org/10.1007/978-1-4842-8876-4

On Windows and Mac, you can simply download Docker Desktop from the Docker website (`docker.com`). Installation for both is fairly straightforward, though, on Windows, depending on your operating system and hardware setup, it may require that you enable certain low-level features on your PC.

Docker also has desktop packages for Linux, but configuring those is more system-specific. Additionally, on Linux, there is a separation between Docker Desktop and the Docker Engine. Both allow containers to run, but they are managed independently and don't share containers between the two. It is generally a good idea to only run one of them at a time. Usually, you would want to run Docker Desktop on your desktop and the Docker Engine on a server. In this book, the server portion will be managed by Kubernetes, so you will not need to work with the Docker Engine directly.

On Windows, Mac, or Linux, Docker is primarily a command-line tool. Therefore, this book will assume at least a basic working knowledge of how the command line works. However, to help you get started, some basic information is available in Appendix A.

If you are on Linux and prefer just doing command line or are installing Docker onto a server, you can install the Docker Engine using `apt install docker.io`. The service daemon will auto-start when the Docker command is first run.

B.2 Using Podman

While I highly recommend Docker Desktop, if you are more keen on open source software, the Podman system is available for both Mac and Linux (available from `podman.io`). Podman is command-line compatible with Docker and runs entirely in userspace, with no daemon running when used on Linux. To install Podman on Linux, just do `apt install podman crun`.

Under Mac, Podman has to run under a virtual machine. To install Podman on a Mac using Homebrew, just do `brew install podman`. To use Podman on a Mac, you also have to run the virtual machine, which involves running the commands `podman machine init` and `podman machine start` before starting.

After that, Podman runs almost identically to Docker, simply replacing the `docker` command with `podman`. This can also be accomplished with a symlink or an alias.[1] For the examples in this book, the only difference between the two is the assumed name of

---

[1] I prefer using a symlink because aliases don't work if you need the command in a shell script.

the container description file: `Dockerfile` for Docker and `Containerfile` for Podman. In this book, we always specify the name of the file explicitly with `-f Dockerfile`, so the same command will work with both systems.

Depending on your setup, another difference with Podman is that, since the containers here are stored on Docker Hub, you may need to prefix the name of container images with `docker.io/` in order for Podman to find them. Some installations of Podman will do this for you, but others will not.

B.3 Using Apple Silicon

If you are running on a Mac that is using Apple Silicon (e.g., an M1 or similar processor), note that all of the examples presented in this book will still work. In fact, both Docker Desktop and Podman for Mac running on Apple Silicon are fully compatible with both x86-64 and arm64 images (see in the following for instructions on making Podman compatible). The main issue is that, by default, Docker will pull and build images for whatever processor you are currently running.

So, if you don't specify otherwise, Docker will build images which are for an ARM processor, not an x86 processor, and therefore may not run on your cluster. To prevent this, be sure to specify the platform in your `Dockerfile`. This means that anytime you have `FROM name-of-base-image`, you need to replace that with `FROM --platform=linux/amd64 name-of-base-image`. If you *wanted* to specify an ARM processor, you would specify the platform as `linux/arm64`.

To use x86-64 images with Podman under Apple Silicon, you need to do a few additional steps, but it isn't hard. After you do `podman machine start`, you have to install the x86 compatibility. You can do that with the following series of commands:

```
podman machine ssh
sudo -i
rpm-ostree install qemu-user-static
systemctl reboot
```

Then, you will need to wait a few minutes for the machine to restart. After that, you are ready to run Docker images for either ARM or x86!

B.4 Installing `kubectl`

If you run Docker Desktop, the `kubectl` command is now standard with Docker. In fact, Docker Desktop can run a single-Node Kubernetes environment on your desktop for testing out Kubernetes applications. The application described in Chapter 10 is compatible with this system, with the (perhaps obvious) exception that the Ingress runs out of `localhost`, not an externally facing load balancer. However, even though you can install everything locally, I still recommend running the examples through Linode. With Linode, not only do you have access to a multi-Node cluster, but you are working with the exact same environment you will get when working with production clusters, including the ability to access it from an externally facing IP address.

However, if you are using a Docker alternative like Podman, you can also download `kubectl` separately. `kubectl` is available from your normal package providers, but it is also available as a direct download from the Kubernetes website at `kubernetes.io`. Essentially, you can directly download the `kubectl` command from the Kubernetes website and then move it into a directory in your command path.

For Linux, you can get `kubectl` with `apt install kubernetes-client`. For Mac, you can install it with `brew install kubectl`. For Windows, you can install it with `choco install kubernetes-cli`.

B.5 Installing Helm

If you want to use Helm to install additional Kubernetes components, you will need to install the command-line controller for it. Information about Helm can be found on Helm's website at `helm.sh`. You can install Helm on a Mac with `brew install helm` and on Windows with `choco install kubernetes-helm`. The Linux install is more complicated, and I will simply refer you to the website.

APPENDIX C

Common kubectl Commands

In addition to the basic commands and command structure discussed in Chapter 7, there are several handy kubectl commands to keep in mind. This is not anywhere near a complete reference, but rather a handy guide for those few odd commands that you need on a regular basis. Additionally, I am not including any commands that would be better implemented by creating YAML manifests and applying them like normal.

C.1 List Kubernetes Resources and What API Version Defines Them

It's always a pain to remember what all the resources are called. Thankfully, there is a command that lists them all for you!

```
kubectl api-resources -o wide
```

This not only lists the resources available, but it also gives you (a) the `apiVersion` to use with them and (b) their short names as well. Perhaps you are tired of typing `kubectl get persistentvolumeclaims`. The preceding command will tell you that you can shorten that to `kubectl get pvc`.

© Jonathan Bartlett 2023
J. Bartlett, *Cloud Native Applications with Docker and Kubernetes*,
https://doi.org/10.1007/978-1-4842-8876-4

C.2 Fire Up a Shell on a Pod

There are many occasions where you might need to run a shell in your Kubernetes cluster. Before the advent of containers, it was fairly easy to get on to a server using SSH and debug what issues were happening straight on the server. With containers, there is not an operating system running an SSH server. However, if your Pod has a container with a shell installed, you can get a shell by running the following command:

```
kubectl exec -it MY-POD-NAME -c POD-CONTAINER-NAME -- /bin/bash
```

If you are only running one container in your Pod or are fine with just getting the first container in the Pod, you can leave off the `-c POD-CONTAINER-NAME`. The `-it` switch allows interactivity with the command. Everything after the `--` is the command to run on the container. The `/bin/bash` command usually is a lot nicer interface than just running the standard `/bin/sh`.

You can also use this as a template for running other commands on your containers, but usually people just shell in first. If you need to run a long-running command in a container (watching system processes or resources or something), and you are worried you might be disconnected, the `screen` command will allow you to detach from your terminal and reattach later without interrupting any processes. However, the `screen` command will probably need to be installed on your container separately.

You can also run a separate debug container on your Pod as well using the `kubectl debug` command. This launches a new container with an image you choose onto your Pod for debugging, connected to the process space of the container in the Pod you specify. The command for this is as follows:

```
kubectl debug -it MY-POD-NAME --image MY-IMAGE --target CONTAINER
```

The filesystem of the attached container is available at `/proc/1/root` (except in really unusual configurations). If you wanted, you can do a `chroot /proc/1/root` to get a filesystem matching the original container that needs debugging.

Attaching debugging containers is especially helpful if the container image doesn't provide a shell, if the container image has crashed (making `kubectl exec` not work), or if you want a debugging image with more tools installed.

C.3 Run a Custom Image (and Shell) on a New Pod

Sometimes you need to debug the cluster as a whole. Perhaps you need to have a presence inside the cluster to see why a ClusterIP service isn't responding how you expect. The best way to do this is to fire up a single-use Pod running an image that is pre-equipped with most of the networking tools you might want. You can do that with the following command:

```
kubectl run my-temp-shell --rm -it --image CONTAINER-IMAGE -- /bin/sh
```

You would choose CONTAINER-IMAGE depending on what you want to do. This image should have network tools, DNS tools[1], possibly database tools, and anything else you need to do work in your cluster. Three fairly standard images for this include busybox (a tiny but effective network toolset), nicolaka/netshoot (which has lots of network debugging and performance monitoring tools), and praqma/network-multitool (similar to netshoot but with different tools and a much smaller image). However, creating public Docker Hub images is free, so I would recommend putting together your favorite tools from your favorite distribution that you like to use on your network, creating an image, and using that one. I created one for this purpose, available at johnnyb61820/network-toolkit.

The --rm on this command tells Kubernetes to clean up the Pod when you exit.

C.4 Attaching to a Pod Container

You can attach your console directly to a Pod container by using kubectl attach. The command looks like this:

```
kubectl attach -it MY-POD-NAME -c CONTAINER-NAME
```

This will attach (both input and output) to the given container on the given Pod. Generally I recommend against this for a variety of reasons. First of all, there are already lots of logging and debugging commands, so this one doesn't give you much additional. Second, depending on your terminal (and other configurations), getting out of this can be more problematic than getting in. In short, attaching depends on a lot of specifics of your shell and the remote container, and you will get more predictable and consistent results using the other means of Pod debugging available to you.

---

[1] Note that, when looking at DNS on Kubernetes, you should use nslookup, not dig.

C.5 Getting Logs for a Pod

Pods can log either to a file or to STDOUT, but, typically, Kubernetes assumes that they are logging their main application data to STDOUT. To get these logs, run the following:

```
kubectl logs POD-NAME
```

If a Pod has more than one container, you can select that container with the -c CONTAINER-NAME flag. If you add the -f flag, it will tail (i.e., follow) the log file until you terminate the command.

C.6 Reboot All Pods in a Deployment

Sometimes something changes in the network, and you just need to reboot everything in a Deployment. Kubernetes has a command just for this!

```
kubectl rollout restart deployment YOUR-DEPLOYMENT-NAME
```

This will restart all of the Pods under the Deployment YOUR-DEPLOYMENT-NAME. This also works for DaemonSets and StatefulSets. You can check the status of your restart with this:

```
kubectl rollout status deployment YOUR-DEPLOYMENT-NAME
```

C.7 Forwarding a Local Port to a Port in the Cluster

If you need a port from the cluster exposed on your localhost, you can use the following command:

```
kubectl port-forward service/MY-SERVICE LOCALPORT:REMOTEPORT
```

This will make LOCALPORT on your localhost forward to the REMOTEPORT port on the Service named MY-SERVICE. Note that this syntax for specifying the Service is a little different. Additionally, you can target pods directly as well by specifying pod/MY-POD. If you need the port bound for your whole machine (and not just localhost), add the flag --address 0.0.0.0 to the command.

The command will proxy until the command is terminated.

C.8 Show Node Health

To show the health (CPU/memory) of all your Nodes, run

```
kubectl top nodes
```

You can do the same with pods, and either show all of them or specify the Pod you are interested in.

C.9 Show All Kubernetes Events

To get a sense of the action going on within the cluster, run the command:

```
kubectl get events
```

This will tell you things like when an image is being pulled, when a Pod is being created, etc.

C.10 Show a Secret

Oftentimes you will need to see a secret. These can be straightforwardly obtained by doing a kubectl get on the secret. However, these are base64-encoded, so you will have to decode it to read it. So, if your secret is named MYSECRET and is stored in the key MYPASS, you can retrieve it with the following:

```
kubectl get secret MYSECRET -o 'go-template={{.data.MYPASS |
base64decode}}'
```

C.11 Force-Terminate a Pod

You can always terminate a Pod with kubectl delete pod PODNAME. However, sometimes this isn't fast enough. Kubernetes likes to give Pods time to clean up after themselves, and maybe you're in a hurry. To force the immediate termination of a Pod, you can issue the following command:

```
kubectl delete pod PODNAME --grace-period=0 --force
```

C.12 Some Handy Switches to Remember

The following switches are handy on a variety of different `commands`:

- `-o wide`: This yields additional fields when getting information about a resource. It is especially useful when getting Pod information, as it returns the Pod's internal cluster IP address as well as the Node that it is located on.

- `-n NAMESPACE`: This can be used to select the particular namespace that your command is associated with.

- `-A`: This tells `kubectl` to look in all namespaces when using a `kubectl get` or `kubectl describe` command.

C.13 Accessing the Underlying Node

Depending on your cloud provider, accessing the underlying Kubernetes Nodes may be trivial or difficult. If you set up the cluster yourself, you probably already have credentials. However, if the cluster is set up automatically (such as with Linode), chances are you don't have direct access to the Nodes. In most cases, though, giving yourself access is simple enough.

The DaemonSet deployment shown in Figure C-1 will install a Pod on every Node running a base Debian install (or whatever image you want). However, that Pod will be running in a privileged security context, sharing the host's process space, IPC space, and networking space. The host's entire filesystem will also be mounted into your Pod container at `/node-fs`, so you can access all of the Node's files. It additionally mounts the `/dev` directory as `/dev` because some of those files are picky about where they exist on the filesystem. This gives you essentially complete access to the Node.[2]

It is not advisable to run Pods that are this wide open normally, but, if you do need temporary access to the underlying Node, this is a straightforward way of doing it. I would suggest removing the DaemonSet with a `kubectl delete` immediately when you

---

[2] In fact, if you want it to behave identically to a login shell (i.e., so the paths on your shell match the Node), you can perform `chroot /node-fs`, and now your root directory will be the Node's root directory, and you will no longer have access to the rest of the Pod filesystem.

are finished. Once running this DaemonSet, you can do `kubectl get pods -o wide` to see which Pod is running on which Node. Then you can do a `kubectl exec` to get access to the Pod (see Appendix C.2).

```
apiVersion: apps/v1
kind: DaemonSet
metadata:
  name: privpod
spec:
  selector:
    matchLabels:
      mydaemon: privpod
  template:
    metadata:
      labels:
        mydaemon: privpod
    spec:
      hostNetwork: true
      hostPID: true
      hostIPC: true
      containers:
        - name: privcontainer
          image: johnnyb61820/network-toolkit
          securityContext:
            privileged: true
          command:
            - tail
            - "-f"
            - /dev/null
          volumeMounts:
            - name: nodefs
              mountPath: /node-fs
            - name: devfs
              mountPath: /dev
      volumes:
        - name: nodefs
          hostPath:
            path: /
        - name: devfs
          hostPath:
            path: /dev
```

Figure C-1. *A DaemonSet with Full Access to the Underlying Node*

More on Kubernetes Storage

While storage is an important topic, unfortunately it is full of details that would interrupt the flow of the main book, are somewhat out of scope for the book, and are largely cloud-specific. However, I did want to cover some of the basics for how Kubernetes handles storage beyond what was covered in the main text.

The two types of storage that were focused on in the main text were `emptyDir` volumes, which simply requested a local, empty volume for sharing between containers within a Pod, and PersistentVolumeClaims, which, the way we used them, requested physical storage from the cloud infrastructure using the cloud's default mechanism. In this appendix, we will discuss a little bit more about storage and some additional options that you have for storage management.

D.1 StorageClasses

When you create a PersistentVolumeClaim, you can tell Kubernetes additional information about what physical needs you have for the storage. Depending on the cloud platform, you might have options for fast storage, slow storage, shared storage, etc. A StorageClass allows you to preconfigure different storage options together into a named configuration. By separating the *name* of the configuration from the implementation details, you can separate out the management of the details of the storage allocation and the needs of the programmer.

If you don't specify a StorageClass in your PersistentVolumeClaim, Kubernetes uses the default StorageClass. While the cluster administrator can specify a default StorageClass, most clusters come with a standard preconfigured default StorageClass. If you aren't going to use the cloud's preferred StorageClass, it is best to specify one explicitly.

243

© Jonathan Bartlett 2023
J. Bartlett, *Cloud Native Applications with Docker and Kubernetes*,
https://doi.org/10.1007/978-1-4842-8876-4

Linode comes with two predefined StorageClasses—`linode-block-storage` and `linode-block-storage-retain`. Both of these are identical, except that `linode-block-storage-retain` will not delete the underlying volume when the PVC itself is deleted (as a safety precaution). The `linode-block-storage-retain` StorageClass is the default StorageClass on Linode.

Defining a StorageClass is very cloud-specific. Essentially, you associate a StorageClass name with a *provisioner*, which is a cloud-specific driver for creating volumes. You can then specify a list of provisioner-specific parameters that the provisioner should use when creating a volume and a list of mount options that the containers should use when mounting the volume. You can also specify whether, when an associated PVC is deleted, the volume itself should be deleted or retained.

Once a StorageClass is defined, it can be set on a PVC by using the `storageClassName` field.

D.2 File System Expansion

Some provisioners support file system expansion, which is the ability to resize PVCs dynamically. If your provisioner supports this, you can get a larger volume simply by changing the PVC definition and applying it. If your cluster and StorageClass support the so-called online file system expansion, then this can be done even while the filesystem is mounted to a Pod.

Depending on the type of storage, you may need to perform manual steps to expand the volume as well. On Linode, for instance, while expanding the PersistentVolumeClaim expands the *available storage*, you have to issue another command to the filesystem to tell it to actually take advantage of the new storage space. Additionally, you have to do this on the Node itself, as the Pod doesn't have sufficient privileges (or even access to the disk) to do this.

Therefore, you need to first identify the physical device that needs expansion. The most reliable way to do this is to `kubectl exec` into a shell on a container that has the volume attached. Then, run the command `df -h` to see a list of mounted filesystems, as well as the device files that are supplying them. Take note of the name of the device which is providing your filesystem's storage (we will say it is `/dev/MYDISK` for this example).

Note that the device file listed will be the device file on the *Node*, not on the Pod. Therefore, you need to access the underlying Node to work on it. Log off of the Pod, and then run `kubectl get pod PODNAME -o wide` to see which Node it is running on. Then, you need to use the procedure in Appendix C.13 to log in to the underlying Node. Once on the Node, you can run the following command:

```
resize2fs /dev/MYDISK
```

This tells Linux to detect the new size of the disk and inform the filesystem structure to take advantage of the new size. If the command tells you, "The filesystem is already X blocks long. Nothing to do," then that means that your Kubernetes cluster doesn't support *online* volume expansion, and you will need to unmount the drive (by deleting the Pod using it) and then remount the drive (by launching it again) first. As of this writing, this is required on Linode. Alternatively, if restarting the Pod does not work, you can also try restarting the Node itself.

D.3 Preprovisioned Storage

In addition to dynamically allocating storage with a StorageClass (or even the default StorageClass of your cluster provider), in most Kubernetes environments, you can define preprovisioned storage outside of Kubernetes and then import a reference to that storage as a PersistentVolume. The details of the PersistentVolume configuration are specific to the cloud and storage type, but, just like everything else in Kubernetes, you need to give it a name.

Once created, this PersistentVolume can then be utilized by your PersistentVolumeClaim. In the PVC, you need to do two things:

1. Set the field `volumeName` to be the name of your PersistentVolume.

2. Set the field `storageClassName` explicitly to be "" to prevent the default StorageClass from being used.

Alternatively, you can set the PersistentVolume to be part of a StorageClass using the `storageClassName` field. In this way, rather than a PVC for the StorageClass causing the cloud provider to dynamically create storage for you on-the-fly, the StorageClass can simply grab the preprovisioned volume that best matches the PVC. I don't personally recommend this, but it is available.

D.4 StatefulSets

While StatefulSets were mentioned briefly in the main text, we didn't dive very deep into them. StatefulSets can be used (a) when the order of Pods needs to be explicit and/or (b) when Pods created from a template need attached storage. Think about a replicated database cluster with many read-only replicas (see Chapter 16). In such a cluster, we have an ordering problem—the master database needs to boot up first, before the replicas. Additionally, for large databases, every Pod will need provisioned storage, since the size of the database will probably be larger than what the Nodes can handle by themselves.

On the surface, StatefulSets look a lot like ordinary Deployments. However, there are four main differences:

1. StatefulSets require a headless service to be created to manage the DNS for the Pods (see Chapter 10).

2. Each Pod is created in-order with a reliable name for the Pod. The next Pod replica will not be built until the prior one is ready.

3. Each Pod can have templates for PVCs so that PVCs are dynamically created for the Pod as well.

4. When updating deployments or scaling down the replica count, the Pods are destroyed in reverse order of their creation (most recently created is destroyed first).[1]

Each Pod will have a local hostname of `SSNAME-IDX`, where `SSNAME` is the name of the StatefulSet and `IDX` is the index number of the Pod (starting with 0). The Pod can find its own name through the standard hostname function (from a shell script, it is simply the command `hostname`). If you need to dynamically find the name of the service, you can find the fully qualified hostname by running the command `hostname  -f`. If a Pod wants to find another Pod in the StatefulSet, that Pod will have the hostname `SSNAME-IDX.`
`SERVICENAME.NAMESPACE.svc.cluster.local` (though, if it is in the same namespace, you can leave out `NAMESPACE.svc.cluster.local`). This is why the headless Service is needed—so that the Pods can find each other.

---

[1] Note that this does not happen on StatefulSet *deletion*. Therefore, if you want to delete a StatefulSet in a graceful manner, it is usually best to first change the replica count to zero, wait for the Pods to terminate, and *then* delete the StatefulSet.

The way that this works is that the startup script can be tailored to do different actions depending on which index number of the StatefulSet it is running. If we think about replicated databases, the master database does a different startup procedure than the replica databases. So, the script will check the hostname to see if it is index 0, and, if so, it will start itself as the master database. Otherwise, the script will attempt to connect to the master node, which it knows is at index 0. The magic sauce here is that Kubernetes is starting up your Pods in-order and giving them reliable hostnames so that the Pods can find each other in their startup scripts and know which role they are playing based on their index number. This can enable any amount of complex startup behavior.

Additionally, as mentioned, we can give each Pod some additional storage using PVC templates. Essentially, each replica is auto-creating a PVC based on this template, which can then be mounted into the Pod.

An example StatefulSet is shown in Figure D-1. This StatefulSet doesn't do anything important—it just creates a running Pod that you can log into (see Appendix C.2) and look around and see how it is configured. Note that the replicas field actually gives you one more Pod than it says. This is because, in the usual way of setting up StatefulSets, the first Pod is a "master," not a replica. So you will always get a first Pod (index 0) and then however many replicas you request after that.

```
apiVersion: v1
kind: Service
metadata:
  name: my-ss-service
spec:
  clusterIP: None
  selector:
    app: my-ss
---
apiVersion: apps/v1
kind: StatefulSet
metadata:
  name: my-ss
spec:
  serviceName: my-ss-service
  selector:
    matchLabels:
      app: my-ss
  replicas: 4
  template:
    metadata:
      labels:
        app: my-ss
    spec:
      containers:
        - name: shell
          image: debian
          command:
            - sleep
            - infinity
          volumeMounts:
            - name: my-ss-claim
              mountPath: /my/data
  volumeClaimTemplates:
    - metadata:
        name: my-ss-claim
      spec:
        accessModes:
          - ReadWriteOnce
        resources:
          requests:
            storage: 1Gi
```

Figure D-1. *An Example StatefulSet*

D.5 A Few Additional Details

There are a few more details we need to talk about concerning storage, and they don't really fit in elsewhere. The first is that each PVC has a list of `accessModes` defined which describe how the PVC can be mounted. The usual configuration for this is a single entry of `ReadWriteOnce`, which means that the PVC can be mounted to exactly one Node. Usually, this means it should also be only mounted to a single Pod (though it can be mounted to multiple containers in that Pod). However, there are some situations where you might want to share a volume with other Pods on a Node, though this would mean that you would need to do some advanced scheduling techniques to get all of the Pods running on the same Node. If you want to ensure that a PVC is only mounted by a single Pod, you can set it to `ReadWriteOncePod`.

The other options are `ReadOnlyMany` and `ReadWriteMany`, which allow the volume to be mounted on multiple Nodes. Only some types of storage support this, such as NFS volumes. Note that even if a PVC or PV supports more than one access mode, all Nodes that have the volume mounted must have it mounted in the *same* access mode.

The other detail to mention is the `reclaimPolicy`, which is what Kubernetes does with the underlying provisioned volume after a PVC or PV is deleted. There are two options, `Retain` or `Delete`. If set to `Retain`, the underlying cloud volume is preserved even when it is removed from Kubernetes. The `Delete` option tells the cloud provider to go ahead and delete the volume when the PVC or PV is deleted.

The primary difference between the two Linode-supplied StorageClasses, `linode-block-storage` and `linode-block-storage-retain`, is that the latter is set to have a `reclaimPolicy` of `Retain`.

APPENDIX E

More on Pod Scheduling

Pod scheduling refers to the placement and running of Pods into Nodes by Kubernetes. This was largely ignored in the main text for the sake of having straightforward chapters, but it is an important subject nonetheless.

E.1 Readiness Gates

The first aspects of Pod scheduling we need to cover are Kubernetes' readiness gates. A readiness gate tells Kubernetes whether or not a Pod is capable of running. Readiness gates come in three flavors: startup probes, readiness probes, and liveness probes. A startup probe tells Kubernetes how to tell if the container successfully started up. We don't want half-started Pods being added to a service, so a startup probe will let Kubernetes know if the container (and therefore the Pod) has finished starting.

Liveness probes are used to tell if a container is in total failure and needs to be restarted. While Kubernetes can itself check to see if the process stopped, there are other total failures you might need to check for. For instance, many processes can deadlock without the process dying. If you can probe for such a case, you can add a liveness probe so that Kubernetes will know when your container is having sufficient problems that it needs a total restart. Liveness probes do not begin until after the startup probes have completed.

Readiness probes are a little different. Readiness probes tell Kubernetes if the Pod is ready to receive traffic. You can use a readiness probe to temporarily pull a Pod out of service if, say, it is currently overloaded but you expect it to recover.

When the readiness probe fails, the Pod is removed from any Services, but kept alive. When the readiness probe succeeds again, the Pod is placed back into its Services.

Probes are configured on a per-container basis. Probes come in a few basic flavors: commands, HTTP requests, and TCP connection checks. Probes can be configured with a wide variety of timeout values as well.

251

© Jonathan Bartlett 2023
J. Bartlett, *Cloud Native Applications with Docker and Kubernetes*,
https://doi.org/10.1007/978-1-4842-8876-4

```
apiVersion: v1
kind: Pod
metadata:
  name: test-pod
spec:
  containers:
    - name: webserver
      image: my-example-image
      startupProbe:
        exec:
          command:
            - ./checkme
        periodSeconds: 10
      livenessProbe:
        tcpSocket:
          port: 80
        periodSeconds: 30
      readinessProbe:
        httpGet:
          port: 80
          path: /my/path
        timeoutSeconds: 20
        periodSeconds: 60
```

Figure E-1. *An Example Probe Configuration*

Figure E-1 shows an example (fake) Pod definition with different types of probes attached. On startup, it executes the `./checkme` command every ten seconds until it succeeds. After starting up, it will terminate the Pod if the TCP port stops accepting connections, and it will take it out of temporary service if the HTTP request takes too long to process (more than 20 seconds).

Note that readiness gates can also be used to supply some amount of implicit ordering between Services. If Service B requires Service A to be started first, you can set up readiness gates on the Pods for Service B to check to see if Service A has fully started. Usually, you want Services to *not* need such implicit ordering, but that is how you would implement it if it were necessary. It is preferred that Services that have required orderings are taken care of by StatefulSets (see Appendix D.4).

E.2 Pod Topology: Affinities and Anti-affinities

Pod topology refers to which physical Node each Pod is placed into. By default, Kubernetes will schedule a Pod to run wherever it will fit. It doesn't ask you where you want it to go—it assumes that sort of decision-making is beneath you. However, although it is bad to micromanage Pod topology, there are often times when you at least have some preferences about which Pod goes where. For instance, you wouldn't want all of the Pods in one Service to be scheduled to the same Node, because then your entire Service will be subject to the failure of that one Node.

The two basic ideas for Pod topology are Pod affinities and anti-affinities. Pod affinities tell Kubernetes which other Pods a particular Pod should be near, and Pod anti-affinities tell Kubernetes which Pods a particular Pod should not be near. The list of Pods to be near (or not-near) is defined by a standard label selector. What qualifies as "near" is whether or not the labels on the *Node* are equal, known as a topologyKey. An example topology key (which is also the most well-supported) is kubernetes.io/hostname, which should be set to the name of the Node. Other relevant topology keys can be found in Chapter 17.

Figure E-2 shows a Pod that should run on the same hostname as a those with the label mylabel=myvalue but should not run on the same hostname as those with the label myotherlabel=myothervalue. A typical use case of Pod affinities is to use an anti-affinity for a Pod with its own label to prevent it from being run on the same Node as another Pod from the same Deployment.

Note that you *can* require these rules (instead of prefer them with a weighting), but this would mean that if Kubernetes could not meet your requirements, the Pod simply would not be scheduled.

E.3 Node Tainting and Cordoning

Kubernetes has a system of *taints* and *tolerations* which are used to preferentially allow or disallow a Pod on a Node. While affinities are based on what *other* Pods are running on the Node, a taint is more direct. It is also useful for making exceptions to DaemonSets, so they don't run on *every* Node. However, the full tainting system of Kubernetes is outside the scope of the present book, except for one specialized taint—marking a Node as being unschedulable.

```
apiVersion: v1
kind: Pod
metadata:
  name: my-pod
spec:
  containers:
    - name: my-container
      image: my-image
  affinity:
    podAffinity:
      preferredDuringSchedulingIgnoredDuringExecution:
        - weight: 10
          podAffinityTerm:
            labelSelector:
              matchLabels:
                mylabel: myvalue
            topologyKey: kubernetes.io/hostname
    podAntiAffinity:
      preferredDuringSchedulingIgnoredDuringExecution:
        - weight: 20
          podAffinityTerm:
            labelSelector:
              matchLabels:
                myotherlabel: myothervalue
            topologyKey: kubernetes.io/hostname
```

Figure E-2. *An Example Pod Affinity and Anti-affinity*

If you require downtime for a Node, either for hardware maintenance, scheduled reboots, or just consolidation of your cluster, you can tell Kubernetes to stop scheduling new Pods on that Node. This is done with a special taint: node.kubernetes.io/ unschedulable. You can set this taint with a special kubectl command. To tell Kubernetes to not schedule any new Pods to MY-NODE, simply type the following:

kubectl cordon MY-NODE

This doesn't do anything to Pods already on the Node but just prevents scheduling new Pods. You can reverse this by doing the following:

kubectl uncordon MY-NODE

While a Node is cordoned off, you can ask Kubernetes to remove Pods running on it using the following command:

kubectl drain MY-NODE

This will cause Kubernetes to attempt to gracefully shut down all Pods on that Node and start them up elsewhere. Depending on your cloud architecture, and which specific Pods are running on this Node, it could cause some amount of downtime. However, Kubernetes will try to warn you if there are Pod types that it thinks may be harmed by shutting them down. In this case, you can either terminate the Pods directly (using `kubectl delete pod`) or you can specify the additional override flags that `kubectl` will suggest to you to ignore the warnings and tell Kubernetes to go ahead and drain the Node.

Additionally, when running under Linode, you can request that Linode recycle a Node. This will cause it to drain the Node, turn off the Node, and then start a brand new Node in its place. It is probably good to recycle all of your Nodes occasionally, if only to be sure that your cluster is always in a state that can be recycled successfully.

APPENDIX F

Troubleshooting Kubernetes Clusters

In the first line of *Anna Karenina*, Leo Tolstoy says, "Happy families are all alike; every unhappy family is unhappy in its own way." While I'm not sure about the truth of that statement, it does point to an important fact about troubleshooting—there are just a lot of things that can go wrong, and general principles are hard to find. Nonetheless, I don't want to leave you without any tools in your toolkit for diagnosing a problematic configuration. Starting out in any new technology can be scary, and, when you run into issues, having somewhere to start looking is helpful.

Before we get into any specific techniques, however, there are a few things you should always do:

- Don't panic. Everyone has had difficulty with solving cluster problems before. You aren't the first one. Get out of "panic mode" and get into "thinking mode."

- Imagine yourself to be the cluster. What information might you be missing to do the job properly? What might have been specified incorrectly? Imagine how the parts fit together (go back and see Chapter 8, especially), and then imagine what might be preventing them from fitting together correctly.

- Check your spelling/typing. If you entered the command wrong, it probably won't work. Also be careful that your computer didn't autocorrect something, especially if you are copying/pasting any code. Be sure that you are using the correct punctuation and the correct number of dashes and that you are using straight single and double quotes (not those fancy curly ones that are used by word processors).

257

© Jonathan Bartlett 2023
J. Bartlett, *Cloud Native Applications with Docker and Kubernetes*,
https://doi.org/10.1007/978-1-4842-8876-4

- Did you substitute all the values correctly? If the command is `kubectl describe pod NAME-OF-POD`, did you remember to *replace* `NAME-OF-POD` with the Pod you were wanting to look at?

- Did you miss a step? All the steps are important. You may want to reread the chapter to make sure you didn't forget one.

- Stop and think—what was the last thing that I *know* worked? What were the steps that I took since then? Which one, specifically, is likely causing the problems?

- If this is just a test system, don't be afraid to just wipe it out completely and start over. I did that several times writing this book! If you do that, you might go through the steps more slowly the next time and verify the success of each step as you go. Perhaps your problem occurred earlier than you thought.

- Ask online. If you're stuck, go to the Internet! Asking in forums or searching for your error message in a search engine will oftentimes give you the missing information you need.

In addition to those, this chapter has specific suggestions for different issues you may face getting everything in this book working.

F.1 Connecting to the Cluster

If you are having trouble getting `kubectl` to connect to your cluster, here are some suggestions:

- If this is a brand new cluster—wait! It can sometimes take several minutes for a cluster to come up. Go have a cup of tea and come back.

- Make sure the `KUBECONFIG` environment variable is set to the right file. Additionally, make sure the variable is *exported* to the environment so `kubectl` can pick it up.

- Try running with the flag `--kubeconfig /PATH/TO/ KUBECONFIG` added.

- Run `kubectl config get-contexts` to make sure the current context matches up with your cluster.

F.2 Pods Are Not Starting

If you have created a Deployment but your Pods are not starting up, try these ideas:

- Run `kubectl get pods` to see your list of Pods and which ones are failing.

- Run `kubectl describe pod FAILING-POD` to see the details of a Pod that has a non-successful status. The "events" section usually will tell you what, specifically, is happening.

- Run `kubectl get events` to see what else is happening in the cluster (note that this doesn't show you error events, unfortunately).

- Run `kubectl top nodes` to see if there is an overutilization issue on one of your Nodes.

If the error is with pulling images, be sure that the image is available to the cluster. This means

- The image is on a repository that is in a registry that can be reached by Kubernetes.

- The location of the image is properly specified (including the location of the registry if it isn't Docker Hub).

- If it is a private repository, you have specified appropriate `imagePullCredentials` to pull the image.

- If you built the image from a different CPU architecture than what your Nodes are running, that will prevent the Pod from being able to pull the image (most common case—building the image using a Mac with Apple Silicon (resulting in a `linux/arm64` image) and deploying to Linux x86 (needing a `linux/amd64` image)).

When I first started messing around with Kubernetes, I expected the cluster to know about container images that I built locally on my laptop and had a hard time figuring out why Kubernetes couldn't find the images! It didn't occur to me for a while that `kubectl` was only a simplistic pathway to Kubernetes and didn't give the cluster access to things I was storing on my laptop.

If the image is in a private repository, as long as there is nothing actually secret there, I would try out a public repository to see if it isn't a problem with your credentials.

Another common issue with Pods not starting is resource issues. Be sure you haven't set resource requests on your Pods that go beyond (or even near) the size of the Node they are running on, as this will prevent them from being scheduled. This is especially problematic with third-party services installed from remote YAML URLs or Helm Charts. If the requested Pod is bigger than the Node itself, even adding more Nodes won't help.

The most annoying issue to diagnose is the infamous CrashLoopBackoff. This means that the container is *starting*, but the main process is crashing very soon afterward. The problem here is that, when a container crashes, you can no longer `kubectl exec` into it, so it is more difficult to debug. Hopefully there are enough logs so that `kubectl logs -p PODNAME` will tell you what is going on, but that isn't always the case.

Oftentimes these are the result of misconfigurations, so I would check to see if all of the environment variables it needs are set and that they have the correct values for your configuration. Basically, think of all of the things the Pod needs to start up successfully and which of those things might be failing.

One thing you can sometimes do is to modify the container's startup command to run `tail -f /dev/null`. This basically makes the container run forever doing nothing. Then, you can `kubectl exec` into the container and run the "real" command manually and debug what is happening. Alternatively, you can use the tricks in Appendix C.2 to launch a new debugging container that has the original filesystem mounted.

F.3 Pods Not Behaving as Expected

The first thing to do if a Pod is not behaving as expected is to check the log file using `kubectl logs NAME-OF-POD`. Log files should always be your first spot to check. Also use `kubectl describe pod NAME-OF-POD` to get information about any events associated with the Pod.

As long as the Pod is running, you can get a shell on a Pod container using the technique shown in Appendix C.2. This will allow you to do troubleshooting on the Pod itself. This requires deeper knowledge of the command line, but it is certainly worth knowing. Appendix A gives many important commands and files that, while they won't tell you everything you need to know, may be enough to point you in the right direction.

F.4 Pods Can't Reach Service

If you have created a Service and the Pods can't reach it, there are several things that could have gone wrong. For many of these, you may want to be running a troubleshooting Pod in your cluster to see what is going on (see Appendix C.3).

- Is the Service up? Run `kubectl get services` to make sure that Kubernetes actually knows about the Service.

- Does the Service have any Pods attached? If you run `kubectl describe service MY-SERVICE`, it should have Pod IP addresses listed under "Endpoints." If you run `kubectl get pods -o wide`, it will show you the IP address of each Pod, so you know which one it is referring to. If there aren't any Pods attached, check to make sure the labels on the Pods match the ones specified by the selector on the Service.

- Is the port correct? The previous commands will show what port(s) the Service is using. Try connecting to one of the Pods in the cluster through your troubleshooting Pod and see if you can connect to that port (you will have to know its IP address in the cluster to do this). If you can't connect to the port on the Pod, the Service can't either.

F.5 Ingress Is Not Getting an External IP Address

The Ingress is controlled through a separate Ingress Class. Here, we installed the `nginx` Ingress Class. If you didn't receive an external IP address, that is likely because the Ingress Class didn't pick up on your Ingress configuration. This usually comes from just a few causes:

- You didn't add an `ingressClassName` to your Ingress spec.

- You misspelled the Ingress Class (should be `nginx`).

- You didn't install the Ingress Class (see Section 10.7).

- You didn't wait long enough for the Ingress Class to allocate an IP address (usually takes a few minutes).

F.6 Going Forward

As you build more advanced clusters, more and more difficult things can go wrong. However, it's never bad to go back and check the basics.

Index

A

Ad hoc interactions, 148
Alpine Linux, 13, 38
Alpine package management, 221
Alpine version, 38
Amazon's S3, 187
Apache HTTP server, 109
apiVersion, 88
Apple Silicon, 233
Application-level diagnostic commands
    ab (in apache2-utils), 227
    curl (in curl), 227
    mysql in (mysql-client), 227
    psql in (postgresql-client), 227
Application policies
    ad hoc interactions, 148
    authentication protocol, 148
    authorization control, 149
    coding style, 150
    early stages, development, 148
    error message protocol, 149
    logging format, 149
    message formats, 149
    pagination, 150
    response time, 150
    source of truth, 149
    subsystems, 149
Applications installation
    Apple Silicon, 233
    development package manager, 231
    Docker, 231, 232
    kubectl, 231, 234

package management, 231
    Podman, 232, 233
Architectural diagram, 146, 147
Architecture values
    goal, 205
    integrity, 212
    observability, 207
    predictability, 210, 211
    repeatability, 211, 212
    scalability, 205, 206
    security, 212–214
    testability, 209, 210
    traceability, 207–209
Authentication, 160–162, 166
Authentication API, 163
Authorization, 160–162, 166
Autoscaler, 131
Autoscaling, 128–131
Autoscaling Pods, 129
Availability zones, 197–199, 202

B

Base Linux distribution, 35
broQue, 179

C

CentOS/Fedora/RHEL Package
    Management, 222
Channels, 168
Cloud architect, 177, 178, 182, 206

263

D

faulty hardware, 2
  infrastructure, 1
Wi-Fi router, 38
Windows operating system, 2
Workload types, 72
Work queue, 168–170, 182

Y, Z

YAML, 106, 118, 125, 127–129, 133, 136,
        137, 140, 141, 145–147, 150,
        153, 154

configuration file
    format, 85
configuring clusters, 95
documents, 86, 87, 93
file translated into JSON, 86
indentation
    whitespace, 86
key/value pairs, 85
numeric data, 86
provided file, 85
sample, 85
version-controlling, 95

Printed in the United States
by Baker & Taylor Publisher Services